The Presence of the Past in Children's Literature

Recent Titles in
Contributions to the Study of World Literature

The Presence of the Past in Children's Literature

Edited by
Ann Lawson Lucas

Prepared under the auspices of the
International Research Society for Children's Literature

Contributions to the Study of World Literature, Number 120

Westport, Connecticut
London

In memory of my dear uncle, Colin Lawson

Library of Congress Cataloging-in-Publication Data

The presence of the past in children's literature / edited by Ann Lawson Lucas.
    p. cm. — (Contributions to the study of world literature, ISSN 0738–9345 ; no. 120)
    Includes bibliographical references and index.
    ISBN 0–313–32483–2 (alk. paper)
    1. Children's literature—History and criticism. 2. History and literature. I. Lawson
Lucas, Ann. II. Series.
PN1009.5.H57 P74   2003
809'93358—dc21   2002029771

British Library Cataloguing in Publication Data is available.

Library of Congress Catalog Card Number: 2002029771
ISBN: 0–313–32483–2
ISSN: 0738–9345

First published in 2003

Praeger Publishers, 88 Post Road West, Westport, CT 06881
An imprint of Greenwood Publishing Group, Inc.
www.praeger.com

Printed in the United States of America

Copyright Acknowledgment

The editor and publisher gratefully acknowledge permission for use of the following material:

An earlier version of Chapter 13 by Celia Keenan was previously published in Valerie Coghlan and Celia
Keenan, eds., *The Big Guide 2: Irish Children's Books* (Dublin: Children's Books Ireland, 2000); the
chapter appears here by kind permission of the editors and publisher.

Contents

Illustrations

Acknowledgments

Without the great diversity and quality of expertise evident to the reader in the work of the contributors, this book would not have come into being. I am deeply grateful to them, too, for their unfailing helpfulness, conscientiousness and patience in periods both of delay and of haste. Before my correspondence with this worldwide web of stalwarts started, there had already been a deal of work done by the ever-prompt, ever-committed, ever-shrewd team of editorial advisors, all past or present presidents of the International Research Society for Children's Literature (IRSCL), and two of them also recent editors of the society's volumes of selected Congress papers. I cannot thank warmly enough my good friends and colleagues Sandra Beckett (in Canada), Maria Nikolajeva (in Sweden — sometimes) and John Stephens (in Australia), who also undertook to give specialist advice to individual scholars on the revision for publication of some of the essays. All three have always been towers of strength. Here in Britain, I am particularly grateful to George Talbot, my friend and colleague in Italian and Head of the Department of Modern Languages at Hull University, who has helped enormously with the camera-ready technology necessary for this publication. Alan Deighton, another friend and colleague in a department which abounds with unusual scholarly resources and progressive expertise (including in Children's Literature), gave much invaluable and learned assistance when my minimal German fell short of the task.

   In this territory of Children's Literature studies (still on the academic margins in some countries like Britain), we sometimes feel like eccentric pioneers on dangerous ground; reliably cheering us on to reach the next frontier, very many—too many to name individually—are the friends and colleagues from around the globe who lent support and encouragement in the preparation of both the 13th International Congress of IRSCL and this volume which derives from it. As well as my modest but heartfelt thanks, may they all reap generous rewards for their scholarship, their creativity, their vigor, and above all for their international commitment and solidarity.

   Finally, I wish to express my warmest gratitude also to the British Arts and Humanities Research Board for its sponsorship through the Research Leave Scheme which made the completion of several major projects, including this volume, possible.

Introduction

The Past in the Present of Children's Literature

Ann Lawson Lucas

In the last years of the old, Western millennium and the first years of the new one, we have been made momentously aware of Time. Through the modern miracle of worldwide television, millions of people all around the globe became conscious both of the international celebrations to mark the extraordinary (but man-made) occasion and also of the international inconsistencies which characterize the ways in which we reckon time past and passing. We came to acknowledge the variety, the unreliability, the own-culture-centeredness of our calculations and concepts of time; even the Christian (or once Christian) world could not decide with clarity and unanimity when to commemorate the event which gave rise to the Western calendar. Time is a mystery as yet only partially fathomed by humankind, whether in terms of physics or metaphysics, but it ineluctably shapes our lives and thoughts; like the striking and the snuffing of a match, it kindles us and extinguishes us, and it asserts the rhythm of our brief experience of the world.

Of poetic and philosophical necessity, time is one of the great perpetual themes of literature. In their works writers have always been obliged to represent this *sine qua non* of life, and for some—from Homer to Dante to Proust—it was a foremost preoccupation; indeed it was one that had been expressed in carved stone and hieroglyphics, from the Andes to Egypt to Easter Island, from time immemorial. With the development of modern science, writers have added to the religious, practical, philosophical, symbolic and emotional treatments of time a new kind of intellectual enquiry and even playfulness in experimental, exploratory works, so that twentieth-century Western literature at least (I cannot speak for the others) has given a special place to our doubts and theories about the very nature of time.

The relatively young genre of children's literature is as equal as any to the challenge. Indeed, time is one of its most prominent themes, whether one thinks of sumptuous re-creations of the past in historical novels, or uncertain, sensitive meditations on the meaning of present, impermanent experience; the young, like adults, want to know about the past—in its unregarded personal minutiae as well as in all its panoply and pomp—though first they must learn of its very existence; they easily wonder, too, whether the past is gone forever or is sometimes (always?) with us. The concern with time is notable—unlike, say, the topics of animals or fairies—for its prominence in both children's and adults' books; it provides a kind of intellectual and imaginative connective tissue throughout our lives' reading matter. This volume explores many of the ways in which children's writers have sought to present the theme and concepts of time past. The work is not concerned with the history of children's literature, a different matter altogether, although some of its phases can be detected through references to changing treatments of time and changing preoccupations within the recurring theme of time. The "present" of this introduction's title is (in keeping with contemporary pluralism) not the fixed time zone of our Now; it is the present of any age. The present, indeed like the past, is always with us. But if our understanding of the present is limited and fragile, our relationship with the past is ten times more tenuous while simultaneously both crucial and vital. Is history "bunk"? That once debunking and shocking remark now carries a lapidary truth enshrined in modern writing which recognizes the complexity of our relationship with the past and our perceptions of it. We are now aware that we, consciously or unconsciously, "construct," create or "invent" the past. The catastrophe in Iraq's museums and libraries (like the destruction of Dubrovnik) has reminded us that we also destroy the past, including the evidence of past civilization. In so doing we destroy ourselves, for the past is our identity, our *raison d'être*. A great Italian poet of two hundred years ago, Ugo Foscolo, believed that there is no afterlife other than in the memories and memorializings of those who follow, so these are of utter importance. Created before his birth, the British Museum—the oldest in the world—has chosen appropriately (and poignantly) to celebrate its 250th anniversary with an exhibition devoted to memory. One of the defining human experiences, memory is conveyed to our young by the oral telling of tales, by written stories and by pictures representing—and re-presenting—the past of human events and of human imagination.

This volume is composed of chapters developed from a small number of selected conference papers which were delivered at the 13th Biennial Congress of the International Research Society for Children's Literature (IRSCL), held in 1997 in the historic city of York, England (the first visit of the Congress to Britain for 20 years). The IRSCL has two missions. The first is to promote serious research and scholarly writing in the field of children's literature, and the second is to provide an international forum for this to happen cooperatively and comparatively, so encouraging the crossing of political and cultural boundaries. Because child readers are not (yet) deeply imbued with a sense of national confines as barriers, children's books travel the world in a perhaps surprisingly untrammelled way (despite publishers' resistance to translation in some countries, including Britain). Some of the greatest works of children's literature—*Alice, Pinocchio, Tom* and *Huck, The Little Mermaid, Twenty Thousand Leagues under the Seas, Treasure Island*—as well as others appropriated by the young—*The Arabian Nights*—have all but lost any national or regional connotation or at least are not hampered by one in their permeation of world culture. On the other hand, children are fascinated, with an unprejudiced eagerness, by stories and information which are "foreign": internationalism is actively nurtured by those stories that present otherness as of central interest and motivation, like the realist treatment of Abroad in the series about twins of different lands which was published in mid-twentieth-century Britain, and like the foreign fantasies of Andrew Lang's *Fairy Books* of 50 years earlier. The IRSCL, then, has a well-travelled literature to discuss and, in response, has developed well-travelled literary history and criticism to match.

The York Congress welcomed participants from 28 countries including Russia, China and Japan, South Africa, Australia and New Zealand, North and Central America, the Faroe Islands, Finland, Poland, and Slovenia, and from the Middle East both Israel and Egypt were represented. In a sense, even more remarkable was the large number of participants from the British Isles where the study of the subject is generally fragmented, interested academics isolated and major fora few and far between. The disproportionate number of British contributions selected for this volume (by chance, certainly not by partisan design) may perhaps encourage a greater international participation by British scholars in a field which thrives so vigorously in other countries. Of the hundred or so papers presented, these 23 chapters cannot adequately convey the breadth of diversity or the depth of common ground, but it hints at the variety of international crossovers that IRSCL exists to encourage. The book's contributors come from 11 countries and, far from exclusively blowing their own national trumpets, these scholars also study and compare the literatures of others. The British and German contributors investigate each others' literatures, from Canada and the USA there are long-distance views of French and English writers, an American author is the subject of a Japanese academic, while the making of Portuguese myths is examined by a Belgian researcher. By contrast, it is the impermanence of populations and boundaries that is implicit within an Israeli scholar's consideration of the painful European past. We were not concerned exclusively with real, literal history and geography, of course, but with those of imagined lives and worlds, including the fantastic. Moreover, the passing of time—along with the occurrence of "time-slip"—in literary history itself is denoted by intertextuality. Books carry the literary genes of past writings, and some of our contributors are concerned with the evolution of the literary family tree, and with the treatment of old themes taken from past masters. As a force for the creation of international bonds which are cultural and aesthetic in nature, the great literary archetypes are hard to excel, like that ancient Robinson Crusoe, of

York, Mariner, traveller, citizen of the world's narratives, who had a prominent role to play in the conference programme.

If place was an unspoken or sometimes secondary theme of the Congress, it was time, history, the past that were our overt concern. How does children's literature treat such complex, protean, incomprehensible subjects which, because they are too gigantic for the human brain to encompass fully, are especially susceptible to subjectivity—and therefore, among more attractive things, to prejudice and partiality? That subjectivity may be intensified, often beneficially, because the passing of time entails our own passing and the knowledge of loss, giving rise to deep emotion. This volume is concerned with writers, not of the very beginnings of children's literature but, of the nineteenth and twentieth centuries. The historical novel in the West was the brainchild of Romanticism, with its exploration of the inner world of feeling, and it grew to full vigor in the course of the era of imperialism and the exploration of the physical world. From the late eighteenth century on, children's books burgeoned, partly in response to these cultural and political influences. After Darwin, Freud and Einstein, the time-theme became less sure of itself, capable of mercurial change, quicksilver slipperiness, plural interpretation. Is there more than one kind of time? Do we simultaneously inhabit more than one period of time? How much of the past is in me? How much of me will inhabit the future?

Many of the different significances of the past for children's writers are discussed here. The collection is intended to provide an impression of all the dominant themes and approaches which were present in the conference program, and to suggest the many ramifications of the subject as a whole and how these have changed over time. Once, the historiographical end of the spectrum was clearcut, "factual," reliable, while the fictional treatment of the past might instead be imaginative, unfettered, romantically fancy-free; now these roles, it is argued here, have been reversed in a literary dialogue on the very nature of history — and indeed of fiction. The volume starts with the application of literary theory to our theme as well as a detailed, systematic analysis of examples of the juvenile historical novel. Here too is an investigation of fashions in criticism and in publishing and the pressure they bring to bear on writers: how critical judgment is also subject to the ravages of time and how it affects both the content of books and the response of readers. While the works considered by the contributors all belong to the last two centuries, the subject-matter of those works ranges far, far back in time, to medieval Europe and to the Ancient World of the previous millennium. The history that comes down to us from distant times is often perceived in a manner yet more simplified than is recent history, simplified but also perhaps magnified in grandeur. Three chapters examine the creation and development through literature of national myths based on political history, while a fourth considers the legacy of another sort of archetype, the myth of literary origin which bequeaths centuries of international intertextuality. This is the case of Defoe's castaway with all his essential connotations: islands, solitude, self-reliant industry, exploitation of—or oneness with—nature, adventure, the Other, which over time are reworked the world over by writers who fit the myth to the tenor of their times and places. The greatest literary archetypes possess the immortality of at least hemispherical universality. The patriotic myth, while capable of frequent rebirth to serve new causes, is geographically defined, and yet a local saint may herself be an example of a greater symbol; she is also the female warrior in shining armor, who champions the good variously for Renaissance chivalric poets (Ariosto) and postmodern fabulists (Calvino) alike, as well as for children's Golden Age adventure novelists (Salgari). My examples are European, but there is no great historical or literary connection between Northern France and Italy; it is a question of the international power of ideas and images which recur. This image also illustrates other cultural flexibilities offered by the past; it is not the preserve of one age-group and it may be presented as either factual or fictional.

The historical novel and the adventure novel are sometimes one and the same; both flourished separately and together in Victorian and Edwardian Britain—and indeed still do—but both chapters concerned with this field show how there was a timely shift in the treatment of the past. By the end of the nineteenth century, the earlier realist (albeit often romanticized) vision was giving way to an evocation of historical times which was dependant on an element of fantasy; by the late twentieth century, in many works by writers such as Philip Pullman (winner of the Whitbread Prize for Literature in 2002), fantasy had become a leading feature, political history had virtually disappeared, and all that remained of historical "reality" was a form of social history: Revolution and Restoration had given way to Ruritania (celebrating its hundredth birthday), but Ruritania with a democratic dimension. On the other hand, Victorian adventure novelists like Captain Marryat, Ballantyne, Kingsley and Henty often chose their plots, and the geography of their plots, prompted by the contemporary patriotic and colonialist spirit. Henty, indeed, was frequently the narrator of contemporary, as opposed to past, history. The era of imperialism was the spur to a vast (jubilant, yet dutiful) children's literature of its own; today, it is the (tragic, shameful) consequences of imperialism that preoccupy writers for young and old alike. In an effort to express the pain, even for the young to know and feel it, or in an effort to make amends, writers from here to the Antipodes seek words and pictures to do justice to the horror of that past without doing harm to present children. Through a sequence of studies included here, we observe how children's writers, in presenting the past, often communicate opinions. These opinions tend to be relevant to their own era rather than the one described; such narrators are indeed didactic for they aim to teach a better future (but in the future their work may appear both anachronistic and old-fashioned as society comes to need new opinions). First with the representation of Saint Joan by French and by English interpreters—her own countrymen and her countrymen's enemies—or by Catholic monarchists on the one hand and secular Republicans on the other, and then with the differing perceptions of colonists and colonized (or rather their descendants), we see the emergence, and socio-political significance for children's literature, of differing and conflicting points of view. This literature of times past which has a present hidden agenda is seen to employ history not merely for decorative or narrative or pedagogical purposes; as a result it becomes less distanced, less impartial, more nuanced by latterday emotions, whether of allegiance or grief or guilt. Conversely, admiration of the glamor of past cultures is associated more clearly with that literature in which no conclusions are drawn or implied for the modern world.

As it happens, it is also in the context of colonialism that this volume develops its consideration of literary form. We see how, in a writer like Hugh Lofting, past colonial history, recent personal experience and present literary imagination may combine to create atemporal Never-Never Lands. But in this section, we move from fictional narratives to historiography, the supposed representation of the true, the factual reality of the past, as distinct from imaginative re-creation. Teaching the "facts" of history in nonfiction invites pictorial illustration; the visual texts of colonial times, once decoded, are however pregnant with political and social instruction designed to underpin the structures of Empire and of inequality. (Is it the case that, in changing societies, nonfiction has an even greater capacity than fiction for becoming embarrassingly dated? Of course it is a fate heartily to be desired for earnest didacticism the assumptions of which are now repugnant to the educated reader or teacher. But *caveat scriptor!* — today's good intentions are tomorrow's odious prejudice.) Pictures as texts to be read and interpreted are indeed the central focus of the chapter on Australian publications, and altogether four of the volume's contributors concern themselves with pictorial communication, the meaning and the power of visual images, so distinctive a feature of children's literature.

The seven parts of this book are arranged in an order approximating to the chronology of the different periods of time evoked in the works under discussion. World War II and especially the Holocaust filled several substantial conference sessions; in the volume's section devoted to the war and its repercussions, further variations in terms of literary form make their appearance. Two of the three chapters are concerned with autobiographical writing, in numerical terms a minor form within the general framework of books for the young, yet two examples discussed here have an exceptional power. Moreover, one of the autobiographical works is a (once private) diary, one which—made public—has provoked admiration, horror, emulation. It is, too, the diary of a child, Anne Frank; this is children's literature in several different senses, and wholly unlike the norm. It is clearly no accident that personal testimony looms so large in the context of one of the most extreme experiences of atrocity in a century scarred by real, lived atrocities beyond our most horrific imaginings. By the same token, fiction falls short of its duty in relating the same subject matter; here is a case in which, despite some good intentions, the historical aspect of fiction is seen to be partial (in both senses), a case which may contribute to the contemporary belief that "true history" is a contradiction in terms or is at least not a realizable literary form. This section also contributes to a *leit-motiv* running through this book, which is specific to, or of more emphatic concern in, writings for the young; it can be expressed in the general question: "How does one tell children about the worst aspects of human life?"

The Second World War changed everything, not only in Europe, not only in the West, not only in the northern hemisphere. For many the world and society had to be rebuilt; much of the past was gone—its material evidence obliterated—except in memory, and memory as a device in literature increased in significance as the twentieth century progressed. Alongside the postwar atmosphere of joyous relief and optimistic innovation, there was a sadder, more doubting, more nostalgic culture which was sensitive and speculative. Nowhere is this culture expressed more pervasively and persuasively than in narratives for children written in the aftermath of the war, and typically written—it seems from this volume's showing—in England and by women. There is an extraordinary paradox amply evidenced here; men's absence from normal work during the war and the need for women to take their place, along with the intense relationships and emotions of wartime, had the effect of emancipating women, who were suddenly able to pursue professional and social roles on their own account. Yet afterwards, a number of educated, middle-class women began to write with yearning about the past; in children's stories their chosen literary locus was frequently the (grand) house and garden, that is to say the traditional domain of women, the conservators of wholesome family life and sometimes—it has to be said—of social snobbery. To be fair, the source of this nostalgia was doubtless an anguished awareness of the deep damage done, both societal and individual. Moreover, the families and the children populating these novels are usually anomalous, and uncomfortable because of that. Paradoxical also in the ideas they develop, these narratives draw from a traditional setting thoughts about time (perhaps even more than about the past) which are innovative and unsettling. Literary experiments in time were not new; in England, E. Nesbit, H. G. Wells and J. B. Priestley had established substantial reputations much earlier, reputations resting in part on their enquiries into the nature of time. But it was in the 1950s that the time-slip story began to be a distinctive sub-genre of narratives for children. On the whole it is a backward-looking literature, a product of the age of anxiety. Its most positive quality, though, is its endorsement of experimental thoughtfulness and questioning. However, in an age of advancing science and technology (but also of the irrational threat of debased science in the atomic bomb), this play of literary intellect hints at unfathomable mysteries; it says, "There are more things in heaven and earth, Horatio,/ Than are dreamt of in your philosophy." Subsequently it would lead to the playfulness of the avowedly postmodern, with its self-conscious awareness of form and language and the literary heritage, and its eschewing of realism.

The mysterious and inexplicable experiences described in time-slip novels, in which the past is not simply a painful or curious memory but is indeed present, have to take place within realistically represented settings which speak of normality. But, perhaps also as a consequence of wartime restrictions and then of the high hopes of new peacetime, in tandem with quiet, local realities, there was magic in the air: there emerged a new thrusting form of fantasy which invented empires and dynasts. Bearing as little resemblance to the real world as possible, this was a literature, not of the parochial, but of the universal, the titanic, the mythical. In the real world, the sound barrier had been broken, the space-race entered, the Cold War battle of gigantic wills entrenched, and one branch of the fantasy kaleidoscope was itself technological, its preferred time zone the future. Yet, just as it was in the other branch, derived from ancient folklore, legend and myth, the past was present here too. Science-fiction fantasy reacted overtly against the past, while the new-Arthurian moral universes enshrined, theologized the past.

The two World Wars had shaken the very roots of society which, through a long, agonizing series of rebirths and false dawns, began to reinvent itself. In many parts of the world the principal beneficiaries of this process were women and children (in others they are still the principal victims) and in the last 50 years the cultural histories of women and of children, like the social ones, have been significantly intertwined. Women writers for children now make a major contribution worldwide. In the same period many Western children's books have addressed social issues, including gender and inequality and relationships, all with the aim of having a constructive effect on social progress. Naturally these narratives (or plays or verses) look above all to the future. All the chapters in our final section, in which fantasy dominates, have something to say about womanhood and male-female relations but, perhaps because our overarching theme is the presence of the past in children's literature, the gender roles described are far from fully representative of the range of this international debate or of the vision of the new woman widely treated (or still even mistreated) in the broad sweep of modern writings for the young. Indeed the men, women and gender relations deployed in the works discussed in this section are a strange, exotic, anomalous and necessarily quirky assortment: necessarily because these are works of fantasy. It might be assumed that fantasy writing would generally be socially progressive, even utopian (though the original Utopia is hardly encouraging), but instead I would argue that much fantasy—and currently *The Lord of the Rings* comes readily to mind—is deep-dyed conservatism with a fancy cloak. Whatever the protestations, both *Dan Dare* and *Earthsea* probably serve to reinforce the unreconstructed social traditions: the past is present indeed. In our chapters on fantasy, it is only among the latterday witches that we find some suggestion of imaginative social progress, sometimes linked to the greatest anxiety for the twenty-first century, the fear of environmental collapse and the present need to nurture and conserve nature. Yet if new witches may both conserve nature and be benignly subversive as priestesses of the Alternative, they are still inevitably and literally eccentric, not the norm, and that condemns all their activities including environmental protection to inhabit the twilit sidelines; this is womanhood as well-meaning, bizarre and ineffectual. In the past reality of history, a saint who saved her king and country was burned as a witch; she was tellingly condemned for her unnatural practices as, when she went to war with a mob of ruffians in chain-mail, she wore men's clothing. At least that's changed, in life and in literature, but the idea of the unusual woman as witch dies hard.

Perspectives on the past, the presence of the past in our present or in some earlier present, the presentation of the past by writers for children — all these permutations combine within the theme of this volume. Its chapters illustrate the variety and vigor of the genre of children's literature worldwide (with some unavoidable emphasis on works written in English, albeit from a variety of continents and cultures — North American and Australian as well as British and Irish), and the perpetual and inventive self-renewal of children's literature is also amply evidenced. In terms of socio-political commentary, however, this volume makes for sobering reading; past conflicts, barbarities and inequalities are recurrent themes. So what of the future? Can the writers and critics of children's literature turn away from the past and perceive some hopeful sign beckoning in the new millennium? In the afterword our final contributor elaborates two cases of major significance, one for the world of scholarship and criticism, the other, though directed to that same community, also holds deep meaning for anyone prepared to listen to the voice of reason. In relation to academic methods—and, it is surely fair to say, fashions (which are outside the purview of the very finest criticism, by definition universal and durable)—the afterword argues passionately for historicism in critical thought, as opposed to the application of anachronistic concepts and standards to the assessment of literary works of the past. (It may give present comfort to castigate the perpetrators of misdeeds not recognized as such in their day but, in itself, it is no proof of an advanced sense of justice.) Instead, condemnations are for the here and now, while understanding is the watchword of the (historicist) scholar. And the afterword's clarion call of relevance to everyone, which also reasserts a primary aim of the International Research Society for Children's Literature, is encapsulated in the final word of Jean Perrot's title: "Unite!" It expresses IRSCL's mission to advance the cause of internationalism, now more than ever urgent in our dangerous world. But the partner of unity (and community) is the courage to be independent, nay idiosyncratic, while recognizing the absolute right of others to be equally so; in place of autocratic, homogenizing "political correctness," let us stand together to foster—through reading and writing—tolerant and flexible minds and lives, and the diversity which they imply.

NOTE

To facilitate the uninterrupted reading of the text of this volume, non-English book titles quoted in the chapters are provided with a plain translation in square brackets on their first appearance. This does not necessarily imply that a translation of these works has been published.

Part I

Presenting the Past — Writers, Books, Critics: Theoretical Approaches

1

Fiction Versus History: History's Ghosts

Danielle Thaler

The historical novel incarnates the joining of fiction and history; but how does this union take place? The historical novel is based on an illusion, namely, the belief that history can be rewritten with the help of characters who have never existed and with whom the reader will be able to identify. This is even more true of historical fiction for young people—a revived literary genre which proposes to its readers heroes of their own age—since children are largely absent from the scene of history. How then can historical fiction for young people promote the child and the young adolescent to the rank of hero while history ignores them? Without presupposing what might make up the distinctiveness of historical fiction for young people, we must ask what role a meeting between the child or the young teenager and an historical figure is going to play in this confrontation between historical fiction for young people and history. By focusing on the possible relationships that link the historical characters to the child and the adolescent, I hope to contribute to an analysis of their historical status and also make a first attempt at drawing up a typology of historical fiction written for young readers.

After examining a group of historical novels written for young people by French authors, most of which have been published or even reprinted during the last 30 years, I have been able to distinguish three broad categories, which I term "The impossible encounter," "The refused encounter" and "The encounter."

THE IMPOSSIBLE ENCOUNTER

The encounter between the hero and the historical individual cannot take place as at least one of the two protagonists misses the summons. This absence is not without meaning. It can, in fact, reflect a concept of history that is more concerned with daily life than with the game of political strengths or the praise of famous men.

A World without Children?

The world of history is basically an adult sphere. How many children and young adolescents can history offer as examples to today's young readers? Very few. In *Le Rubis du roi lépreux* [The leper king's ruby] of 1968, Huguette Pirotte marvels at young Baudoin IV, King of the Franks in Jerusalem, who is defending his kingdom which is under threat of attack by the great Saladin. One possibility would have been to follow the trail leading to the childhood of the historical characters, but rare indeed are the writers who might follow a path that leads more towards biography. Preference tends to be given to historical characters whose childhood remains mysterious, as shown by L.-N. Lavolle's choice in *L'Acrobate de Minos* [Minos' acrobat] of 1983.

Does this mean that historical novels for young people avoid a rule which supposes that young readers should be given heroes of their own age as often as possible, or is there a suitable age to enter history? It should be noted that the novelists have a marked preference for 15-year-old heroes, as was revealed by a study of a group of historical novels for young people. For example, that is the age of nearly all Odile Weulersse's young heroes and heroines. We should point out that the historical novel is primarily a novel for adolescents or pre-adolescents because this is the moment when an awareness of history begins to develop in the reader. And if 15 seems to be the ideal age, it is because it is a threshold age, when everything can go through abrupt change, an age that opens out into the adult world. Given that, it is hardly surprising to observe that the historical novel for young people is often a novel of initiation in which the hero casts off the last traces of his childhood, asserts his autonomy and develops an individual conscience with regard to the world he is passing through.

A World without Historical Characters?

Few historical characters dominate the stage in historical fiction for young people, which thus follows Mérimée's advice to avoid bringing to the forefront of history individuals whose lives "are too well known [for you] to be able to change or add anything to them."[1] Among recent examples of writing, Soncarrieu is the only one to my knowledge who dares to choose Magellan as a protagonist (for his novel *Le Premier Tour du monde* [The first voyage round the world], 1986). This reluctance seems to be characteristic of historical fiction for young people; in this it differs from historical novels intended for older readers which certainly never hesitate to thrust the most famous historical personages into the limelight.

Novelists for young people prefer to confine their historical characters to the back recesses of the novel, which they come to haunt like ghosts invited to return periodically to the scene, in order to give an historical flavor to fiction that otherwise might lack it. This, then, seems to be the main function of these famous figures, reduced to the level of foils and supporting roles. Often they even vanish from the universe of the novel and only the mention of their names will jog the reader's memory and bring to mind that they were the key figures of an age. Of course there are unavoidable names whose historical weight is sufficient to conjure up a period or date a plot; only the most famous can act as markers and chronological milestones: Bonaparte, Richelieu, Louis XIV, Julius Caesar and the like. In *Embuscade à la pierre clouée* [Ambush at the riveted rock] of 1989 by Noguès, Richelieu does not appear once in the story; nevertheless, it is he who condemns the hero to failure in a novel of betrayal in which political values triumph over the heroic and romantic values embodied by Damiano the bandit. It seems like history's revenge over fiction or a summons to reality; fiction cannot in the long run outstrip history.

A Novel of Everyday Life

There is room for the child in the historical novel, but in an historical novel firmly turned towards the recounting of a daily life that spares neither children nor adults — the adults being recruited particularly from the lower levels of society, the class from which historical personages are absent and to which even the echo of their names filters down in weakened form. No event of an historical nature comes to disturb the course of an adventure being lived out in everyday life. People suffer from cold and hunger. They fight over a piece of meat or bread. And everything that happens to the characters born of the author's imagination bears witness to the atmosphere and way of life of the period depicted. That is why we may wonder if all these figures might not be historic in the sense that Lukacs meant,[2] since they are characters whose existence is not historically attested but who assume a condition in which we can recognize an historical reality.

THE REFUSED ENCOUNTER

The expression "refused encounter" is chosen because it suggests an intention on the part of the author, one that is more or less conscious, more or less constant, apparently to avoid—as far as possible—too restricting an encounter between the world of history and the world of childhood and adolescence: a strange contradiction in a genre that sets out to narrate history to the young generations. No doubt it is a question of leaving enough autonomy to the fiction without forbidding it to flirt with history or to spare childhood its upheavals and burnings. Bertrand Solet's 1988 novel, *En Egypte avec Bonaparte* [With Bonaparte in Egypt] shows that even when the conditions for a meeting are present, it may be put off or never take place. The title is deceptive, for young Laplume and Bonaparte experience their campaign in Egypt separately, each in his own way. Even though in young people's fiction the leading roles are held by children or young teenagers, let us remember that the latter are excluded from factual history and to involve them in the great upheavals that have disrupted our civilization would, paradoxically, and because of a series of improbabilities, amount to removing credibility from the historical nature of the work. This is not to question the validity of the documentation on which these novelists base their work, but it defines a tendency that would favor history as a framework for adventures that could occasionally take place elsewhere, at another time.

Procedures and Examples

Let us start with a paradox in which the meeting definitely takes place but is not narrated. Here, it is the reader whom the narrative ellipse deprives of an encounter with the great figures of history, it is the reader whose expectations are unfulfilled. For what reasons? The procedure is used, for example, by Jean-Marc Soyez in *Le Complot de La Bible-d'or* [The Golden Bible plot] of 1989. Soyez sends his hero, Thierry Bonivet, to Cardinal Du Bellay; even if he does not spare his young character a long wait, the reader will nevertheless not see the slightest hint of a fold in the famous cardinal's ecclesiastical robes. There can be no better example of a willingness to pass over an encounter scene during which the historical character is generally required to sacrifice a bit of historical truth and his own prestige to validate all the better the hero's triumph.

Another procedure, also used by Soyez in the same novel, seems to confirm this idea. "Jacques Cartier will come by tomorrow."[3] This sentence allows us to hope for an appearance of the famous sailor in the following chapters, but this promise is never kept. It illustrates one of the possible options in the historical novel for juniors within its self-imposed limits; the author proposes to bring back to life important figures from the past, but the better known a personage is, the less chance he has to appear in the narrative. Here, fiction is vying with history but it avoids encroaching too far into its territory.

These "ghosts of history" seem to exist on the frontier of a universe that the child-hero is only very rarely invited to cross. They are there, behind the curtain, behind the door, or else at the back of the crowd, but always beyond reach. It is Amerigo, a little ten-year-old boy, who is present, but from afar, at the return of Columbus's ship *Nina* to the port of Lisbon on 4 March 1493, and Sophie, the narrator of *La Seule Amie du roi* [The king's only friend] of 1995, who catches a glimpse of King Louis XVII busy reading but who will never go near him. Can this reluctance to bring historical figures to the forefront be interpreted as a new attitude towards history?

The Status of the Child and the Adolescent

In this type of novel, it is unavoidable that the novelist endows his child and teenaged characters with the leading roles, but what is their attitude towards history to be, how are they going to live it? Strangely, two different ideas about this coexist.

In the first, the child and the teenager are witnesses and observers of history. Thus, Alice Piguet, in *Temps d'Orage* [Stormy times] of 1970, is careful to keep her two little girls outside of the political events that dominate Paris in the reign of Charles IX, away from the Saint Bartholomew massacres, even if Henriette Pamiers sees them from an upper window. Is this an attempt to spare children's sensitivities? Not to pass over the events in silence, but not to involve in them the heroes with whom young readers will identify? To maintain a certain distance between the brutality of the event and the conscience of the reader? The author is mainly seeking to give an account of the daily life of a period by recounting the friendship of two little girls, one of whom is Protestant and the other Catholic. While this novel defends tolerance, it also maintains the illusion of the existence of two historical worlds, one belonging to the great figures of history, full of blood and tumult, and one belonging to ordinary people who are little inclined to take part in convulsions that do not concern them.

In the second concept, the child and the adolescent are active mainly because they are at the vortex of a whirlwind of adventures that sometimes leads them to a meeting with history. In Noguès' *Mon Pays sous les eaux* [My country under water], published in 1988, Peet contributes to the defeat of Louis XIV in the Low Countries. Often, the child and the teenager find themselves entrusted with missions as messengers or they replace faltering or wounded adults. Géraud Mounier in *Au siège de La Rochelle* [At the siege of La Rochelle] of 1995 manages to transmit a message from the Governor of L'Ile de Ré, which is being attacked by the English, to Cardinal de Richelieu, whom he will never see except from afar. The young hero carries out a mission that a soldier at the end of his strength has not been able to accomplish. This is where their contribution to authentic history lies. But even if there are still kings and countries to be saved, the authors often make a pact with history, even to the point of inventing plots that give the best part to the adolescent. Fiction seems to be seconding history, but it is always a history that misleads, a history that is deceptive.

The Status of the Historical Figure

Alice Piguet's novel *Temps d'Orage* develops a pessimistic view of its historical characters by which, without being accused of all evils, they are made responsible for the country's misfortunes. Hubert-Richou's novel shares in this condemnation: "The twists and turns of politics will cause the wretched people to suffer for a long time yet."[4] Perhaps that might explain why those historical characters are relegated to the sidelines and involvement with them is avoided. Their words are reported, their actions are cited, but they hardly have any right to live in fiction's domain. Just as they place the child and teenaged characters on the frontiers of history, these novelists keep their historical characters on the edge of fiction. As these characters exist above all to be objects of conversation, they are singularly lacking in substance; it seems to me that they fully deserve the epithet "ghosts of history" used earlier.

THE ENCOUNTER

The third type of situation under consideration is the one in which the meeting between the child or adolescent and the historical personage is allowed to take place. Historical fiction's odds are then doubled; to endow fictional characters with an historical appearance and to create a novelistic dimension for historical figures of primary importance. If by chance the narrative were to fail to satisfy this condition, the charm would probably be broken; the novel would lose its credibility by being unsuccessful at creating the illusion upon which it is all based. It therefore needs historical characters who talk, feel and think and child and adolescent characters who are involved in the life of the city. In a certain sense, each of them must borrow from the other in order to exist.

Fiction to the Aid of History?

As in some of the preceding novels,[5] there emerges here a will-centered, civic-minded concept of history. The finest example illustrating this is to be found in the novels of Odile Weulersse who, even as she brings ancient civilizations back to life, often presents her readers with young heroes who are not only headstrong and resourceful but who also have a well developed civic sense. Hence, in one of her most popular works, of 1985, *Le Messager d'Athènes* [The messenger from Athens], the personal fate of young Timokles intersects the course of history at a powerful moment in the history of ancient Greece, and the young hero must follow a path that leads him to save Athenian democracy and Greece from the Persian invasion, even if he does not take part in the decisive battle of Marathon which brings the novel to a close.

This type of historical fiction shows a preference for moments of great crisis in which the hero's destiny is at stake at the same time as the destiny of a nation or a regime. We might wonder if, behind the principle requiring the course of history to remain untouched, there is a suggestion of a defence of the established order. It is true that the historical novel, whether it is intended for adults or for younger people, is recognizable more easily in the characters who serve the existing power, on which they thus confer greater legitimacy. It would be very difficult to find in historical fiction for young people any adolescent or child characters who are in rebellion against the established order unless it is already contested and threatened. This means that young heroes can join the ranks of the rebels and the revolutionaries of 1789, 1848 or the Paris Commune but never, to our knowledge, the groups who oppose a Louis XIV or a Bonaparte.

The Encounter: The Child, the Adolescent and the Historical Figure

One of the primary functions of the meeting between the two characters is to stress the role played by the intervention of the historical figure, that is, to insure the young hero's salvation. It is a scene of redemption but also one of acknowledgment and consecration which simultaneously puts an end to the distress of the young hero by sweeping away the obstacles that might still lie before him and by brushing aside the final threats that were lying in wait for him. However, it also brings to an end the story of an initiation that finishes with a kind of enthronement that, in its own way, announces the end of childhood and the integration into the world of adults. If the story can then come to an end, it is because the hero is in the process of finding his place in society which, through the agency of the historical figure, recognizes his talent, his difference and his personality. The encounter with Lorenzo de' Medici in Noguès' *Silvio ou l'été florentin* [Silvio, or The Florentine summer] (1969, 1983), saves the young boy from prison but at the same time consecrates his talent as a painter. In other words, he has finished with childhood and has now found his niche.

This pattern can undergo many variations and the meeting scene can serve many other purposes, but it seems to me that its basic value is acknowledgement. The meeting builds a bridge between fiction and history by summing up, if not the stakes in the conflict, at least the state of the forces that are present.

The Status of the Child, the Adolescent
and the Historical Figure

It has already been stressed that the child and the adolescent are no longer locked into passive roles on the stage of history and—by joining a cause that goes beyond themselves: the safety of a nation, of a regime, of a great personage—they become actors in their own destinies. One dimension these characters acquire has been less emphasized; in the novels where the meeting takes place, the young hero functions like a double of the historical figure for whom he becomes a kind of agent. Resorting to the fictional character allows authors to avoid multiplying the appearances of the historical figure on the novel's stage while at the same time they are unwinding the thread of history. This is perhaps why the meetings are often brief, accidental and unforeseen, although inevitable.

It is not simply a matter of considering the scenes where an historical figure entrusts a mission to the young fictional hero, as in *Le Vœu du paon* [The peacock's vow] by Noguès (1987): Raymond Blasco and Raymond de Mirepoix, two essential figures in the resurrection of Catharism, appear unexpectedly to ask the two heroes of the story to bear a message suggesting a raising of the Chateau de Monségur from its ruins.

The word "double" is used in the sense that the fictional character becomes an incarnation of the historical figure with whom he consorted. Huguette Pirotte turns her young hero, Gui de Montlhéry, into a real copy of Baudoin, the leper king of Jerusalem (*Le Rubis du roi lépreux*). This is the way that the child or the adolescent protagonist finds a part of his identity in the historical model with which he can identify. Here, the historical figures acquire a breadth and a psychological density that they did not have in the other novels and they need this if they are going to be a match for characters who have no existence outside of the story and are not limited by what history teaches us. The salvation of fiction depends on their ability to exist in the universe of the novel. So these characters, as Umberto Eco reminds us, are going to accomplish actions inscribed in encyclopedias alongside of actions imagined by the novelist.[6] King Baudoin of Jerusalem therefore enters into a campaign against Saladin but at the same time becomes a friend to the hero of *Le Rubis du roi lépreux*. Great historical figures are thus condemned to compromising with their own history in order to gain a foothold in the novel. In fact, it is astonishing to see how certain historical characters become so entangled in fiction that the novelists who make use of them manage to avoid the historical scenes which brought them fame.

The three approaches identified show that there exists a variety of combinations which in a sense favor a type of adventure novel in an historical setting, for it is perhaps the pattern that best corresponds to a certain "re-creative" idea of literature for young people ("re-creative" in the highest sense of the term). It is also the model that most easily offers the young hero a role equal to the hopes of young readers. The "real historical novel" has not been abandoned in the least; we find attention paid to the daily life of people in earlier times, a fact that can situate the child and the adolescent in the centre of the historical universe, to the point of making them historical figures in the sense that Lukacs intended; because of this, the novel gains in authenticity what it loses in flamboyant deeds.

Historical fiction for young people therefore follows in the footsteps of the adult historical novel, the only difference being that it often chooses a hero of its readers' age, who has a mentality and a psychology close to those of our children and teenagers. As for the historical figure, young people's historical fiction differs from the adult historical novel in two ways: a more noticeable reluctance to build the narrative around a great figure in history and a strong hesitation at thrusting historical personages into the arena of fiction. Most often these figures do in fact remain on the periphery of the story and when they do enter into the universe of the novel, it is almost always to remain in the background, in the shadow of the child and the adolescent. This concession is the means by which the work can reach its reader and, through its story, lightly touch upon history.

NOTES
The author wishes to thank Alain Jean-Bart for his participation in this project.

    1. Quoted by Michel Raimond in *Le Roman depuis la Révolution* (Paris: Armand Colin, 1981), p. 23.

    2. Georges Lukacs, *Le Roman historique* (Paris: Payot, 1972).

    3. Jean-Marc Soyez, *Le Complot de La Bible-d'or* (Paris: Hachette, 1989), p. 9.

    4. Gérard Hubert-Richou, *Au siège de La Rochelle* (Paris: Hachette, 1995), p. 29.

    5. Soyez, *Bible-d'or* and Jean-Côme Noguès, *Mon Pays sous les eaux* (Paris: Editions G. P., 1971).

    6. Umberto Eco, *Apostille au "Nom de la Rose"* (Paris: Grasset, 1985), p. 86. (Published in English as "Postscript" to *The Name of the Rose*, translated by William Weaver, New York: Harcourt Brace, 1984.)

REFERENCES
Children's books
Brisou-Pellen, Evelyne. *Les Portes de Vannes*. Paris: Hachette, Le Livre de Poche Jeunesse, 1993.

Chérer, Sophie. *La Seule Amie du roi*. Paris: L'Ecole des Loisirs, Neuf, 1995.

Hubert-Richou, Gérard. *Au siège de La Rochelle*. Paris: Hachette, Le Livre de Poche Jeunesse, 1995.

Jay, Annie. *Complot à Versailles*. Paris: Hachette, Le Livre de Poche Jeunesse, 1993.

Lavolle, L. N. *L'Acrobate de Minos*. 1966. Paris: Editions de l'Amitié, G. T. Rageot, 1983 [reissued Paris: Rageot-Editeur, Cascade, 1991].

Noguès, Jean-Côme. *Embuscade à la pierre clouée*. Paris: Editions de l'Amitié; G. T. Rageot, Les Maîtres de l'Aventure, 1989.

―――. *Mon Pays sous les eaux*. Paris: Editions G. P., 1971. New ed. Paris: Flammarion, Castor Poche, 1988.

———. *Silvio ou l'été florentin*. 1969. Paris: Editions de l'Amitié; G. T. Rageot, Les Maîtres de l'Aventure, 1984.

———. *Le Vœu du paon*. Paris: Gallimard, Folio Junior, 1987.

Pays, Jean-François. *La Dernière Charge*. Paris: Société Nouvelle des Editions G. P., Bibliothèque Rouge et Or, 1963.

Piguet, Alice. *Temps d'orage*. Paris: Editions G. P., Bibliothèque Rouge et Or, 1970.

Pirotte, Huguette. *Le Rubis du roi lépreux*. Paris: Rageot, Bibliothèque de l'Amitié, 1968.

———. *Le Perroquet d'Américo*. Paris: Rageot, Bibliothèque de l'Amitié, 1971.

Solet, Bertrand. *En Egypte avec Bonaparte*. Paris: Hachette, Le Livre de Poche Jeunesse, 1988.

Soncarrieu, Gérard. *Le Premier Tour du monde*. Paris: Hachette, Le Livre de Poche Jeunesse, 1996.

Soyez, Jean-Marc. *Le Complot de La Bible-d'or*. Paris: Hachette, Le Livre de Poche Jeunesse, 1989.

Weulersse, Odile. *Le Messager d'Athènes*. Paris: Hachette, Le Livre de Poche Jeunesse, 1985.

———. *Tumulte à Rome*. Paris: Hachette, Le Livre de Poche Jeunesse, 1997.

Criticism

Bator, Robert, ed. *Signposts to Criticism of Children's Literature*. Chicago: American Library Association, 1983.

Eco, Umberto. *Apostille au "Nom de la rose."* Paris: Grasset, Le Livre de Poche, Biblio Essais, 1985. Translated as "Postscript" to *The Name of the Rose* (New York: Harcourt Brace, 1984.)

Hunt, Peter, ed. *International Companion Encyclopedia of Children's Literature*. London: Routledge, 1996.

Lukacs, Georges. *Le Roman historique*. Paris: Payot, 1972.

Nélod, Gilles. *Panorama du roman historique*. Paris: Editions SODI, 1969.

Nikolajeva, Maria. *Children's Literature Comes of Age: Toward a New Aesthetic*. New York: Garland Publishing, 1996.

Raimond, Michel. *Le Roman depuis la Révolution*. Paris: Armand Colin, 1981.

"Le Roman historique." *Revue d'Histoire Littéraire de la France* 2–3 (mars–juin 1975).

Soriano, Marc. "Histoire et littérature pour la jeunesse." In *Guide de la littérature pour la jeunesse*. Paris: Flammarion, 1975.

Vérot, Marguerite. "Un Roman historique nouveau." In *Tendances actuelles de la littérature pour la jeunesse*. Paris: Magnard, L'Ecole, Lecture en Liberté, 1975.

Vindt, Gérard et Giraud, Nicole. *Les Grands Romans historiques*. Paris: Bordas, 1991.

2

From Literary Text to Literary Field: Boys' Fiction in Norway between the Two World Wars; a Re-reading

Rolf Romøren

Books written specifically for adolescent boys used to be immensely popular in Norway, the period of their greatest flourishing falling between the two World Wars. They became a vehicle that brought children's literature to an expanding public (and market) of pastime readers. But schools and public libraries, not to speak of academia, were wary of popularity and skeptical towards this expanding genre, as they were to girls' books. After the Second World War such books were no longer read for a number of reasons, including changing attitudes and ideologies of gender and race, as well as changes in the book market and in literary institutions.

To understand the rise and fall of this genre, it is necessary to look beyond the texts themselves, even though these challenged literary taste in many ways by reflecting modernity (inventions and discoveries), and by making use of formulaic elements, not to mention fantasy. I shall try to contextualize the genre, and will argue that boys' fiction can be examined profitably with reference to the concept of "cultural field," introduced in the works of the French sociologist and anthropologist Pierre Bourdieu.[1]

Beginning with a brief discussion of some central aspects of Bourdieu's theory and analysis of the concept of cultural field, I will consider the actual reception of boys' fiction between the two World Wars, and then compare this to the assessment of the same books in the 1960s and 1970s in the context of the history of Norwegian children's literature. This leads to a final discussion of patterns of historical narrative as they relate to the history of boys' books and the cultural field.

BOURDIEU AND THE CULTURAL FIELD

Literary criticism, as well as the shaping of a literary history, involves not only establishing a system of differences between writers of different moral and aesthetic quality, but also determining at the outset which are the "quality" writers who constitute the relevant canon. Literary histories inevitably also become narratives. Matters of aesthetic discrimination and canon-formation are vital to the establishing of such a dominant genre as the boys' book was in the market of the 1930s. What is observed here may well be what Bourdieu calls "the symbolic production of the work, that is, the production of the value of the work or, which amounts to the same thing, of belief in the value of the work." Answers to the questions, "Who is a good writer?" and "How did boys' fiction obtain, defend and eventually lose its position?" may thus be sought in the perspectives and arguments of Bourdieu, who in his works considers both competing relations between agents and positions within a system, and the dynamic and historical changes in the same system. In *The Field of Cultural Production* (1993) and most extensively in *The Rules of Art* (1996), Bourdieu does this when studying Flaubert's work in relation to the emerging modern cultural institutions of France in the nineteenth century.[2]

The Concepts of *Field* and *Habitus*

Two of Bourdieu's key concepts, that of *field* (French *champ*) and *habitus*, are deeply interdependent. A *field* may be defined as a competitive system of social relations which functions according to its own specific logic or rules. "A field," Bourdieu writes, "is a space in which a game takes place (*espace de jeu*), a field of objective relations between individuals or institutions who are competing for the same stake."[3] What, then, is at stake at this site of struggle or battlefield? It is Bourdieu's assumption that the aim of the agents is to rule the field, to become the authority which has the power to confer legitimacy on or withdraw it from other participants in the game. Such a position of dominance is achieved by amassing the maximum amount of the specific kind of symbolic capital current in the field. Cultural (or more specifically literary) fields have their own specific mechanisms of selection and canon-formation. To obtain legitimacy, agents in the field have to use many and varied strategies.

These strategies are rarely perceived as such by the agents themselves, but are instead what Bourdieu terms a *habitus*, a sort of internalized "feel for the game." The habitus of the agents may be seen as the totality of general dispositions acquired through practical experience of the field, which in turn generates new practices and perceptions. It must be admitted that Bourdieu's concept of habitus is a very difficult and elusive one. The reason may simply be his very ambitious balancing between subjectivism and objectivism. Instead of tracing the motives for actions within the cultural field in individual biography, the focus is relational: it is shaped and exercises its influence according to its position within the field. Thus the habitus of male journalists and critics, female librarians and teachers, male and female academics may be very much alike in the interplay of the cultural field.

If we turn to the literary field of the 1930s, we may observe how the production of boys' fiction and the production of the value of boys' fiction are relational: there was a battle going on between the established publishing houses rich in both economic and symbolic capital, and there were modern pretenders trying to build up their own symbolic and economic capital by different means. Like children's literature in general, boys' fiction is part of a subfield on the verge of what Bourdieu calls the *field of restricted production* where high art and serious literature dominate, and where the competition between agents is based primarily on symbolic profit. But children's literature and boys' fiction are also situated near the *field of large-scale production*, sometimes referred to as mass or popular literature, heavily dependant on economic success. In a way we may trace the habitus of the pretenders, with their dual address, through an institutional perspective as well. On the one hand, the producers of boys' fiction (writers and publishers) were seeking acknowledgment in the form of symbolic capital from the literary establishment of critics, librarians and teachers. On the other hand, there is a subordination to the demands of economic capital, not to speak of those of the readers themselves. It is likely that we shall also see how the habitus of the historian of children's literature seems to have been relational as well, shaped in close connection with the canonizing efforts of the general or adult literary field in the 1960s and 1970s in an attempt to raise the prestige of the subfield of children's literature.

As already indicated, in a cultural or literary field competition often concerns the authority inherent in recognition, canon-formation and prestige. In all parts of the cultural field symbolic and cultural capital counts, of course, but even more so in the subfield of restricted production, with its "production for producers." In this part of the field Bourdieu often finds what he calls "an economic world reversed," based on the logic of "winner loses," since financial success may well become a liability, for example, if an author of serious literature writes a best seller.

BOYS' FICTION IN THE LITERARY FIELD
OF THE 1930s

How did the competing participants discuss boys' fiction in the 1920s and 1930s, and what were their positions? A study of the files of Windju Simonsen—the leading publisher of boys' fiction between 1926 and the outbreak of World War II—as well as of the firm's series of boys' books themselves (107 volumes) readily discloses the struggle going on to obtain dominance in the field, and the polarization between symbolic and economic capital. Windju Simonsen specialized in children's literature, competing with the larger and more established publishing houses, which based their accumulation of symbolic capital on the production of serious literature for adults, while at the same time an important part of their commercial basis was the less prestigious production of children's literature.

What we see in this period is the expansion of production that was less dependant on cultural and pedagogical institutions, and more dependant on the market. But to call this production purely commercial would be jumping to conclusions. It is rather a question of production without a security net, which was made possible, especially in the 1930s, by the increase in children's pastime reading. The agents in the field do demonstrate artistic ambitions as well. The many boys'-book competitions at the time were of course motivated by the publicity they generated and its positive effect on the market. On the other hand, the Windju Simonsen files show that the assessments of the juries not only refer to what they expect will fascinate the young readers, but to aesthetic and moral values as well.

Correspondence between editors and authors reveals different positions within the field: if the publisher is reluctant to accept a manuscript, he advises the author to turn to other publishers, either those rich enough (in economic as well as symbolic capital) to practise the system of the "economic world reversed," or those with lower artistic ambitions in the subfield of large-scale production, or even those publishing boys' magazines.

Newspaper reviews of children's literature were then rare and superficial, but well-established and celebrated male critics had a soft spot for boys' books. This is illustrated by the reception of one well-known boys' book from another non-establishment publisher, Nationalforlaget [The National Publishing House]. The book, *Panterfolk og Graabein* [Panthers and Wolves], was published in 1929. It is a mystery novel, or detective story, written by a well-known journalist and author of travel books and detective stories, Trygve Hjorth Johansen.[4] The Panthers and the Wolves are two rival gangs, the Panthers consisting of a colorful thieving gypsy tribe, while the Wolves are characterized as ordinary criminals, led by the thoroughly corrupt and highly unsympathetic Swede, Mr. Nelson. The boy heroes of the story are confronted with the rival gangs, and they side with the gypsies, since one of them is unjustly prosecuted for murder. The book is highly readable even today, due partly to the remarkable portrait of the gypsy boy Kaschmir, a half-Norwegian literary relative of Huck Finn, and partly to the imaginative language and unmistakable anti-establishment tone of the book.

There follow some brief assessments of the book from different positions within the literary field: those of the publisher, the critics, and a contemporary writer and editor. As for the reputation of the book in literary history, contemporary assessments differed immensely from that of Sonja Hagemann, the distinguished historian of children's literature, some thirty years later.

The position of the publisher can in this case be observed in some of the advertising material. Not surprisingly, the large number of copies already sold forms an important argument. But an added parenthesis—"(even though the Association of Booksellers do not dare sell it!)"—lends a subversive flavor to the book. The explanation for this is that the publisher, Nationalforlaget, having learnt modern publishing methods in America, refused to adapt to the established system of regulation in the Norwegian market, and was therefore to some extent boycotted and even considered "lowbrow." But popularity and subversiveness, traits linking book production to the subfield of large-scale production, are supplemented by statements of literary quality. The language of *Panterfolk* is, according to the advertisements, "lively and artistic" and demonstrates "an outstanding sense of style."

Established critics in the Oslo newspapers, mostly male journalists who very rarely focused on childrens' literature, were unanimous in praising the book for its extraordinary suspense, as well as for the lively and artistic language and the author's outstanding sense of style (as mentioned in the publicity). A few years later, in 1936, there was an extensive debate on boys' books in the leading Oslo newspaper *Dagbladet,* in which respected authors and critics took part. Nils Johan Rud, the author, publisher and editor, concluded:

Are the snobs inside and outside the Norwegian Authors' Association aware of the fact that we have a living writer of boys' books highly comparable to the canonized classics . . . ? Do the acknowledged cultural magazines know that we have an author who addresses the precious man in the boy, an author internationally esteemed even, . . . who is successful in the Danish, Swedish, Czech, Hungarian, Italian, German, French and English languages? His boys' books are sold in twelve different countries. In Germany they have printed close to a hundred thousand copies, and this month his splendid book, *Panthers and Wolves*, was released by one of England's largest publishers. (Translated from *Dagbladet,* 21 October 1936)

Rud's comments indicate some of the different positions taken within the cultural field, and how agents expose their "feel for the game" (*habitus*), as well as the fundamental conflicts of the field itself. (More could be said about other prominent opinions, such as those of professional groups dominated by women — librarians, who were tolerant towards boys' fiction, and pedagogues and child psychologists, who were mostly very critical. These will be documented in a future treatment.)

BOYS' FICTION IN THE NORWEGIAN LITERARY HISTORY OF THE 1960s AND 1970s
Sonja Hagemann (1898–1983) wrote about *Panterfolk og Graabein* in her history of children's literature in 1973:

Apparently the writers of children's literature in the 1920s and 1930s regarded criminal acts as a legitimate means of creating suspense. This is thoroughly demonstrated by Hjorth Johansen's book *Panthers and Wolves* (1929). The book was apparently written quickly off the cuff, prompted by a boys' book competition organized by the National Publishing House. . . . It is a wild story, containing safe-crackings, robberies, poisoning and murder, and appealing to boys' sense of exitement with both logic and fantasy. The plot is complicated and unrealistic, all sorts of horrors being heaped up. The book, being of surprisingly low literary value from the hands of Hjorth Johansen, may serve as a paradigm of the sort of boys' books flourishing in those years. This is literature without merit ("low literature") for children, based on technical writing skills and a certain ingenuity. (Translated from *Barnelitteratur i Norge 1914–1970,* p. 84)

Hagemann, the pioneer woman critic who, between 1965 and 1974, wrote the first extensive (three volume) history of Norwegian children's literature, was originally a graduate in economics. Her stated ambition was to describe children's literature as part of social history in general, and of education and child-rearing in particular. But the genre of literary history itself, and the fact that she also sought to obtain an academic degree in literature, made her develop her habitus in other directions as well, especially in her last volume, covering the period from 1914 to 1970. Like many other literary historians after the Second World War she became dedicated to the task of (re)shaping the national identity.[5]

Hagemann took on the task of defining a national canon of children's literature, paying special attention to writers who were also recognized and established as writers of adult literature. (A majority of the writers who wrote for children had won esteem as writers for adults as well.) Her definition of the "Golden Age" of children's literature around the end of the previous century combined both perspectives; following the moral and aesthetic preferences of the already declared Golden Age of adult literature a couple of decades earlier, she defined the aesthetic norm for children's literature as "critical realism."

As for the development of children's literature in Norway, Hagemann's Golden Age was inevitably followed by a period of decline and a restoration. Boys' fiction (and girls' fiction as well) served Hagemann as the ultimate example of the moral and literary decay of the inter-war period of decline. These genres were (literally speaking) foreign to the canon-formation she was trying to establish. This seems evident in the English summary of her Volume III:

A fairly thorough analysis is given of *authors worthy of being mentioned*, not underestimating their importance as exponents of tendencies within children's literature of this epoch. They are markedly Norwegian. Some *authors of less importance* are briefly mentioned as representatives of literary trends collected from children's literature of the Western world. To a certain degree these are *alien elements* in Norwegian children's books, at their best distinguished by the suspense of the work itself, not by suspense brought about from more or less improbable exterior occurrence. (p. 294, emphasis added)

To be fair to Hagemann, the traditional task of all national literary histories has been to establish a national canon. The problem is of course that you cannot do this without indirectly defining the "otherness" of other literatures—either as containing "alien elements" or being literatures of "less importance" or even "literature that removes itself from reality" (p. 296), central premises in Hagemann's aesthetics. In Hagemann's case this resulted in an elimination of both boys' and, to an even larger extent, girls' books.

BOYS' BOOKS IN THE HISTORICAL NARRATIVE
OF CHILDREN'S LITERATURE

All histories become narratives in one way or another, and in this case the narrative conforms to the pattern of the Bildungsroman, with its narrative structure Home–Departure–Adventure and Trials–Homecoming. The important part here is the idea of the return home, which I regard as a pre-modern and religious concept of story, with roots going back to the Bible (The Prodigal Son) and certain fairy tales, like Little Red Riding Hood.[6] (As we know, the Adventure and Trials in this context may be said to smack more of Trials and Tribulations, as in John Bunyan.)

According to Habermas, the hero of Goethe's defining Bildungsroman, *Wilhelm Meister* lives in a modern universe, and has to adapt to that condition, but he is nevertheless bound to pre-modern ideals. That is exactly Hagemann's dilemma when describing adventurous boys' fiction as a sort of moral and aesthetic decline, in contrast to the preceding Golden Age period. The subsequent return home in the postwar period meant a return to more stable moral values and to "artistic" writing for children, which meant more realistic and mimetic modes and less formula and fantasy writing. This was due to dramatic changes within the Norwegian book market as well. From the 1960s onwards, Norwegian "serious" fiction was heavily subsidized,[7] which gave children's literature a more secure place within the field of restricted production. Thus Sonja Hagemann's narrative aimed to win for children's literature—as well as research into children's literature—the same degree of recognition (Bourdieu would say "consecration" and "prestige") as the revered adult literature.

This is an ambition not unknown in our own time, most recently evidenced by Maria Nikolajeva's study *Children's Literature Comes of Age* (1996). It is a fascinating thought that the growing independence from pedagogics and the corresponding aesthetic liberation which she has described have their parallel in the development of the independence of the cultural field—and the development of the aesthetics of modernism more than a century before—as described by Bourdieu. But the narratives differ: Hagemann's Bildungsroman is that of returning home to the mimetic and realistic novel with an explicit moral. Nikolajeva and Bourdieu (in *The Rules of Art*) seem to be telling another type of (hi)story; it takes the form of the more modern *Entwicklungsroman*, not ending with the reconciliation and homecoming, but rather with the gaining of independence and a new identity, that of modernism—where the writer presents the reader with a crooked mirror. In the words of Maria Nikolajeva, "modern children's literature, like modern literature and art in general, is not a mirror which reflects reality precisely as it is (or is supposed to be); it is rather a crooked mirror which distorts reality, divides it into hundreds of puzzle pieces which readers are challenged to put together" (p. 98).

It is clear that this ambition has affected the trajectory of boys' fiction from the 1920s to this day. In my view, boys' fiction cannot be satisfactorily interpreted either within the metaphorical frame of the classic and ethical Bildungsroman or within the metaphorical frame of the aesthetically and ethically liberated and modernist Entwicklungsroman. The real challenge, therefore, is to account for the fascination these partly canonical and trivial, partly traditional and "realistic," and partly subversive books had for their readers. To do this one must scrutinize not only the books themselves, but their fate ("trajectory" is another of Bourdieu's concepts) within the whole system of "the symbolic production of the work" or "the belief in the value of the work" (*The Field of Cultural Production*, 1993, p. 37). With Bourdieu this issue can be viewed as a

struggle between positions and dispositions within the cultural field of the time—
and ever after.

NOTES

Throughout, unattributed translations are my own.

1. It can be argued that Bourdieu's works have clear affinities with other contextual
studies of literature, such as J. B. Thompson's "depth hermeneutics," in *Ideology and
Modern Culture: Critical Social Theory in the Era of Mass Communication* (Cambridge:
Polity Press, 1990), pp. 281–91, and the "new historicism" of Steven Greenblatt's essay
"Towards a Poetics of Culture," in H. A. Veeser, *The New Historicism* (New York:
Routledge, 1989), pp. 1–14.

2. I do not have the space here to expound Bourdieu's general philosophy of
science, as set out in *An Invitation to Reflexive Sociology*, with Loïc Wacquant (Chicago:
University of Chicago Press, 1992), or the more popular *Distinction: A Social Critique of
the Judgement of Taste* (Cambridge, Mass.: Harvard University Press, 1984), or the very
lucid analysis of academic life and culture in *Homo Academicus* (Cambridge: Polity
Press, 1989). The latter analysis would be very helpful in understanding the efforts of
researchers in children's literature striving to obtain status and recognition within this
subfield of academic research—as well as for understanding the traditional split between
the "book people" and the "child people" within the subfield of children's literature itself.

3. Pierre Bourdieu, *Questions de sociologie* (Paris: Minuit, 1980), p. 197.

4. Hjorth Johansen wrote five novels for boys, the trilogy about the gipsy boy
Kaschmir, and two sea novels. In addition he wrote detective stories, essays, books of
travels and other records from all parts of the world.

5. Evidently this is an international phenomenon. An outstanding example is R. W.
B. Lewis, *The American Adam* (1955).

6. Benneth A. Brockman has written an interesting article on the literary "taming" of
the subversive romance of Robin Hood, performed by the humanists in the sixteenth
century, a process which forged it into a Bildungsroman. From the fairly clear original
conception of Robin Hood as a rather brutal yeoman outlaw—the kind we would expect
from our knowledge of actual medieval brigands—he was turned into a prince of thieves
and a courtly gentleman. The article bears the significant title "Robin Hood and the
Invention of Children's Literature," in *Children's Literature*, vol. 10 (New Haven: Yale
University Press, 1982), pp. 1–17.

7. At the time when Sonja Hagemann wrote her literary history, from the end of the
1960s onwards, a public cultural fund was established in Norway to purchase 1,000
copies of new Norwegian fiction for libraries, thus encouraging the subfield of small-scale
production of both children's and adult literature.

REFERENCES

Bourdieu, Pierre. *Questions de sociologie*. Paris: Minuit, 1980.
———. *Distinction: A Social Critique of the Judgement of Taste*. Cambridge, Mass.:
Harvard University Press, 1984.
———. *Homo Academicus*. Cambridge: Polity Press, 1989.
———. *An Invitation to Reflexive Sociology*, with Loïc Wacquant. Chicago: University
of Chicago Press, 1992.
———. *The Field of Cultural Production*. Cambridge: Polity Press, 1993.
———. *The Rules of Art*. Cambridge: Polity Press, 1996.
Brockman, Benneth A. "Robin Hood and the Invention of Children's Literature." In
Children's Literature, Vol. 10. New Haven: Yale University Press, 1982: 1–17.

Cawelti, John G. *Formula Stories as Art and Popular Culture.* Chicago: University of Chicago Press, 1976.

Greenblatt, Stephen "Towards a Poetics of Culture." In *The New Historicism.* Ed. H. A. Veeser. New York: Routledge, 1989.

Hagemann, Sonja. *Barnelitteratur i Norge 1914-1970.* Oslo: Aschehoug, 1974.

Hjorth Johansen, Trygve. *Kaschmir.* Oslo: Nasjonalforlaget, 1930.

———. *Panterfolk og Graabein.* Oslo: Nasjonalforlaget, 1929.

Nikolajeva, Maria. *Children's Literature Comes of Age. Towards a New Aesthetic.* New York: Garland Publishing, 1996.

Thompson, J. B. *Ideology and Modern Culture: Critical Social Theory in the Era of Mass Communication.* Cambridge: Polity Press, 1990.

Zipes, Jack, ed. *The Trials and Tribulations of Little Red Riding Hood.* New York: Routledge, 1993.

3

Historical Friction: Shifting Ideas of Objective Reality in History and Fiction

Deborah Stevenson

As with children's literature as a whole, the treatment of history in books for children has been subject to changes in approach. Scholarship for juvenile history has become more sophisticated, for example, now requiring source notes and often drawing on original sources and interviews rather than entirely depending on histories written for adults. Perhaps the most noticeable recent trend in fiction and nonfiction has been a challenge to old textbook viewpoints of chauvinism of all kinds and to utter certainty in the rightness of received history, a shift that has resulted in changing emphases in biographies, war chronicles that include perspectives other than those of the victors, and historical fiction that finds drama in the domestic as well as the military.

A new trend, however, seems to be starting. Jim Murphy's *The Great Fire* (1995) uses four different eyewitness accounts of the Chicago Fire of 1871 to analyze not only a significant historical conflagration but how and why that event became historicized as it did. Steven Jaffe's *Who Were the Founding Fathers? Two Hundred Years of Reinventing American History* (1996) explores the continual reification of the creators of America by subsequent generations. Lori Lee Wilson's *The Salem Witch Trials* (1997) appears as the first entry in a series titled "How History Is Invented," a bold statement on the nature of historiography unprecedented in American children's literature. Nonfiction for children is beginning tentatively to examine the process of history-making itself, to examine historiographic questions of objectivity and subjectivity, and to call into question the existence of a completely knowable history.

Earlier trends have paved the way for some of these changes. The insistence of writers such as Jean Fritz on the nonfictionality of history and on the necessity for research in primary, not just secondary, sources and the increasing demand for the inclusion of notes and source citations in histories for children have also shaped the concept of history in children's books. If history were pure and objective mimesis, secondary sources should be as effective as primary. These changes have resulted in an approach simultaneously more scientific and more admitting of the impossibility of scientific accuracy. It eventually leads, as it does in the histories discussed here, to considering the very creation of history. Murphy describes history that was first believed and then disbelieved, history whose causes are the teller more than the events.[1] Jaffe emphasizes the Founding Fathers' self-creation as historical figures in addition to later generations' reinventions. Wilson examines how written histories influenced views of the past even more than events did, pointing to different strands in the witchcraft argument and their effect on historical views over the years. They all examine how history was created through individual viewpoints, and how those viewpoints are not necessarily reconcilable.

Louis Mink suggests that this failure of historical narratives to "aggregate into more comprehensive narratives" has been the cause of conceptual discomfort, and that "the traditional way of avoiding it, and very analgesic it has been, too, is to distinguish between 'objectivity' and 'subjectivity.'"[2] Juvenile history has begun to join Mink in questioning this convenient and misleading dichotomy. More than a mere acknowledgment of a subjectivity, this approach suggests the absence of anything but subjectivity. In an era when questions of false memory and the problems of personal history have become both a legal issue and a matter for study, the reliability of individual accounts of public history can hardly remain unchallenged. Children's literature has been uneasy with many forms of equivocality and ambiguity; few histories have discussed discrepancies between their accounts and other juvenile histories, and in general such books have wished simply to ignore the unreconcilable aspects to which human histories are prone. These newer histories not only account for discrepancies between books but also set up paradoxes within themselves. Historical theorists William H. Thornton and Songok Han Thornton offer the idea that "our own pluralist position could carry the motto 'in mendacio veritas,' meaning in practical terms that the best antidote for one willful bias is a broad exposure to contrary biases"; drawing on Norman Mailer's assertion that "sometimes the only way you can tell the truth is by a comparison of the lies," they state that "that methodology is precisely the project of postmodern historiography."[3] So too does the acknowledged multivocality of narratives such as *The Great Fire* mean that their internal contradictions may remain similarly unresolved in texts—and in readers.

Narrative style may increase in importance as such histories require evaluation of varied reports rather than attempting to crown one account as the truth. Currently, nonfiction for children tends to be judged differently than fiction. Lackluster writing is often forgiven if facts are valid and clearly arrayed;

conversely, brilliant writing in a nonfiction book rarely receives specific qualitative attention. Nonfiction (aside from folklore and poetry, which are treated quite differently) rarely wins "open" awards that do not specify genre; in a recent discussion on the Usenet newsgroup rec.arts.books.childrens, some participants opined that nonfiction simply was not literature. It is certainly often treated as if it were not.

These newer histories overtly place history into the category of narrative, emphasizing the story in history. Hayden White points out that "histories gain part of their explanatory effect by their success in making stories out of mere chronicles."[4] As Natalie Zemon Davis notes in *Fiction in the Archives* (1987), the emplotment of fact in fictional form is hardly a bastard recent invention but rather an old tradition that perhaps suggests a fundamental way in which narrative shapes human understanding. And if facts are indeterminate, reporting the facts is not sufficient for merit in a nonfiction text. It is notable that Jim Murphy and Albert Marrin, two of the major figures in the new history, do not just organize and research well but also write with distinction.

Ultimately, this trend means that children's literature is witnessing if not the actual death, at least the serious illness of the concept of "Universal History," which, in the words of Louis Mink, believes "that past actuality is an untold story and that there is a right way to tell it even though only in part."[5] These texts demonstrate an erosion of the faith in the Rankean concept of the past "as it really happened."[6] History is at best now global cartography, where an exact reality cannot be conveyed on two-dimensional paper and chroniclers resort to the Mercator projection, which includes gross distortions but nonetheless offers information sufficient to chart a course.

This approach brings with it possible obstacles and limitations. Perhaps this historiographic tack will become an historical equivalent of postmodern irony, which practice in children's literature seems less often to be a questioning of narrative reality than to be a formulaic inversion that is itself becoming the norm. Lesser practitioners may consider the acknowledgment of subjectivity and emphasis on story license to return to the fictionalized histories of the past.

One might also hypothesize that such extension of possibility means that all well-written histories are created equal. That is both extreme and incorrect. I do not expect that some beautifully written Holocaust revisionist history for children is going to appear, but even if it did, the notion that facts are elusive and no one is in complete possession of them does not preclude the possibility of some claims simply being wrong. These histories are not considering all viewpoints as equal—Wilson nowhere suggests or implies that Cotton Mather may have been right about the Salem Village witches—they are merely suggesting that none of them possesses complete objective truth. In answer to what Bernd Engler terms the "notorious question of what historical representations are representations of if they are far from being representations of some universally comprehensible historical reality,"[7] they offer written history as a metaphor for the past, as a self-aware representation of a kind of understanding of another time. They work in the space between "history," meaning the past, and "history," meaning a written account of a time gone by.

Nor do historians writing for children seem prepared to take the final step of examining their own historiographic role. Neither Jaffe nor Murphy points out what subjectivity might mean to their own examinations; Jaffe does not consider how he himself uses the Founding Fathers, nor what effect his history, like those he describes, might have on future histories. In some senses this literature's refusal to make its investigation complete leaves it wanting things both ways— other histories are suspect, but not this one. It is doubtful, however, that any of these authors intend to privilege their work at the expense of their sources. This self-exemption is more a result of an essential belief in the pragmatic utility of their endeavors that historiographic theoreticians either do not support or cannot reconcile with their philosophy. As with cartography, contemporary children's history believes in its practical usages regardless of the inherent flaws of its recording. It is also quite likely that these authors are aware and hopeful of the possibility that an alert young reader may use the implications of their texts to question those texts themselves.

Fiction, dedicated as it tends to be to presenting individual and idiosyncratic accounts of human existence, is certainly a genre dependent on the vagaries of individual viewpoint. Yet contemporary American children's fiction, historical or not, rarely challenges narrative and authorial authority. Works of fiction treat this viewpoint as an objective, if not necessarily complete, account of the facts, and historical fiction seems particularly intent to establish its version as The Truth rather than to challenge the possibility of truth at all. Unreliable narrators are scarce to nonexistent; self-questioning texts rarer still. And perhaps for good reason—young and inexperienced readers often have difficulty understanding that which is not made manifest; they often fail to comprehend dramatic irony. In general, narrators tell the truth, and texts assume the truth to be accessible.

This is not to say historical fiction for children is changeless; it is not. Formerly unchallenged heroes are viewed more equivocally, those previously unheard of are now treated as heroes, and some protagonists may not be heroes at all. Microhistory is gaining ground on macrohistory, and the accounts now are of ordinary folk who may never have met anyone famous. Books such as Patricia MacLachlan's *Sarah, Plain and Tall* (1985) argue for the expanding of history with previously untold stories. Historical fiction for children has long embraced a sort of Sherman and Mr. Peabody historicism (a term I take from the old time-travel cartoon involving those characters), where the protagonist child encounters a famous historical personage and provides a small but crucial part of a significant event. While this pattern has a certain predictability, it also establishes the precedent for focusing not entirely on the Great Man, but on the lower soldier in the ranks, the working boy, the Johnny Tremain.[8] Historical fiction has indeed embraced the broadening of the notions of history with a vengeance, with notable works such as *My Brother Sam Is Dead* (1974) undercutting received versions of history, while countless others including *Sarah, Plain and Tall* and *Lyddie* (1991) depict the lives of the marginalized as important aspects of the past, whether real historical figures appear in the texts or not.

The genre nonetheless seems unmoved by the newer currents in history. Effects of postmodernism are difficult to detect in juvenile historical fiction; the texts remain cohesive and constructed. Even the less linear formats of author Paul Fleischman in his *Bull Run* (1993), a series of soliloquies, or his *Dateline: Troy* (1996), a retelling of classic history offset by news reports of parallel contemporary incidents, are unusual mainly by contrast with other examples of this very conservative genre. Even Michael Dorris' *Morning Girl* (1992), which depicts the rich life of the Taino Indians "discovered" by Columbus, makes its ironic point overt with the inclusion of Columbus' dismissive summation of the people he had encountered. There is only one recent work of historical fiction that I know of in which the historical truth remains unstated; this is Gudrun Pausewang's *The Final Journey* (1996), which is not American and which treats a topic—the true fate of those riding in cattle cars to a concentration camp—the global knowledge of which is sufficient to override the difficulty young readers have in inferring truths from context.

And, unlike historiography, historical fiction seems determined to avoid the question of subjectivity. Like history, works in the genre depend on historical facts; historical fiction is supposed to get its history "right." Its "right" may challenge a previous orthodoxy of belief (*Morning Girl* undermines the Columbus-as-hero doctrine, *My Brother Sam Is Dead* challenges the glory of the American revolution), yet the belief in historical fact *qua* fact is if anything stronger. The problem with those orthodox beliefs, such books suggest, is that they were based on incomplete facts, and these narratives intend to tell the rest of the story. Now that the story is complete, we finally understand the real or full historical truth. There is no acknowledgment of the possibility that a full picture is unobtainable and that the rest of the story too is incomplete (for instance, *Morning Girl* evades the issue of the Taino practice of slavery by never mentioning it). Historical fiction seems either to be conveying orthodox history or to consider itself to be *repairing* history—in essence, creating a new orthodoxy while clinging firmly to the Rankean doctrine of history.

Many such books engage in disguised time travel, where the protagonist corrects his era or his era's thinking by introducing contemporary viewpoints; as James Kerr points out in his discussion of Sir Walter Scott, "the classical historical novel has as its object not history, but ideology."[9] While some of this ideological work comes merely from the selection of certain events for literary treatment and the focus on certain aspects of those subjects, some of it comes from overt editorializing and alteration. The chances are slim, for instance, that a contemporary American author would willingly create a frontier protagonist who believed unquestioningly in manifest destiny. To meet contemporary definitions of the "good guy," protagonists must be produced and viewed anachronistically. To the historical novelist, "history becomes at once his alibi and his enemy."[10]

"Everyone knows," says Mink, "that what makes a story good is different from what, if anything, makes it true";[11] more and more, however, the merit of the story itself constitutes truth of a kind, offering a reality preferable, in some eyes, to the nonfiction that impedes wholehearted belief with its more conservative attributions, reservations, and contradictions. Historical fiction for children acts as history improved, a superior replacement for the real but flawed thing; it creates history that history has not been sufficiently generous to supply of its own accord. Its practitioners often describe its creation in terms of opposition to nonfiction history, and they bemoan the drawbacks of nonfiction treatments— often while simultaneously wishing their books to be mistaken for historical reality. Patricia Clapp talks of the necessity for historical fiction to "stick to the facts" and unblushingly terms her piece on historical fiction "Letting History Speak for Itself"; Joan Blos happily attests to the fact that some young readers believe her *A Gathering of Days* (1979) to be a real diary.[12] This is a genre based on an unacknowledged irony: it intends to sharpen the sense of historical realism by producing imaginary history.

Yet this implication of the unreal nature of accounts of history is common to both these genres; as Joan Blos notes, both her fictional history and objective documentary are narrative performances. The responses to this implication simply differ, with historical fiction choosing to recast history in the fictional mode it considers more real and the newer histories drawing attention to the unreality of such cohesive and reconciled accounts. Both of these genres seek a new form of history, rejecting straightforward, unquestioning Great Men and Deeds and Dates historicism. Both history and historical fiction have been reluctant to admit the author's lack of authority.

Some contemporary theorists will go so far as to say the only difference between history and fiction is intentionality—it's a history if that's what the author thought it was. Scholarship on adult texts intimates that the two genres increasingly overlap. The distinction between them may become vaguer as the divisions continue to blur; writers will probably begin to acknowledge their own ambivalent intentions and catalogers will grow ever more frustrated.

This eventuality would seem to be a long way off for children's literature. In the meantime, however, the genres are starting to trade places. History is offering possibilities, while fiction offers certainty. Though unprepared to take the final step and challenge its own authority, history is undercutting the authority of narrative while historical fiction still clings to it, asserting itself as more real than fact because it is a better story. The suspension of disbelief for fiction expands to suspend all equivocality; fiction exists to create belief while history begins to constitute itself as making cohesive belief impossible. The change in historical fiction has been the embrace of relativity, the idea that someone else is going to see a different part of the past, but history begins to suggest the possibility of complete subjectivity—that no one is seeing the past quite right and that the stories will not match up. Books such as *Morning Girl* are devoted to telling how history lies, whereas the new historiographical nonfiction is telling where it lies.

Even while fiction makes its claim for a finite and knowable past, history asserts its subjective and shifting nature. Fiction tells the previously untold story, but nonfiction begins to address the problem of its quixotic task: telling the ultimately untellable story that is history.

NOTES
    1. Jim Murphy, *The Great Fire* (New York: Scholastic, 1995), pp. 75, 76.

2. Louis O. Mink, "Narrative Form as a Cognitive Instrument" in *The Writing of History: Literary Form and Historical Understanding,* ed. Robert H. Canary and Henry Kozicki (Madison: The University of Wisconsin Press, 1978), p. 142.

3. William H. Thornton and Songok Han Thornton, "Toward a Cultural Prosaics: Postmodern Realism in the New Literary Historiography," *Mosaic* 26, 4 (Fall 1993), p. 123.

4. Hayden White, "The Historical Text as Literary Artifact," in *The Writing of History: Literary Form and Historical Understanding,* ed. Robert H. Canary and Henry Kozicki (Madison: The University of Wisconsin Press, 1978), p. 46.

5. Mink, "Narrative Form," p. 143.

6. From Leopold von Ranke (1795–1886), sometimes called "the father of objective history."

7. Bernd Engler, "The Dismemberment of Clio: Fictionality, Narrativity, and the Construction of Historical Reality in Historiographic Metafiction," in *Historiographic Metafiction in Modern American and Canadian Literature,* ed. Bernd Engler and Kurt Müller (Paderborn: Ferdinand Schöningh, 1994), p. 25.

8. Esther Forbes' enduringly popular Newbery Medal-winning novel, *Johnny Tremain,* features a young apprentice silversmith in revolutionary-era Boston.

9. James Kerr, *Fiction Against History: Scott as Storyteller* (Cambridge: Cambridge University Press, 1989), p. 3.

10. Ibid., p. 2.

11. Mink, "Narrative Form," pp. 129–30.

12. Patricia Clapp, "Letting History Speak for Itself," in *The Voice of the Narrator in Children's Literature: Insights from Writers and Critics,* ed. Charlotte F. Otten and Gary D. Schmidt (Westport, Conn.: Greenwood Press, 1989), p. 273; Joan W. Blos, "'I, Catherine Cabot Hall. . . .' The Journal as Historical Fiction," in *The Voice of the Narrator,* p. 281.

REFERENCES

Blos, Joan W. *A Gathering of Days: A New England Girl's Journal,* 1830–32. New York: Scribner, 1979.

———. "'I, Catherine Cabot Hall. . . .' The Journal as Historical Fiction." In *The Voice of the Narrator in Children's Literature: Insights from Writers and Critics.* Ed. Charlotte F. Otten and Gary D. Schmidt. New York: Greenwood Press, 1989: 278–81.

Clapp, Patricia. "Letting History Speak for Itself." In *The Voice of the Narrator in Children's Literature: Insights from Writers and Critics.* Ed. Charlotte F. Otten and Gary D. Schmidt. New York: Greenwood Press, 1989: 269–75.

Collier, Christopher and Lincoln, James. *My Brother Sam Is Dead.* New York: Four Winds, 1974.

Dorris, Michael. *Morning Girl.* New York: Hyperion, 1992.

Engler, Bernd. "The Dismemberment of Clio: Fictionality, Narrativity, and the Construction of Historical Reality in Historiographic Metafiction." In *Historiographic Metafiction in Modern American and Canadian Literature.* Ed. Bernd Engler and Kurt Müller. Paderborn: Ferdinand Schöningh, 1994: 13–33.

Fleischman, Paul. *Bull Run.* New York: HarperCollins, 1993.

———. *Dateline: Troy.* Cambridge, Mass.: Candlewick, 1996.

Forbes, Esther. *Johnny Tremain.* Boston: Houghton Mifflin, 1943.

Jaffe, Steven H. *Who Were the Founding Fathers?: Two Hundred Years of Reinventing American History.* New York: Holt, 1996.

Kerr, James. *Fiction Against History: Scott as Storyteller.* Cambridge: Cambridge University Press, 1989.

MacLachlan, Patricia. *Sarah, Plain and Tall*. New York: Harper, 1985.

Mink, Louis O. "Narrative Form as a Cognitive Instrument." In *The Writing of History: Literary Form and Historical Understanding*. Ed. Robert H. Canary and Henry Kozicki. Madison: The University of Wisconsin Press, 1978: 129–58.

Murphy, Jim. *The Great Fire*. New York: Scholastic, 1995.

Paterson, Katherine. *Lyddie*. New York: Dutton, 1991.

Pausewang, Gudrun. *The Final Journey*. New York: Viking, 1996.

Thornton, William H. and Thornton, Songok Han. "Toward a Cultural Prosaics: Postmodern Realism in the New Literary Historiography." *Mosaic* 26,4 (Fall 1993): 119–42.

White, Hayden. "The Historical Text as Literary Artifact." In *The Writing of History: Literary Form and Historical Understanding*. Ed. Robert H. Canary and Henry Kozicki. Madison: The University of Wisconsin Press, 1978: 41–62.

Wilson, Lori Lee. *The Salem Witch Trials: How History Is Invented*. Minneapolis: Lerner, 1997.

Zemon Davis, Natalie. *Fiction in the Archives*. Stanford: Stanford University Press, 1987.

Part II

Myths Modernized:
Adapting Archetypes from Fact and Fiction

Photo 4.1
The second battle, from Maurice Boutet de Monvel, *Jeanne d'Arc*, Paris: Plon, Nourrit, 1896, pp. 26-27.

4

In and Out of History:
Jeanne d'Arc by Maurice Boutet de Monvel

Isabelle Nières-Chevrel

In 1896 Maurice Boutet de Monvel published *Jeanne d'Arc* [Joan of Arc],[1] later considered to be his master work. It is a family rather than just a children's picture book, even if, in his foreword (*Avant-Propos*), Boutet de Monvel addresses himself directly to children and although many child groupings are present in the illustrations. The book takes its place among a hundred other biographies dedicated to Joan of Arc in the last third of the nineteenth century. The medieval heroine stood at the heart of a national ideological debate, as she was claimed in turn by the Catholic monarchist Right and by the secular republican Left.[2]

Why might Boutet de Monvel have created an historical picture book, the only one in the entire collection of his work? Did the great children's book illustrator have a new light to shed on this historical character? And why are we still interested in this book when nearly all the others have been forgotten?

My answer is that Boutet de Monvel does not only show a real concern for historical precision, but that he also offers a vision of Joan of Arc which is above the ideological appropriations of both political camps.

AN HISTORICAL PICTURE BOOK

Despite Boutet's independence, *Jeanne d'Arc* is nevertheless set within the political debates of its time. With the Franco-Prussian War of 1870–71, France had lost Alsace and part of Lorraine to Germany. Through the ensuing years the rhetoric of revenge was developed: France, by means of a just war with Germany, intended to retrieve the lost provinces. In addition, France had been a republic for 20 years; established in 1875, the new regime had to fight at length strong royalist and anti-republican opposition.

The Catholic right wing held Joan of Arc as a heroine of the "true France." As Joan had driven the English out of France, it was now necessary to drive the Prussians out of Alsace and Lorraine. At the same time, Joan of Arc was also a patriotic character for the secular and republican left wing, being seen as a daughter of the people who, betrayed by the Church and by her king, was delivered into the hands of the enemy. At a time of great political tension, the most famous character of the Hundred Years War was thus an acclaimed symbol for both sides of the political divide.

In his foreword, Boutet de Monvel reminds readers of the circumstances of Joan's mission: a century-long war with the English, France's national independence threatened, a defaulting monarchy. He contrasts the indolence of the Dauphin with the energy and the faith of Joan of Arc, a little peasant girl from Lorraine, by framing his foreword with two illustrations that affirm the divine inspiration of the girl and the triumph of her arms: the sword and spear of the warrior, the distaff of the shepherdess, the standard of faith. He portrays Joan as a model of piety and courage. The end of the foreword is aimed at children to make them remember Joan of Arc "on the day when your country has need of all your courage" (p. 4). On which day? For what purpose? The frontispiece explains what the *Avant-Propos* leaves unresolved. It shows Joan leading modern French soldiers into battle, wearing uniforms which would still be worn to fight against Germany in 1914. But the book itself does not repeat this initial patriotic message.

What can we sense in this book of the political debate surrounding Joan of Arc? Boutet de Monvel builds his work on the image of a young girl of humble origin totally moved by her faith. He does not dispute her hearing Voices and shows us her own vision of the archangel Michael. The people do not doubt her mission and any reservation is attributed to the king and to the doctors of the Church. All through the book, Boutet de Monvel spares the Church's responsibility as much as history allows and concentrates his attacks on the king's court. However, one can observe a significant discrepancy in the coronation scene. The text describes Joan of Arc as throwing herself at the king's feet, "embracing his knees and weeping copiously" (p. 31), while the picture carefully separates Joan and the king, each kneeling before the double authority of God and the Church.

The mission entrusted to Joan by the archangel ended with the coronation. By going beyond that, did Joan cause her own downfall? This interpretation, supported by the most conservative Catholic tendency, was replaced in the last years of the century by the idea of a Christlike dimension to Joan's destiny, taking her through martyrdom to sainthood. Everything leads us to believe that this interpretation is Boutet de Monvel's. When Joan tells the people that she has been "sold and betrayed" and that she will soon be "delivered over to death" (p. 35), we may notice that the stained-glass window dominating the scene shows

Christ's nativity. The picture book is not the work of a militant and the unavoidable element of modern reinterpretation remains unobtrusive.

Boutet de Monvel strived to stay true to history, in both words and drawings. He gives his narrative a cautiously medieval tone and moreover makes use of the works of historians. He cites several of Joan's own utterances and mentions the written sources provided by the trial records, "the journal of the siege" (p. 15) and "the old chronicle" (p. 31). The court clerks, represented doing their task, appear to be writing precisely what we are reading. As an illustrator he shows a high degree of accuracy in the representation of interiors, of arms and shields, as well as of costumes (photo 4. 1). The conception of the book is based upon very precise historical information. The only anachronism is in the gesticulation of the characters. He depicts some of Joan's gestures: the arm thrust toward the theologians of Poitiers, the arm raised to oppose the battle chiefs (photo 4. 2). Such gestures would have been impossible in a medieval representation because they would have indicated the folly or the immodesty of Joan.[3] Boutet de Monvel's attention to medieval culture is referential, not aesthetic. The aesthetic models are not generally to be found within medieval iconography, but, for example, in Puvis de Chavannes among contemporaries, and in Piero della Francesca among the old masters (of the early Renaissance); similarly, the rich brocades are inspired by William Morris, and the battle scenes by Paolo Uccello.[4]

Boutet de Monvel's intellectual requirements saved him from the medieval gimmickry of the time which was fatal to his contemporaries, whether painters or illustrators. His extreme stylistic care prevented him from falling into the pathos which is all too inviting in a treatment of Joan of Arc's life.

THE PROGRESS OF AN ILLUSTRATOR

Boutet de Monvel viewed his book as an artist and it is enlightening to contrast his *Jeanne d'Arc* with two of his previous works, *Chansons et rondes pour les petits enfants* of 1883 [Songs and roundelays for little ones] and *Chansons de France pour les petits Français* of 1884 [French songs for the children of France]. In these two picture books, he perfected his unique style: the immobility, the long flowing array of characters, the play on colors and variation of form, the foreshortening and absence of perspective, the placing of the inset within the picture, and the combined vision of two facing pages. In *Jeanne d'Arc*, he re-used and elaborated upon two devices employed in the earlier works: the elaboration of variety in costumes and the setting of the text within the illustrated pages.

He liked uniforms because they give an aesthetic homogeneity under the cover of a simple referential fidelity. Around Joan, whose clothing prevalently has a blue tint, he plays with variations for the costumes of the four groups portrayed: the courtiers, the churchmen, the soldiers and the people. The rich material of the court people stands in opposition not only to Joan's dress but also to the plain clothing of the people and the garments of the ecclesiastics. He never uses a color at the maximum intensity. He avoids the bright red which should have been given to the cardinal during the coronation ceremony, and all reds in the picture book are either dark or muted. He makes it possible for the soldiers to be seen alongside the different fabrics, contrasting the warm tints of the clothing to the grey netting of the chain mail and also to the volume of a helmet reflecting the light. Some pages play with the encounter of the different groups, others with the variations occurring within the same group. The most remarkable example is in the trial scene, where the artist experiments with the color of the dresses, as well as the posture—and even the placement of the hands—of the characters (see photo 4. 2).

In order to allow text and illustration to cohabit within the page, he re-used the technique of the inset adopted previously in his song compilations. These insets are usually horizontal rectangles resting on the lower margin of the picture, which echo the oblong shape of the book. A few insets laid vertically seem to interrupt the story and mark transitions, except for the first one which has the obvious role of a cover; there we do not see what Joan is seeing, namely the apparitions of Saint Margaret and Saint Catherine.

Boutet de Monvel explores two new ways of using the inset. One inset mimes the stairs climbed by Joan to reach the king. What can appear banal becomes subtle when, in the basilica, the "stair" shape underlines the presence of three spaces: the congregation's, Joan's and that of God. The second innovation appears at the end of the first battle. This is the anchoring of the inset on the image's upper margin. The same arrangement is repeated at the end of the second battle, for Joan's capture, during the four scenes in prison and, finally, when she is put to death. The result is that the space above Joan shrinks. This lay-out seems to demonstrate what is stronger than Joan: the death of men, captivity, the vice in which she is caught, the stake. With this book, the artist discovered a use of space which he had not explored previously. It was his first narrative work and thus the first one allowing a graphic expression of emotions.

In conceiving an historical picture book, Boutet de Monvel was confronted with problems that were new to him. First, he needed to organize the sequential progression to create a continuous narrative. The stages in Joan's life cannot be rendered by a series of vignettes, a method he used to illustrate the fables of La Fontaine. Group scenes and battle blows require quite a different breadth. On the other hand, the battles—great subjects for historical painting—imposed on him the need to solve a fundamental problem: how to translate motion graphically? This was a definite challenge for an artist who based his aesthetic on immobilizing gestures.

The narrative continuity is ensured by the text, and the pictures work as a series of paintings. The artist avoids perspective and clearly prefers frontal scenes. The procession before Orléans made it possible for him to arrange the crowd in a lateral movement, but he could not go any further. Crowds and war require other solutions to achieve disorder within the structure of lines. He attempted a first kind of response in the entry into Orléans with the high position of Joan in the center, the accumulation of characters, the double diverging and converging movements toward Joan. But Boutet de Monvel's best solutions are to be found in the battle scenes. With images striped by banners, swords and spears, he structures disorder and reconciles dynamic and mass effects, discovering at the same time the benefit he had gained from the double-page construction of the book.

During the first battle, the French are retreating in disarray when Joan rushes to restart the assault and to bring them to victory; the retreating movement on the left-hand page runs into Joan's advancing movement on the right-hand page. The banner crossing over the frame of the page shows her courage and the certainty of the victory. In the second battle, the movement goes across the entire double page stretching from right to left—which means, in a sense, driving the English army out of the picture. The double-page arrangement opposes the right-hand page, structured by the three horses in the foreground, to the collapsing of bodies on the left-hand page (see photo 4. 1). In the last battle, the shock comes this time from the left and the collapsing takes place on the right around Joan, her body out of balance, ready to fall. The banner does not, this time, cross over the limits of the frame.

These three battles call for two remarks. They are sanitized battles. Only one screaming and bloody face can be found in the second battle. It is a kind of self-censorship (already found in the song-books), but it is also an aversion of the artist for all that is shapeless. One must also note that the first two battle scenes—which are victories—are followed by two mourning scenes: Joan overwhelmed by those "who died without confession" (p. 20), and Joan comforting a dying soldier. Here the artist takes advantage of the structure of the book. The thrill of victory hides its misery, its price in deaths. To turn the page is to unveil what the patriotic exaltation tries to hide. There is no such scene after the third battle, because this time it is Joan's own death which will follow. Why a picture book on Joan of Arc? Perhaps to let children see what they are not told: that after heroism one finds mourning, and that being chosen means being alone.

VOCATION AND ISOLATION

It is not so much Joan's heroic glory nor her exemplary nature that the artist foregrounds, but her isolation. The choice of the format is significant. Boutet de Monvel chooses an oblong format (24.8 x 32 cms), slightly larger than that of his previous books (23 x 27), but not as huge as the picture books of *Job* (36.2 x 28.2) or the *Jeanne d'Arc* by Funck-Brentano (37.5 x 30).[5] There is an ideological value to the choice of format. The vertical format is that of glory, of the hero standing, of the full-length portrait and of statues. The oblong format, on the contrary, inserts the character within space. In Boutet de Monvel's book, there is no full-length portrait of Joan, only one equestrian statue on the frontispiece. Moreover, sometimes one must seek Joan in the picture, without always being certain of identifying her within the group.

The book reveals Joan's life between the initial solitude of the meadow and the final solitude of the stake. The very first image shows signs of Joan's destiny. The distaff points to the church and links the shepherdess—without her knowledge—to the choir of the church. The archangel Michael appears only in the following pages, to turn her life into a destiny. Joan does not choose, she is chosen by God.

The signs of Joan being divinely chosen are of course the apparitions which enclose the narrative, but also the light and the Cross. The *leitmotif* of the Cross first appears sketched on the soldiers' clothes or as religious emblems worn by priests. During the trial a divine sign is substituted for these human ones. God's light comes toward Joan and forms a Cross. The clerks who occupied the left angle during the first questioning have moved to the right in order for the Cross to spread over the ground (see photo 4. 2). The artist links light and divine presence. In the basilica, the light comes from a mysterious somewhere else: To the candles' flames on the left-hand page, the artist adds the golden glints on the altar; on the right-hand page, the sun shines to illuminate the stained-glass window as it will illuminate the Cross ten pages later.

Joan's vocation is also a tragic fate and, for the first time in his work, Boutet de Monvel explores the expressive quality of colors and makes use of a "chromatic dramatisation." Purple, color of reference for a bishop's clothing, will become the color of Joan's destiny. Purple is indeed chosen for the book cover and it sets the tone.[6] Quite absent at the beginning, purplish-blue shades progressively take over the last third of the book and reflect Joan's distress: her prayer in the basilica and the announcement that she will soon die, her defeat at Compiègne, her capture (the artist portrays her cornered in the angle of the fireplace), her attempt at escape (the text says "She fell at the foot of the wall and remained there as dead," p. 39), her stay in prison, her trial. The flames of the stake and the light of Joan's faith eventually disperse this color of anguish.

The last picture of the book figures a crown of thorns entwined with a crown of laurel. Glory cannot be separated from martyrdom. In the text Boutet de Monvel tells the heroic destiny of Joan of Arc but in the pictures shows the isolation which is the price to be paid in exchange.

This discussion of Boutet de Monvel's work links three historical periods: I have reflected at the turn of the twentieth century upon a book published at the turn of the nineteenth century, a book which presents an historical character of the fifteenth century. Because he applied artistic priorities to his book, Boutet de Monvel did not fall into the trap of indoctrination and his work still remains alive for us today. The vocation for an extraordinary destiny, isolation and martyrdom do not belong to any particular time and his book can be interpreted in two different ways. It might be read as an illustrated text or flipped through as a story told in pictures, as a series of scenes which are linked together by reminders of a story already known. The latter was probably the approach of many children in and since 1896. Such is reading today. It is not because of his text but because of his pictures that we are still enchanted by Boutet de Monvel's *Jeanne d'Arc*.

NOTES

1.   Maurice Boutet de Monvel, *Jeanne d'Arc* (Paris: Plon, Nourrit, no date [1896]). A first American translation, *Joan of Arc*, was published in 1907 (New York: Century Company), reprinted in 1912, and then in 1916 (Philadelphia: McKay). The book has also been published in England (London: Chiswick Press, 1915) under the title *The Story of*

Joan of Arc, told by Pamela Glenconner. Taken from the French of Boutet de Monvel. Concerning the international fame of the artist, see Friedrich C. Heller, "Maurice Boutet de Monvel als illustrator von Kinderbüchen," *Schiefertafel: Zeitschrift für Kinder-und-Jugendbuchforschung,* Jahrgang VII, n° 1 (April 1984).

2. Gerd Krumeich, *Jeanne à travers l'Histoire* (Paris: Albin Michel, 1993).

3. Jean-Claude Schmitt, *La raison des gestes dans l'Occident médiéval* (Paris: Gallimard, 1990).

4. Pierre Puvis de Chavannes (1824–98) was the foremost French painter of decorative murals of his time; Piero della Francesca (c.1420–92), a leading early Renaissance painter, experimented with perspective and created the series of frescoes on the *Story of the True Cross* in the church of San Francesco in Arezzo, Italy; William Morris (1834–96) sought to revive medieval craftsmanship and impressed his vision on all branches of British design; the Florentine painter Paolo Uccello (1397–1475), preoccupied with patterning and perspective, created his masterpiece in the three panels of *The Rout of San Romano* (c.1455), now located in Florence, London and Paris, the latter in the Louvre from 1861, where no doubt Boutet de Monvel examined it.

5. Fr Funck-Brentano, *Jeanne d'Arc* (Paris: Boivin, 1912).

6. There have also been editions with a beige cover.

Photo 4.2
The trial, from Maurice Boutet de Monvel, *Jeanne d'Arc*
(Paris: Plon, Nourrit, 1896), pp. 44–45.

5

Reinventing the Maid: Images of Joan of Arc in French and English Children's Literature

Penny Brown

Since Jeanne d'Arc was burned at the stake on 30 May 1431 her life and achievements have been interpreted in many different ways, in the light of cultural, political and personal preoccupations, in historical accounts, fiction and the visual arts. The appeal of her youth, integrity and heroism has transcended national and ideological boundaries; she has been appropriated as a symbol of uncompromising courage in England (Christabel Pankhurst's followers wore badges of the suffragette leader in which she looked like Joan of Arc) just as she has for many decades been venerated in France by adherents of both the Left and the Right. Over the centuries she has been variously appropriated by historians and artists as a Renaissance Amazon, as the standard-bearer for Catholicism during the Reformation, as Romanticism's child of Nature and as the symbol of the Resistance during the German Occupation of France in the Second World War, amongst other manifestations.[1] In literature, she has always been a popular and emotive figure: from Shakespeare's "foul fiend of France" (*Henry VI, Part I*) to Shaw's feisty peasant girl defying her learned judges in *Saint Joan*, from Michelet's spirit of France to Jean Anouilh's "lark" who dies to preserve the purity of her individual truth against the forces of oppression and compromise.[2]

Just as her life has been repeatedly reinvented for adults as a perfect subject for romance, so it is also a great story for young readers and especially for young female readers; as in the tradition of fairy tales, Joan is a youthful hero of humble origins who succeeds in changing the course of history. In her short life she argues her cause against powerful and learned adults with childlike forthrightness and simplicity and wins their support; she is responsible for the coronation of her king; she leads an army which obeys her commands, takes part in military exploits extraordinary for her class, age and sex, and so saves her country from a foreign foe; she is adored by the common people but also becomes the object of bitter envy, scorn and hatred, and, finally, is condemned as a heretic and witch by her enemies and put to death. She dies a martyr and, in so doing, achieves eternal fame and glory and subsequently is declared a saint. Her strength, determination and appeal are seen to derive from her youthful innocence, intuition and clarity of insight. Joan transcends the limited role prescribed by her society for her sex and achieves everything and more that a male hero might achieve, challenging the beliefs and interests of patriarchy represented by the Church and State. In the late nineteenth and early twentieth centuries when dynamic, boyish girl characters were gaining in popularity in children's books (Jo in Louisa May Alcott's *Little Women,* and the tomboys of Enid Blyton and Arthur Ransome), Joan represented the epitome of what a young female could achieve and, most significantly, had achieved in reality.

The titles of some of the works devoted to her story in English and French suggest the fascination of the extraordinary: *The Wonderful Exploits of the Maid of Orleans* (1815), *The Maid Marvellous* (1916), *The Girl in White Armour: The True Story of Joan* (1927), *Joan of Arc or the Story of a Girl Warrior* (1929), *La vie merveilleuse de Jeanne d'Arc* [The miraculous life of Joan of Arc] (1940), and *La merveilleuse aventure de Jeanne d'Arc* [The miraculous adventure of Joan of Arc] (1956). Her life is, in all respects, an adventure story, the stuff of myth and fairy tale, and as such is traditionally represented in clear stages, instantly recognizable and memorable (her Domrémy childhood looking after sheep, the hearing of her Voices, her successes in battle, the coronation, trial and death by fire), with particular focus on the three seminal phases of inspiration, military triumph and martyrdom. These have become entrenched in iconography through the centuries, underlining a clearly organized and readily grasped linear progression toward a dramatic culmination; the stained-glass windows at Orléans Cathedral, the hugely popular Epinal prints and generations of school textbooks bear witness to this. The ways in which these stages are represented in texts which recount her life and achievements tell us a great deal about the times in which they were written and the ideologies that the authors wished to promote.

Joan's story has always had its problematic areas, however, which have exercised successive generations of commentators just as they did her judges at Rouen. The anomaly of Joan's defiance of the conventions of feminine behavior and decorum, not only usurping the male privileges of military and political endeavor but also assuming male dress, needed to be addressed and justified in the nineteenth century as much as it did in the fifteenth and sixteenth. The question of whether her Voices were truly divine inspiration, or something more akin to extreme individualistic instinct as Romantic humanists insisted, remains a difficult one to this day.[3] Moreover, a central challenge facing English writers has, of course, been that of making a sympathetic hero of an historical personage whose mission was to thwart English attempts to conquer France. This was more of a problem in the nineteenth century when it was less easy to imagine and accept that one's country could be in the wrong, the perpetrator of politically and morally criminal acts against other nations and humanity itself. This essay explores these questions by considering six areas of Joan's story (her appearance and background, her Voices, the battles, the trial, her death, the role of the English) and the implications of how they were represented in books for young readers in France and England in the nineteenth and twentieth centuries; in particular I focus on Maurice Boutet de Monvel's picture book *Jeanne d'Arc* (1896), with its gorgeous detailed and stylized illustrations in striking flat colors (influenced by Kate Greenaway, Japanese prints and medieval illuminated manuscripts and sometimes referred to as fin-de-siècle Uccello) and Evelyn Everett Green's *Called of Her Country* (1903), a fictionalized romance from an author known for wholesome books for girls.[4]

Because no contemporary image done from life survives, Joan's appearance in portraiture and literary representation has varied according to changing concepts of beauty, dignity and strength. Shakespeare suggested that Joan became beautiful through her communion with fiends.[5] A 1912 French version of her life evokes the prejudices of the day by describing her as tall and stately with black hair and a white skin unusual in a peasant.[6] Evelyn Everett Green, writing in 1903, described Joan in almost pre-Raphaelite terms as "a maiden slim and tall" with long tresses of wavy hair that "looked dark till the sun touched them, and then glowed like burnished gold."[7] Her face is pale with great dark eyes and a sweet, serene expression that renders all who see her "lost in admiration of her beauty" (p. 32). This beauty is not, however, a commonplace earthly one, but is seen emphatically as indefinable and not of this world, which underlines the saintliness, the "something of miracle and mystery" (p. 33) which Green attributes to Joan from the start. It seems that the issue of her looks was always a significant one, physical attractiveness being, for many writers, a necessary concomitant of virtue. Boutet de Monvel adheres to traditional nineteenth-century literary conventions associating goodness, piety and grace with blondness and portrays her initially as a demure young girl with her hair in a bun. Although traditional imaging of Joan has tended to focus on an androgynous figure with her trademark pageboy haircut and apparel, there is frequently, nevertheless, a detectable latent sexuality in the figure of the child/woman ("La Pucelle," the Maid) dressed as a boy as depicted in biographical accounts. This unexpectedly surfaces in Green's description of Joan in an interview with the king as "a slim, boy-like figure . . . , her cheeks a little flushed, her slender fingers tightly entwined, the breath coming and going through her parted lips" (p. 282). In illustrations in later twentieth-century versions, however, Joan is resolutely given the looks of a character from a *Schoolgirl's Own* annual—sturdy and capable with a fresh face and a neat bob—and on horseback she has something of the air of a pony-club heroine, rather than the ethereal beauty of fifty years earlier.

At her trial, Joan's assumption of male attire was one of the most serious charges levelled because it betokened "unnatural" behavior and went against the teachings of the Church. Although this ceased to be a burning issue (literally) in the twentieth century, overt justifications for it are felt to be necessary in earlier texts. Her garb is frequently endorsed by writers as right and fitting for her circumstances according to the dictates of common sense, as a gift from her greatest admirers, the common people (Boutet de Monvel) or as a specific command of her Voices thus, for the believer, placing the issue beyond question. Understandably, recent versions make little of the issue; the Ladybird publication (1971) opted for the Saints as the origin of the idea while the Kingfisher Explorer book (1979), in the "History Makers" series, attributed it in passing to Baudricourt.[8] The fifteenth-century argument that it served to protect her virginity while in the close company of rough soldiers is not aired in children's books, although some French texts do allude to the need for modesty; indeed the issue of sexuality is largely ignored, her enemies scoffing at her lack of experience rather than indulging in scurrilous innuendo. Generally, the assumption of a different mode of dress is used as a device to signal the dramatic change in Joan's life, the plain woollen dress of the peasant girl exchanged for the armor of a warrior, underlining the immense significance of the transformation wrought by divine command. In Green's novel, the shining white armor and white velvet serve to reinforce the notion of purity, thus avoiding any of the complications suggested by transvestism; however, Joan retains her long tresses for a while, even after donning simple male attire, which perhaps added an extra piquancy to the image, while Boutet de Monvel depicts her in silver armor and a beautiful white tabard embroidered with fleurs-de-lys, long scalloped sleeves flowing from her shoulders like the wings of an angel.

All the texts that I have seen emphasize Joan's simple peasant background, happy childhood and participation in the normal female activities of her age and class. Many stress her dexterity in sewing, spinning and household work and depict her both in the text and in accompanying illustrations minding her father's sheep (or cattle), playing and singing with her friends and caring for the young, sick and poor: a quiet, intensely pious "petite fille modèle" (an ideal child), exemplary in every way. Boutet de Monvel describes her as the best girl in the village and portrays her walking barefoot in a meadow, distaff in hand and a cow at her side. It is easy to detect in such images the lingering influence of the Romantics' privileging of a life lived close to Nature as well as the nineteenth-century cult of the family and the child, and the frequent association with sheep is, of course, evocative of the idea of Christ as the Good Shepherd. The portrayal of this part of her life would obviously appeal to young readers. An illustration in a French primary school textbook of 1957 depicts a Disney-like Joan perched on a well with a large distaff in her hand and a rather knowing smile on her face, a very modern-looking house behind her and a variety of sheep, chickens, farmworkers and farming implements on the flower-strewn grass. The caption reads: "Aimerais-tu passer les vacances dans cette jolie campagne et avoir cette souriante jeune fille pour amie?" (Would you like to spend your holidays in this lovely countryside and be friends with this happy young girl?).[9] The deployment of such an idealized pastoral vision and the continuing emphasis on evidence of her "womanliness" thereafter is an obvious strategy to render acceptable the flagrant rejection of contemporary conventions of passive femininity inherent in her story; thus her grief at leaving her home is frequently highlighted and her caring nature is translated into a deep pity for men wounded in battle, whether friend or enemy. In Green's book she tends an English soldier who surrenders admiringly to her gentleness and she is portrayed as being at her happiest when playing with a small child, thus promoting the traditional feminine qualities of compassion and nurturing which Green's young readers might aspire to emulate, even if they are never called upon to save their country. The anomaly of her position as a warrior is further tackled here by means of the lack of understanding and disapproval of Joan's father, who frowns on his daughter's unfeminine ambitions but is reconciled with her later precisely because of her submissive patience and filial affection, although the reader suspects that the tax exemption granted to Domrémy is a contributing factor (p. 295).

Joan's deeply religious nature is an element strongly emphasized even in otherwise secular works in order to explain what has always been claimed to be the impetus for her mission, the Voices of Saint Michael, Saint Margaret and Saint Catherine. Interestingly, a 1987 version of her story by Harold Nottridge in the "Great Lives" series, while remaining conspicuously neutral on the question of the divine inspiration ("A few have tried to paint her as a saint who could see things invisible to the majority of people . . . [W]e do not know exactly what that power was"), nevertheless evokes the image of St. Francis in the assertion that "It was said that birds would feed readily from her hands."[10] The Voices are seen here as projections of Joan's own faith, stressing—as most modern versions do—that she "believed" they were from God and the accompanying illustration shows Joan kneeling, gazing upwards, accompanied only by birds and rabbits. The Ladybird version also suggests projection, but actually depicts the shadowy figures of the saints hovering before her. Green takes a different approach, employing an interesting narrative strategy to underpin her view. Like Mark Twain's text of 1896, *Personal Recollections of Joan of Arc, by the Sieur Louis de Conte (Her Page and Secretary)*, her narrative is mediated through a contemporary follower of Joan, in this case Jean de Metz, an actual historical figure who became one of the Maid's attendant knights. Employing a double distancing device, Green has her narrator first learn of Joan from a friend who has witnessed her interview with Robert de Baudricourt at Vaucouleurs and describes her outlined in a doorway as with a "halo of pure white light" (p. 8). When Jean sees the Maid for himself, he witnesses her communing with her saints in a wood near her home, a heavenly light shining on her face. Although the watching men see only her rapture, the agitation of the horses and the strange spell that seems to still all nature and keeps the men "as in a dream bound hand and foot by invisible bonds" underlines the mystery before them and creates a fairytale feel which contrasts with the later image of her as a witch (p. 32). The repeated references to the wonderful expression on her face, the "holy joy" in her eyes and the fact that all who encounter her are, like Jean, instantly enthralled with "mysterious rapture" and converted to her cause, reinforce the assumption of her saintliness.

In France in the late nineteenth century there was a clear division between commentators who defended the divine origin of Joan's mission and those who, influenced by the Romantics, interpreted her convictions as emanating from intense personal conviction. Although less extreme in children's books, the same division is apparent. The former, inspired by Michelet's eulogistic view of Joan in his *Histoire de France* [History of France] of 1844, present her, especially in school books, as exemplary of Catholic girlhood and employ a number of devices to endorse her (and their) belief.[11] An overtly religious text of 1909 by the Chanoine (Canon) Montet entitled *La Bienheureuse Jeanne d'Arc* [The Blessed Joan of Arc], insists that "tout est miracle dans la Mission de Jeanne: vouloir l'expliquer autrement, c'est se condamner à l'absurde" (everything about Joan's mission is miraculous: to try to explain it otherwise is to enter the realms of the absurd) and it emphasizes the personal sacrifice made by Joan to do God's bidding.[12] Joan's initial fearfulness and reluctance but eventual dutiful obedience to the command she believes to come from God further justify, of course, her assumption of such an abnormal role. Illustrations play a particularly important role here; in his *Avant-Propos* [Foreword], Boutet de Monvel asserts that Joan was born specifically for her mission and his second illustration depicts her as a demure young woman in peasant dress — but with a halo, and holding a lance and banner, while a distaff and a sword lie beside her on the ground. One foot rests on a lion and her face is upraised in a ray of light. In illustrations in nineteenth- and twentieth-century French books, the figures of the saints themselves tend to appear in clear and authorititive form. Boutet de Monvel affirms his viewpoint early on. His foreword is accompanied by a picture of Joan in peasant dress with a sword upright in her hand standing in front of an androgynous angel whose hands rest protectively on her shoulders. Her first experience of her Voices is rendered explicitly as a visitation: Joan is shown kneeling in amazement before a beautiful hovering Saint Michael in golden armor surrounded by a dazzling aura of tongues of flame. Later, when Joan is visited in prison by visions of Saint Catherine and Saint Margaret, they are represented as beautiful, tall, identical figures in blue gowns with long blond hair and a starry aura of light and flowers. A plate in a later text, Coutet's *La Vie Merveilleuse de Jeanne d'Arc* (1940), shows a gigantic Saint Michael in full armor dominating the picture, his face obscured by the visor of his helmet, his arms outstretched, one holding a sword and the other pointing, his huge wings drawing the eye upwards as he seems to rise from the center of a tree and hover over the head of a small, frightened female figure, an unconcerned sheep grazing nearby.[13]

A French journal, *Le Petit Parisien*, in an article of 6 May 1894 informed by a lay, Republican viewpoint, took a different line, linking the Voices specifically with Joan's patriotism in an interesting way: "Jeanne, méditant sur la grande détresse du beau pays de France, se dit: 'Oh! si je pouvais être la libératrice'" (Reflecting on the woes of the lovely land of France, Joan said to herself, "Oh! if only I could liberate her") and at this point she hears the divine command: "'Va et délivre le pays!'" (Go, free thy country!). The text affirms: "Il était naturel que les ardentes aspirations de sa jeune âme lui apparaissent comme un appel venu du dehors et d'en haut" (It was natural that the ardent longings of her youthful soul should seem like a call from outside and from on high).[14] The notion of patriotic devotion to duty was clearly a major source of appeal to writers of the nineteenth and early twentieth centuries, perhaps especially to writers for the young.[15] In both France and England, self-sacrifice in the service of one's country was at the heart of the national ethos. For many French writers, Joan became, as Michelet describes her, the personification of France itself and in the latter part of the century, when the nation was still experiencing the after-effects of the disaster of the Franco-Prussian War, in which Joan's birthplace in Lorraine was ceded to Germany, the promise, conviction and heroism which she represented were seen as qualities open to everyone. Statues were commissioned in many parts of France and journals were dedicated to her.[16] Boutet de Monvel, inspired to write his book by Frémiet's statue of Joan on horseback erected in 1875 in the Place des Pyramides in Paris, emphasizes in his foreword the empowering nature of patriotic fervor: "De sa faible main, elle ramassa la grande épée de la France vaincue, et, de sa frêle poitrine faisant un rempart à tant de détresses, elle puisa dans l'énergie de sa foi la force de relever les courages éperdus et d'arracher notre pays à l'Anglais victorieux" (With her frail hand, she gathered up the great sword of vanquished France and, making of her slender breast a rampart against so many woes, from the energy of her faith she drew the strength to lift dashed spirits and to snatch our land from the English victor) (p. 4). He then suggests that his young readers might emulate her: "Souvenez-vous-en, le jour ou le pays aura besoin de tout votre courage" (Remember this when your country has need of all your courage) (p. 4). His title page illustration is an explicit endorsement of this intense nationalistic sentiment, showing Joan in armour leading a group of foot-soldiers with the uniforms and rifles of the 1890s, their banner bearing the names of some of Napoleon's victories, thus conflating France's more glorious moments. Canon Montet goes so far as to claim, in 1909, that the problems of France are the same as those in Joan's day, urging that France can only be saved by the same factors—"la Foi, l'union, le travail, la lutte vaillante et le sacrifice" (Faith, unity, work, valiant struggle and sacrifice)—and seeing Joan as a thoroughly desirable role model for general behavior.[17] This was an ideology shared by religious and secular writers alike and Joan became a valuable symbol and her name a talismanic rallying cry for the cause of national identity. In 1948, shortly after the trauma of World War II and the Occupation, M. M. Martin's discussion of Joan in *Histoire de France racontée aux Petits Enfants* [The history of France told for little children] again links the future of the country with the past, asserting that "malgré ses ruines et ses deuils, la France demeure toujours la même, parce qu'elle reste la patrie de la sagesse et de l'héroisme, de la générosite et du dévouement aux nobles causes" (despite all the damage and the grief, France remains today the same as ever, for she is still the land of wisdom and heroism, of generosity and devotion to noble causes).[18]

Green's *Called of Her Country*, as the title suggests, is also intensely patriotic in spirit. When Joan is shown to accede to the wishes of her king that she should continue to fight her campaign despite her own desire to return to a quiet life in Domrémy, her hesitation and distress not only offer, implicitly, further justification for her assumption of her role (the exceptional situation and the wishes of her king and country demand exceptional behavior) but place the emphasis firmly on the concept of obeying duty before personal inclination. The tricky question for an English writer of whether God was on the side of the French at that time, implied in the acceptance of Joan's mission as divine revelation, is resolved by the use of the French narrator who presents the French view of Joan as the "Angelic Maid, heaven-sent, miraculous, apart from the earth, though living amongst us and leading us to victory" (p. 226).

This novel, like most books for young readers, places more emphasis on the excitement of the battles of Orléans, Patay and Paris than on the details of the trial that followed Joan's capture at Compiègne. Such descriptions are, of course, informed and limited by historical fact, but are always organized around certain key images: Joan's inspirational role as standard-bearer (she is frequently depicted in illustrations in dramatic poses, in armor on horseback, or pointing ahead, urging her troops on); her seemingly miraculous ability to persuade her followers to do her bidding; the fact, reassuring for young readers perhaps and a part of the justification process, that Joan claimed never to have killed anyone herself, the battles being human tragedies in her eyes rather than bloodthirsty triumphs. Important too in text and illustrations are the instantly recognizable symbols, such as the sword of St. Catherine (the discovery of which behind an altar has overtones of the Arthurian Excalibur legend) and her standard, rising above the skirmishes like a magic wand or, as in Boutet de Monvel's dramatically crowded, action-packed pictures, pointing meaningfully heavenward. Her apparent imperviousness to the pain from the wounds she receives which once linked her firmly in people's minds with the saints, now can be seen to link her implicitly with the superheroes popular with today's children.

For obvious reasons, the technicalities of the political and theological arguments at the trial of Joan are, for the most part, omitted or greatly simplified in children's books. The integrity and isolation of Joan, and the almost childlike simplicity and straightforwardness of her answers, are always strongly contrasted, nevertheless, in both text and image, with the intransigence, cruelty and inhumanity of her judges. Boutet de Monvel's illustration of the trial shows Joan as an upright, solitary figure surrounded by grim, hostile seated figures, arm extended and palm held up as though warding off an evil spirit, challenging their authority on behalf of the authority of God. Such a stance, denoting confidence in her mission, is in fact repeated with some variation throughout his book. In contrast, the Kingfisher *Joan of Arc* (1979) shows a vulnerable Joan looking remarkably like Jean Seberg in the 1957 film, curled up in a corner, her manacled hands crossed at her breast, while the judges loom sternly over her. In *Called of Her Country*, which has no illustrations, Joan's downfall and trial are only briefly alluded to in the last chapter, with the excuse that the narrator is unable to describe this period because of his distress, thus maintaining the focus on her positive successes.

The fact of Joan's death has always been interpreted in an inspirational light, as in the lives of saints, rather than as minatory in the tradition of tragedy or the cautionary tales offered to children in the eighteenth and nineteenth centuries.[19]

In Romantic terms, her death also denoted the preservation of the innocence of youth before it became contaminated by the world. Boutet de Monvel gives only the briefest of descriptions of her execution and the accompanying illustration shows a small, vulnerable but dignified figure in white at the stake in a swirl of fire, surrounded by a cage of pikes held by her captors, while on the opposite page her followers are forcibly kept at bay. His text ends with the lament of the English soldiers: "Nous sommes perdus, nous avons brûlé une sainte" (We are lost, we have burnt a saint) (p. 47). Green's Joan seems even more fragile, feminine and childlike, underlining the enormity of the crime being perpetrated against her, the emphasis being on her serene, smiling face and the white dove soaring heavenwards, seen by the narrator himself and interpreted overtly as a sign that her saints are with her to the end. Betrayed by her ungrateful king and country, she has gone on to "receive the crown of glory that fadeth not away" (p. 310). There is, indeed, frequently an implicit analogy with the death of Christ in the representation of her martyrdom: the betrayal by her erstwhile friends, the dove, the friar (or soldier in some versions) who offers her comfort in the shape of a cross, her last words calling on her God. The Ladybird version (1971) sidesteps the gruesome truth of her death by referring to it in a single sentence and reproducing as a final image a photograph of a statue of Joan at prayer, a strategy reminiscent of the end of Jean Anouilh's play *L'Alouette* [The lark] (1953) in which the scene of Joan at the stake is interrupted to play instead the scene of the coronation of the Dauphin, one of her most triumphant moments.[20]

Finally, on the question of blame for her death and the role of the English in her downfall, both French and English writers are, of course, constrained by historical fact but their strategies for dealing with the implications of this are illuminating. In French secular versions, where Joan is seen as the people's champion, a hero to appeal to Republican sentiments, her enemies are the nobility and clergy whose hatred and envy are allied with the weakness and cowardice of the king. Catholic writers too, wishing to claim her for the Church, portray her as worshipped by the common people who recognize her "vertu divine" [divine virtue] and accuse the "mauvais prêtres" [bad priests] of the period of being cynical, self-interested perverters of religion. An English text, in the 1986 "Lives of the Saints" series, stresses the role of the Pope in rehabilitating her against witnesses "who had not spoken the truth."[21] Inevitably the English are seen in French texts as the greater villains. Michelet (1844) presents the English as the victims of overweening pride, while Canon Montet (1909) regards them as solely responsible for the failure of negotiations and hence for the ensuing battles, accusing them of preferring war to peace, and death to life. Depicting such an intransigent and inhuman enemy further enhances Joan's role as inevitable and just, of course. An earlier text by M. Marius Sepet (1868), a fervent panegyric written at the time when the Church was beginning to consider Joan as a possible candidate for sainthood, goes so far as to suggest that England's subsequent troubles, including the Wars of the Roses, were an expiation for their crime.[22]

Evelyn Everett Green deals with the problem of the role of the English in the demise of her heroine in an interesting way. First, as has been seen, the use of

Jean de Metz as narrator facilitates the pro-French, anti-English slant. However, the reactions of the English soldiers in her novel also suggest great admiration and awe for the "White Witch;" miraculously quelled into silence and inertia at her appearance, and allowing her troops to pass, they respond positively to her sensitivity and compassion towards the wounded. The blame for her death is, indeed, laid firmly at the door of her compatriots: "It was Frenchmen who doomed her to this — Frenchmen and priests" (p. 300). The French nobility and clergy are seen as pusillanimous, dishonorable and ungrateful; her king was weak, shameful, idle and base; all of them were unworthy of the Maid. The narrator himself weeps for "the folly, the ingratitude, the baseness of it all" and, to some extent, exonerates the English who, as her enemy, "had the right to hold her as their adversary whose death was necessary for their success" but who would have dispatched her more speedily, and hence more honorably, without the "long-drawn-out agony and mockery of a trial" (p. 300). Later versions are also very critical of the French king and Joan's enemies among the powerful of the land, notably the "despicable" Duke of Burgundy who sold her to the English and the "crafty and deceitful," "dastardly" Bishop Cauchon (Ladybird). Several texts comment on the recognition by an Englishman of her saintliness, followed by a general despair and remorse in the English camp. The frequent assertion of the superstitious nature of the times and the misogyny of the military is also employed to explain the attitude of the English, who are paralyzed with fear by all the hyperbole surrounding the Warrior Maid and hence flee at the appearance of the "witch."

Texts of the period dealt with here, both historical accounts and fictionalized versions, clearly have a political and moral agenda which is generated by the social and cultural climate of the times and, for this purpose, the figure of Joan as the embodiment of patriotic duty, purity, selflessness and all the Christian virtues was an irresistible and universal symbol which transcended national rivalries and became a hero for all seasons, embraced by monarchists and Republicans, the religious and the secular, by Left and Right and by English and French alike. As G. Bruno (the pen-name of Augustine Thuillerie) reveals in her entry on Jeanne d'Arc in her 1877 bestselling didactic work *Le Tour de France par deux enfants* [Two children's journey around France], written when France was desperately in need of symbols to bolster the sense of national identity and pride, Joan as a symbol of "Devoir, Patrie, Humanité" (Duty, Nation, Humanity) was the perfect role-model for the young citizen of the future.[23]

NOTES

1. See Marina Warner's fascinating book, *Joan of Arc: The Image of Female Heroism* (Harmondsworth: Penguin, 1983) for a full discussion of the different interpetations of Joan of Arc. Also Régine Pernoud and Marie-Véronique Clin, *Jeanne d'Arc* (Paris: Fayard, 1986).

2. William Shakespeare, *Henry VI, Part I*, act 3, scene 2; George Bernard Shaw, *Saint Joan* (1923); Jules Michelet, *Histoire de France*, vol. 5 (1844); Jean Anouilh, *L'Alouette* (1953).

3. See discussion of this in Warner, *Joan of Arc* and Roger Odin, *Jeanne d'Arc à l'école: Essai sémiotique* (Paris: Éditions Klincksieck, 1980).

4. Evelyn Everett Green, *Called of Her Country: The Story of Joan of Arc* (London: Bousfield, 1903); Maurice Boutet de Monvel, *Jeanne d'Arc* (Paris: Plon, Nourrit, 1896).

5. *Henry VI, Part I,* act 1, scene 2.

6. Fr Funck-Brentano, *Jeanne d'Arc* (Paris: Boivin, 1912), p. 12.

7. Evelyn Everett Green, *Called of Her Country*, p. 32. Further page references will be indicated in parenthesis in the text.

8. L. Du Garde Peach, *Joan of Arc* (Loughborough: Ladybird, 1971); Brian Williams, *Joan of Arc,* Kingfisher Explorer Books, "History Makers" series (London: Ward Lock, 1979), p. 6.

9. E. Personne, P. Andraud, and G. Marc, *Mon premier Livre d'Histoire* (Paris: A. Colin, 1957), reproduced in Odin, *Jeanne d'Arc*, p. 225.

10. Harold Nottridge, *Joan of Arc,* "Great Lives" series (London: Wayland, 1987), pp. 5, 8.

11. See discussion of this in Odin, *Jeanne d'Arc*, especially chapters 3 and 4.

12. Chanoine E. Montet, *La Bienheureuse Jeanne d'Arc* (Paris: Reulet, 1909), p. 22, cited in Odin, *Jeanne d'Arc*, p. 62.

13. A. Coutet, *La Vie Merveilleuse de Jeanne d'Arc* (Paris: Sirven, 1940), reproduced in Odin, *Jeanne d'Arc*, p. 226.

14. Cited in Odin, *Jeanne d'Arc*, p. 59.

15. Note the success, for example, of the Biggles books and G. A. Henty's novels.

16. Warner, *Joan of Arc*, p. 255.

17. Montet, *La Bienheureuse Jeanne d'Arc*, cited in Odin, *Jeanne d'Arc*, p. 173.

18. M. M. Martin, *Histoire de France racontée aux Petits Enfants* (Paris: Éd. du Conquistador, 1948), cited in Odin, *Jeanne d'Arc*, p. 175.

19. Warner, *Joan of Arc*, p. 265.

20. "La vraie fin de l'histoire de Jeanne est joyeuse. Jeanne d'Arc, c'est une histoire qui finit bien!" (In reality, Joan's story has a happy ending It's a story that ends well!), Jean Anouilh, *L'Alouette* (Paris: Livre de Poche, 1953), p. 180.

21. Nancy Martin, *Religious Stories: The Lives of the Saints* (London: Wayland, 1986).

22. M. Marius Sepet, *Jeanne d'Arc* (Paris: Alfred Mame, 1870), p. 275.

23. G. Bruno, *Le Tour de France par deux enfants* (Paris: Eugène Belin, 1877), pp. 59–61.

REFERENCES

Anouilh, J. *L'Alouette.* Paris: Livre de Poche, 1953.

Boutet de Monvel, M. *Jeanne d'Arc.* Paris: Plon, Nourrit, no date [1896].

Bruno, G. *Le Tour de France par deux enfants.* Paris: E. Belin, 1877.

Coutet, A. *La vie merveilleuse de Jeanne d'Arc.* Paris: Sirven, 1940.

Du Garde Peach, L. *Joan of Arc.* Ladybird: Loughborough, 1971.

Everett Green, Evelyn. *Called of Her Country: The Story of Joan of Arc.* London: Bousfield, 1903.

Funck-Brentano, Fr. *Jeanne d'Arc.* Paris: Boivin, 1912.

Martin, M. M. *Histoire de France racontée aux petits enfants.* Paris: Ed. du Conquistador, 1948.

Martin, N. *Religious Stories: The Lives of the Saints.* London: Wayland, 1986.

Michelet, J. *Histoire de France.* Paris: 1844.

Montet, Chanoine E. *La Bienheureuse Jeanne d'Arc.* Paris: Reulet, 1909.

Nottridge, H. *Joan of Arc.* "Great Lives" series. London: Wayland, 1987.

Odin, R. *Jeanne d'Arc à l'école: Essai sémiotique*. Paris: Éd. Klincksieck, 1980.

Pernoud, R., and Clin, M.-V. *Jeanne d'Arc*. Paris: Fayard, 1986.

Personne, E., Andraud, P., and Marc, G. *Mon premier Livre d'Histoire*. Paris: A. Colin, 1957.

Sepet, M. M. *Jeanne d'Arc*. Paris: Alfred Mame, 1870.

Shakespeare, W. *Henry VI. Part I*. In *The Complete Works of William Shakespeare*. London: The Works Essential Classics, 1993.

Shaw, George Bernard. *Saint Joan*. 1923. In *The Works of George Bernard Shaw*, Vol. 17. London: R. and R. Clark, 1930.

Twain, Mark. *Personal Recollections of Joan of Arc, by the Sieur Louis de Conte (Her Page and Secretary)*. New York and London: Harper and Bros, 1896.

Warner, M. *Joan of Arc: The Image of Female Heroism*. Harmondsworth: Penguin, 1983.

Williams, Brian. *Joan of Arc*. Kingfisher Explorer Books, "History Makers" series. London: Ward Lock, 1979.

6

History and Collective Memory in Contemporary Portuguese Literature for the Young

Francesca Blockeel

When analyzing contemporary Portuguese books for children aged 9 to 14, I was immediately struck by the many allusions to Portugal's history, apparently part of the everyday knowledge of all Portuguese. It is worth pointing out that a boom in youth literature occurred after the revolution of 1974, with some 265 novels written in twenty years. Of these, about 22 percent deal wholly or partly with Portuguese history or culture. To illustrate this theme I will focus on Portugal's first king, a historical but also mythical figure, and assess how he is presented in youth literature, particularly in three novels which I discuss in some detail.

Salient in this respect are two well-known writers for the young, Ana Maria Magalhães and Isabel Alçada, with their very successful series of thirteen books, written in the last decades of the twentieth century and called "Journeys Through Time," in which two youngsters travel through the past to moments of great historical importance, covering the whole of Portugal's history. Because of the success of these books, other publishers launched their own series of historical novels. Magalhães and Alçada also wrote an even more successful series, consisting of thirty-eight adventure stories about five children and their dogs, much in the style of Enid Blyton's classic tales; these Portuguese narratives, however, invariably involve either a historical, a cultural or a geographical aspect of their native land. Once again their success was the stimulus for similar series of culture-cum-adventure books produced by other publishers.

For a better understanding of this strong interest in history it is necessary to consider, albeit briefly, the evolution of nationalist feelings in Portugal. In general, the Portuguese have always been very proud about their more than eight-centuries-old country, their leading position in Europe in the sixteenth century, and their colonial empire covering four continents. This feeling was intensified the twentieth century, the first quarter of which, however, was very chaotic: with the end of the monarchy and advent of the republic, followed by many revolutions and counter-revolutions, patriotic feelings intensified. Nationalist movements thrived and traditions, legends and myths were invented or re-invented. (Eric Hobsbawm's "inventing of tradition" and Benedict Anderson's "imagined communities" come to mind.) The educational guidelines for the mother tongue, history, geography and literature explicitly included the patriotic aim of providing young Portuguese with a collective memory. Children's books mostly dealt with Portuguese popular folk tales, biographies of great Portuguese or facts from national history.

From 1926 until 1974 Portugal lived under a semi-Fascist dictatorship, the "New State," led by António Salazar. Republican patriotism turned into an officially organized, over-exalted nationalism. As Eduardo Lourenço, today the leading Portuguese essayist, points out, Salazar systematically exploited the deeply rooted nationalist feelings of the common man and glorified the past through an authoritarian and filtered version of history.[1] Eventually only one uniform version of Portugal's history remained, most noticeably in the education system: all children, whether living in Portugal or any of its colonies, had the same schoolbooks, transmitting the values of religion, family and nation. For almost fifty years the national conscience was fed by epic tales from a great empire. No wonder Lourenço speaks of the hyper-identity of the Portuguese.[2]

At the end of the 1960s, however, colonial wars and massive emigration created a critical attitude, and ultimately the fall of the regime in 1974. Intellectuals, now attentive to social reality, felt ashamed about their country and its colonial past, and the great heroes of exploration were no longer spoken about. Some years after the revolution, with drastic changes at all levels, the Portuguese felt proud of their country once again, which rekindled interest in historical novels. Various writers, astonished by how little knowledge young Portuguese had of their own history and culture, even spoke of a "lost generation." Magalhães and Alçada overcame this by writing funny and thrilling books in which children learn about their own identity and culture: "It is now fashionable not to speak about certain heroes of Portuguese History. That is perfect nonsense! History is much more easily understood when populated by real persons," says a protagonist of *Uma viagem ao tempo dos castelos* [A journey to the times of the castles].[3]

It is necessary at this point to introduce Afonso Henriques (1110–85), the first king of Portugal and the subject of the novels to be discussed. He symbolizes the "Birth of the Nation," for he not only conquered most of present-day Portugal, fighting the Moors, but also gained independence from neighboring Spanish kingdoms. His story very soon became one of the essential myths of Portuguese culture, so legends thrived, some as old as the twelfth century. No contemporary depiction of him has survived, but the tradition that "he was endowed with gigantic stature, a flowing beard and Herculean strength" still lives on in books for the young.[4] Another very important myth concerns the Battle of Ourique (1139) against the Moors. Nobody knows what really happened, but descriptions of it were embellished to the point that Christ miraculously appeared to give divine blessing to Portugal's independence. Until the nineteenth century, very few Portuguese questioned the belief that they were God's chosen people, promised a grandiose future and charged with bringing faith to other regions, because in school manuals these ideas were mixed in with historical facts. There are two traumatic aspects to Afonso's reign. First, in the Battle of São Mamede (1128) Afonso defeated his own mother, and thus the nation was born out of treachery to a mother. Furthermore, in order to free his country from Castilian dominance, Afonso broke his promise of vassalage to his suzerain, and Afonso's tutor, Egas Moniz, almost lost his life in redeeming the honor of his king.

It thus comes as no surprise to find Afonso Henriques frequently mentioned, or alluded to, in about one quarter of books for young people. While most of these do not detail his deeds or experiences, there are three books in which he is prominently present. They are:

1. *A espada do rei Afonso* [The sword of King Afonso] of 1981 by Alice Vieira tells us about three children who travel through time to the court of Afonso in the aftermath of the conquest of Lisbon (1147). Because of their different ideas they are put in a dungeon, but with their astonishing knowledge about the future, they manage to gain the confidence of the king and be freed.
2. *Uma viagem ao tempo dos castelos* [A journey to the times of the castles] of 1985 by Ana Maria Magalhães and Isabel Alçada tells of two children also travelling through time. They meet Egas Moniz and his family, and unexpectedly get a glimpse of the future king himself, who is, however, not a real protagonist of the story.
3. *O Menino de Guimarães* [The boy from Guimarães] of 1991 by Natércia Rocha is about the friendship between two playmates of the young Afonso Henriques, Ana, a Christian girl, and Sancha, a Muslim girl. The book vaguely suggests that the king had been secretly in love with Sancha, but Sancha flees to her own people once he is grown up and conquers land from the Arabs.

What do we find here about the myths surrounding this epic hero? His physical aspect is treated differently. *Uma viagem ao tempo dos castelos* reflects the stereotype of Afonso the brave and valiant, with a majestic appearance and easygoing manners predisposing him to become king. His sword is bigger than the children have ever seen. In contrast, in *O Menino de Guimarães* the two girls always refer to him as the "boy from Guimarães," even when he is grown-up and is a great leader they admire, indicating the author's aim to portray him as an

ordinary man. Paradoxically, this insistence on calling him "boy" and the fact
that cunning Ana controls the situation detracts from the image of a resolute man
and contrasts highly with the emphasis on his pre-eminent importance as
"Founder of the Nation."

In *A espada do rei Afonso*, the image of a tall, rude warrior, with a dense
beard, a heavy sword, and a voice like a breaking thunderstorm is omnipresent.
But, if the king looks powerful (and thinks he is), he is in no way depicted as an
epic model to follow, because he is presented through everyday situations and
through familiar life. In inventing with humor what history never tells, Vieira
familiarizes the reader not with a hero but with a human figure: rather clumsy and
coarse, he likes to make fun but can be very unpredictable, he quarrels with the
queen, is rather uncivilized as he cannot read or count, and so on. The modern
children are not afraid, even if their lives depend on him. He may be king and
will be forever glorified, as they tell him, but he is in an inferior position because
the children know much more than he does. Not he but they can "get their
meaning to stick,"[5] so he is the one who grows in the story. This inversion of the
child/adult relationship is unique in Portuguese youth literature.

In these three novels the Battle of Ourique is mentioned only in *O Menino de
Guimarães*, but without the apparition of Christ. However, Ana's husband speaks
of five Moorish kings, as in the legend, and concludes that God protected the
Portuguese. Rocha obviously found it necessary to mention the essence of this
once so powerful myth, while the others, writing before her, chose not to do so.

Another important legend depicts Afonso Henriques as the butcher of the
Moors, the "matamoros." In *O Menino de Guimarães* the situation is once again
paradoxical. While the Arabs are presented as other human beings, Afonso is
painted as the legitimated killer of Moors. The only link between the Christians
and the Arabs is the friendship of two women, although Ana is superior to
Sancha. And if Ana fears for the life of Sancha during the conquest of Lisbon,
she has little thought for the other Muslims who perish. The Arab legacy in
Portugal (beautiful cities, poetry, agriculture, medicine) is too dryly presented to
have any great effect. Arab culture is depicted in its strangeness: Sancha is afraid
of the strange perfumes, dislikes the veil, and sticks to the memories of her
childhood among the Christians. Most commonplace ideas of a different and
inferior people are present, reinforced by referring to Sancha at least eight times
as the daughter of "the captive woman" or "the captive Moor."

Alice Vieira openly presents Afonso Henriques as a "matamoros": killing the
"unbelievers"—and, lest we forget, the Castilians—seems to be all he is
interested in. But this involves such exaggeration and humor that the reader
cannot but laugh at the king, as do the three time-travelling children. Moreover,
by playing with narrative frames and skilfully switching between focalizers
(children, Moors, soldiers, crusaders, the queen, people working at the court, and
others), she presents the Muslims through various points of view, never
considering them inferior to the Portuguese. They are depicted as ordinary
people, common men and women who defended themselves courageously but
had another religion — and who is to say that one religion is better than another?
Besides, there is a sensitive appreciation of the Arab legacy in Portugal. A friend

of the three children goes for help with her Muslim friend. While travelling together through the still Arab part of Portugal, she admires the beautiful cities, hears how democratically they are governed, and finds more justice in their system than in Christian feudality. She listens to stories about the myths surrounding the cities and the mysterious names they have, many of which still exist: past and present interrelate. So, by uncovering the horror the Portuguese inflicted on the Arabs, the reader is made to understand and feel proud of how much Portugal has inherited from them.

The traumatic experiences connected with the Battle of São Mamede are also dealt with differently. In *Uma viagem ao tempo dos castelos* the children find the village in turmoil about the outcome of the battle, as many villagers are fighting alongside Afonso. The importance of the battle is explained in all its historical aspects, but the facts are given rather neutrally. Natércia Rocha's story, on the other hand, fiercely defends the king, revealing why he had to fight his mother. First, she had abandoned him as a baby, out of political ambition; secondly, she had usurped power in not calling him to govern; thirdly and most importantly, she was totally influenced by her favorite and his Galician noblemen, who were destroying the dream of an independent kingdom. In Rocha's view, Afonso had no other option than to fight his mother, so there is no reason to feel bad about it. By contrast, in Alice Vieira's book, Afonso himself comments on his mother. He is never plainly negative about her and admits that if he is ambitious, he has inherited that from her. He, with his temper, simply could not let Portugal become a part of Galicia; instead, his goal was a kingdom for himself.

The last myth to be considered here—the episode involving Egas Moniz—is very superficially alluded to by Natércia Rocha, without naming him as such, by saying that it was a normal power game. In this way the episode detracts nothing from the merits of Afonso Henriques. In *Uma viagem ao tempo dos castelos*, Egas Moniz and his family are at the core of the story, and Orlando, the scientist who accompanies the time-travelling children, explains to them how important the king's tutor was. They meet Egas Moniz just after Afonso has broken his word by refusing to pay homage to his suzerain, as Egas had promised earlier. Of course, the breach of honor by the king favors Portugal. Orlando reprimands him, however: a promise is a promise, and he tells him what Egas has in mind, thus passing the historical knowledge on to the fictional children (and the readers, of course), who know that the episode is going to end well, while the protagonists do not.

In *A espada do rei Afonso* the legend is talked about by Egas' son, who profoundly disapproves of his father's deeds; he must have been a fool to accept the situation and force his unwilling children to go to León with a rope around their necks. Not only does Alice Vieira strip the legend of its earnestness and the moral lesson of loyalty, but by giving a voice to children—who have no voice in history—she brings the child-reader much closer to history, their identification with a child being easier than with an epic hero. Turning the episode into a recognizable parent-child relationship, she renders the strangeness of the past familiar.

During the New State regime, literature had to instill in young readers a certain image of the fatherland; they were told only of the splendor and moral dignity of Portugal's history, and were invited to identify themselves with the legendary heroes of the nation. After the revolution of 1974, there was a real effort to deal with history more objectively, to moderate the over-exaltation, but this does not at all mean that nationalism is not present any more, albeit in different ways, as these three books show.

In *O menino de Guimarães*, the author tries to give a less sanctified image of Afonso, but nevertheless he is still glorified and his negative acts are presented as justified. Moreover, the book supports nationalistic feelings, as an analysis of language and of dominant ideological positions between the characters easily reveals. *Uma viagem ao tempo dos castelos* is different, because its first aim is didactic. This story is part of a series to provide children with knowledge about history and culture in a pleasant way. Packaged in a nice adventure story, interesting facts about life in past times, and about historical events or persons, are fully explained and considered from many possible points of view. But as in most adventure stories, rather than introducing new views, this mostly confirms stereotyped conservative values, even if there is some interrogation of the past.

Alice Vieira's book is quite different. She manages to deconsecrate Afonso and present him as an important but human figure, who is no longer the only hero of the story; society in all its layers is the real protagonist. The transformation of historical figures into ordinary people with virtues and faults is a constant paradigm in Vieira's books, making the reader feel involved with history. Hers is no pedagogy of subject-matter, but of learning by perception, aiming at fostering critical minds. She makes the reader feel that "a sense of the past interposes a radical alterity into our own lives,"[6] and that what matters is not dramatic events but the everyday being-in-the-world which defines itself in human communication. An iconoclast of the epic canonic heroes driven by patriotism and religion, Alice Vieira aims at transforming her readers into critical and questioning young Portuguese, giving them the material for the contemplation of self and of otherness. That makes her an outstanding writer; nevertheless, we cannot forget that she seldom stops speaking about Portugal in all its aspects. Interesting facts are integrated, mostly in a carnivalesque way, in spontaneous and varied dialogs, highlighting the important moments of Portugal without ever exalting them. In this way cultural and national identity are even more efficiently, because unconsciously, instilled into the reader's mind.

Since the loss of its colonies in 1975 and its integration into the European Union, Portugal has been looking hard for its own identity. This may explain the many historical novels and the fact that history and culture are so often talked about: authors want to give the young a collective memory. Because of the recent expansion in youth literature, as well as the success of both writers and books, it is probably safe to say that since 1974, without any official pressure, Portuguese literature for the young has been contributing more than ever to the shaping of a strongly developed national conscience. Two other elements reinforce this situation. First, there are currently not many translations of foreign books for young people, and, second, only a handful of Portuguese books in this category deal with other people or countries, 95 percent being focused on Portugal.

NOTES

1. Eduardo Lourenço, *O Labirinto da Saudade* (Lisbon: D. Quixote, 1978, 1992), p. 28.

2. Eduardo Lourenço, *Nós e a Europa, ou as duas Razões* (Lisbon: D. Quixote, 1988), p. 11.

3. Ana Maria Magalhães and Isabel Alçada, *Uma viagem ao tempo dos castelos* (Lisbon: Caminho, 1985, 1992), p. 69.

4. Harold V. Livermore, *A New History of Portugal* (Cambridge: Cambridge University Press, 1966), p. 66.

5. John B. Thompson, *Ideology and Modern Culture: Critical Social Theory in the Era of Mass Communication* (Cambridge: Polity Press, 1990), p. 56.

6. John Stephens, *Language and Ideology in Children's Fiction* (London: Longman, 1992), p. 218.

REFERENCES

Anderson, Benedict. *Imagined Communities: Reflections on the Origins and Spread of Nationalism.* London: Verso, 1983.

Hobsbawm, Eric. "Inventing Traditions." In Eric Hobsbawm and Terence Ranger, eds. *The Invention of Tradition.* Cambridge: Cambridge University Press, 1983.

Livermore, Harold V. *A New History of Portugal.* Cambridge: Cambridge University Press, 1966.

Lourenço, Eduardo. *O Labirinto da Saudade.* 1978. Lisbon: Dom Quixote, 1992.

————. *Nós e a Europa, ou as duas Razões.* Lisbon: Dom Quixote, 1988.

Magalhães, Ana Maria and Alçada, Isabel. *Uma viagem ao tempo dos castelos.* 1985. Lisbon: Caminho, 1992.

Rocha, Natércia. *O Menino de Guimarães.* Porto: Edinter, 1991.

Stephens, John. *Language and Ideology in Children's Fiction.* London: Longman, 1992.

Thompson, John B. *Ideology and Modern Culture: Critical Social Theory in the Era of Mass Communication.* Cambridge: Polity Press, 1990.

Vieira, Alice. *A espada do rei Afonso.* 1981. Lisbon: Caminho, 1991.

7

The Descendants of Robinson Crusoe in North American Children's Literature

Tina L. Hanlon

After Robinson Crusoe left York, England, to see the world in 1651, he was stranded for twenty-eight years on a tropical island near South America. In many contemporary American children's books, Crusoe's descendants do not wander as far from home as he did geographically, but their adventures in various wilderness environments take them much farther away ideologically from the eighteenth-century vision of the natural world, the individual and society reflected in Defoe's classic novel. Among the multitude of stories, poems and films around the world that feature Robinson Crusoe and his descendants, modern Robinsonnades for children focus on dolls, dogs, dinosaurs, and dragons as well as human castaways, and on babies and females in addition to traditional male heroes. Copies of Defoe's novel appear as valued personal possessions in diverse settings ranging from American frontier settlements to spaceships. In *Baby Island* (Ryrie Brink, 1937), a girl lost at sea in a lifeboat expects refuge by nightfall because "the library at home is just full of books about shipwrecked people who landed on tropical islands."[1] Since Crusoe on his island has become an archetype representing the isolated individual's psychological and emotional initiation experiences as well as a physical struggle for survival in an unfamiliar environment, some adaptations depict characters displaced in other secluded locations, such as urban hiding places, or young people who deliberately run away to islands or forest retreats.

In 1985, writing on children's literature, Diane Gunstra identified major elements of this tradition in her article, "The Island Pattern." Although she observes briefly that "the characters and plots change along with their social implications" in modern children's books, her positive emphasis on Crusoe's growing unity with nature and friendship with Friday reflects some of the reasons for the Robinsonnade remaining so popular as an intertextual pattern in children's literature.[2] Crusoe, like many heroes of old and new children's books, leaves home in rebellion against his parents and returns after dangerous adventures develop his self-reliance, respect for the powers of nature, appreciation for human companionship and gratitude for the abundance of God's gifts.

Nevertheless, it is also important to recognize the extent of the ideological distance between Defoe's novel and modern Robinsonnades for children (as many critics have done while discussing books and films for adults). An intriguing, often ironic aspect of intertextuality that is especially pertinent to the Crusoe tradition is the way it appeals simultaneously to our desire for both the familiar and the new. The intertextuality of the Robinsonnade provides a familiar framework within which the most interesting contemporary books for children and young adults are much more subversive than Defoe's and other older novels, without departing from the expected patterns and pleasures of the adventure story genre as dramatically as many satiric, dystopian or tragic Robinsonnades for adults. John Stephens, the literary scholar and specialist in the uses of language, observes that "intertextuality, by making relationships between different cultures and different periods, can act as a critique of current social values."[3] The old myth of a pastoral paradise that nurtures innate goodness, the triumph of the human spirit in adversity, and the return to home and family have remained very common and appealing themes since the Golden Age of children's literature, but modern child characters, unlike Robinson Crusoe, often shed the prejudices of the civilizations they left behind. Although protagonists continue to experience conflicting yearnings for human society and the natural environment, those divided loyalties now have new and heightened significance. As the growing environmental movement strives to gain acceptance by mainstream society, children's books reflect one of the most complex dilemmas of modern life: individuals benefit from contact with nature and the environment must be protected, yet it is increasingly difficult for those who seek it to find unspoiled wilderness, and it is virtually impossible to live in the company of other human beings without encroaching on the natural world.[4]

Recent critics of Crusoe's story view it as a traditionally masculine adventure with dominant themes of capitalism, racism and environmental exploitation.[5] The writer Diana Loxley discusses the use of nineteenth-century Robinsonnades to instill the values of imperialism and colonialism in children.[6] Crusoe's struggle to live off the land teaches him to appreciate his parents' middle-class prosperity and Christian faith, which he had rejected to pursue a life of seafaring and sin. The Swiss Family Robinson, Crusoe's most famous nineteenth-century descendants, become founders of a European colony on their island. They endure even less conflict and soul-searching as the steadfast father teaches four sons how to be good Christian explorers and citizens. In *The Coral Island*, R. M.

Ballantyne's popular mid-Victorian Robinsonnade, three young castaways enjoy boyish adventures without adult supervision until they encounter cannibals and pirates; the book ends by emphasizing the civilizing influence of Christian missionaries in this savage environment. In these older novels, European heroes (usually male) view themselves as masters in the new homes they establish as they are tested by the forces of nature and barbarism. Their love and appreciation for nature grow, but they seldom question the traditional colonial and patriarchal values of European society, including assumption of the right to exploit nature for their own purposes. The scholar Virginia S. Wolf's important essay on the myth of paradise in island novels for children asserts that the reputation of *Robinson Crusoe* has declined because it emphasizes conquest of nature. She writes, "Rather than building a kingdom as Crusoe does, twentieth-century characters discover or transform nature. Thus, the understanding of paradise has changed."[7]

Two prominent American Robinsonnades from the 1930s reflect some of these old prejudices and tendency toward social conformity, although they contain amusing and original twists on the Crusoe formula. In *Floating Island*, Anne Parrish pokes fun at pompous and possessive adults when shipwrecked dolls fuss about salvaging and protecting their private property, yet the only alternative she offers is a distasteful racial stereotype in her depiction of the black cook's preference for jungle life with unruly monkeys, while the white dolls quickly return to rigid domestic roles inside their dollhouse when they prepare for rescue. Although *Baby Island* by Carol Ryrie Brink is noteworthy for portraying brave and independent girls in 1937, it also privileges traditional domesticity and colonialism. The castaway sisters feel compelled to claim the island for themselves and the President of the United States. Both the tomboy and the reclusive man they befriend are influenced less by the island environment than by the four babies and very motherly sister who are shipwrecked there, teaching the sentimental lesson that babies can domesticate the most untamed souls. Later twentieth-century castaways are more likely to depart from the cultural biases of the homes they left behind and form new attitudes toward their environment, rather than attempting to bring civilization to the wilderness.

As the scholar Carolyn Sigler observed, the history of environmental literature has much in common with feminism and the general development of children's literature, which has "a long tradition of nurturing ideologies and issues that the prevailing literary culture regards as subversive or insignificant."[8] Contemporary descendants of Robinson Crusoe represent diverse perspectives within a wide variety of races and species, age groups, and social classes. Some learn new ways of relating to others and of using or preserving resources that would amaze their parents. Among the ten children's novels of the past forty years that I have examined most carefully (not counting the sequels to several of these very popular books), there are four female protagonists, including three Native Americans. *The Island Keeper* by Harry Mazer focuses on an overweight white teenager who runs away from her unhappy, wealthy family to their Canadian lake island vacation home, where she is stranded after a late summer storm destroys her canoe. In *Julie of the Wolves*, by Jean Craighead George, an

Eskimo girl lost in the Arctic survives by living with wolves and then decides that she prefers their company, after finding that her father is involved in destroying animals for sport and profit. Billie Wind in George's *The Talking Earth* is sent to explore her native Florida swamps after scoffing at tribal beliefs about talking animals. She learns that the earth has much to tell us about living if we listen carefully to its detailed messages conveyed by weather, plants and animals. Karana in Scott O'Dell's *Island of the Blue Dolphins*, stranded alone for eighteen years on the Pacific island where she was born, is well-acquainted with its natural resources, yet her development of self-sufficiency requires dramatic departures from tribal custom. Shedding old prejudices and superstitions, such as the taboo forbidding women to make weapons, she frees herself to use all her physical and mental resources to care for herself with nature's help. Eventually she decides to kill only when it is absolutely necessary for food. She also makes friends with unlikely creatures, including the wild dogs who killed her brother and an Aleut daughter of hunters whom she blames for destroying her otter friends and her tribe.

My *Side of the Mountain* by Jean Craighead George, focusing on Sam's flight from a big New York City family to live alone in the Catskill Mountains, is one of many books with white male protagonists, but in the sequel, *On the Far Side of the Mountain*, his sister lives in a nearby treehouse and initiates a trek across the mountain. Wil in Gary Paulsen's *The Island* is another voluntary Crusoe, isolating himself on a lake island for so long that his parents fear for his sanity. Brian in *Hatchet*, also by Paulsen, is stranded in a Canadian forest after a plane crash. Two other young men overcome the racism of their communities while separated from their families. Matt, in Elizabeth George Speare's *Sign of the Beaver*, is an eighteenth-century boy who has been left alone in a pioneer cabin and develops friendships with Native Americans, partly through teaching one to read and sharing the story of *Robinson Crusoe* with him. In a reversal of the relationship between Crusoe and Friday, Matt learns to respect the wisdom of his friend Attean, who teaches him better ways to hunt, fish, use plants for healing, make clothing, find his way in the forest, use resources without wasting anything, and respect the land rather than thinking in terms of possessing it. Phillip in Theodore Taylor's *The Cay* survives a bombing at sea during World War II thanks to an old Caribbean man named Timothy. By showing Phillip how to live on a small raft and then an island, a tiny uncharted cay with very meager resources, Timothy also teaches Phillip to love a black man as a friend and mentor. In *Abel's Island* by William Steig, a spoiled Edwardian mouse swept away by a summer rainstorm must fend for himself on a river island for a year. The young snob overcomes enough of his elitist biases to imitate the survival skills of other animals and accept an old frog as a visitor. Although all these authors are white Americans, only two are women, and attempts to depict cultural diversity realistically have brought controversy to several of them; they all strive to show that all kinds of people share a common struggle for survival on this earth, and we can help each other learn how to survive by considering new perspectives and ways of living.

When Defoe based his novel on newspaper accounts of a real castaway, Europeans were fascinated with travel narratives about unexplored regions of the earth. Although many modern adventure stories depict exotic and uncharted territories on distant planets or imaginary worlds, what was true for Henry David Thoreau's neighbors and readers of *Walden* in mid-nineteenth-century New England is much more true today — that is, attempting to live off the land alone seems exotic and difficult to the average reader in crowded, over-civilized late-twentieth-century America. Thus many writers maintain the Robinsonnade's interplay between romance and realism without sending characters across the globe. In the cases of the mouse in Steig's fantasy or of North American pioneers, short distances can isolate individuals for long intervals. In Catherine Parr Traill's *Canadian Crusoes*, a mid-nineteenth-century landmark of Canadian children's literature noted for its realistic descriptions of the Ontario wilderness, three lost children discover after three years on the shores of Rice Lake that they are only seven miles from home. Some characters who seek deliberately the seclusion in nature that is forced on Crusoe may hide from fellow humans, not from stereotypical cannibals and pirates, but from cannibals or pirates in the form of interfering parents, gossips, reporters, construction workers, police, or conservation officers who enforce society's rules. The use of real locations not so far from home in some of these novels fulfills the environmentalist's desire to instill knowledge of the natural world and a sense of place, to get people involved in dialogues with real places and direct experience with nature.[9]

This immersion in nature has long been described as a return to a simpler life. Joseph Meeker, the influential ecologist and literary critic, argues that the "assumption that nature is simple while civilization is complex is one of the sad legacies of romantic thought. Nature is neither an idyll of simplicity and peace populated by noble savages, as pictured by Rousseau, nor a bloody battlefield where only the most brutal can survive." Meeker's ideas about animal life being more complex than "civilized human life" are equivalent to the differences between Robinson Crusoe's life and his modern descendants' adaptations to their environment.[10] Defoe's detailed descriptions of Crusoe's hard work, which influenced the development of realistic fiction and morally instructive children's literature, focus primarily on efforts to reproduce the kind of home Crusoe knew in Europe. More recent Robinsonnades devote much less space to regrets about the domestic life left behind and attempts to recreate it. Most modern castaways do not salvage huge quantities of supplies from a wreck like Crusoe and the Swiss Family Robinson, or construct such elaborate homes. By accident or by choice, some begin with only a few morsels of food and basic tools, depending immediately on the new environment. Although *Hatchet* and *Abel's Island* show characters longing for favorite foods, hunger helps them understand how food functions in natural ecosystems and they take pride in finding food as other animals do. *The Island Keeper* and *Hatchet* emphasize the daily exertion and self-discipline required to survive at a subsistence level through bad weather, to use every bit of hunted and gathered resources for essential needs.

In conditions ranging from desperate need to emotional and aesthetic contemplation, these characters observe nature more closely than Robinson

Crusoe does, in some cases watching one animal extensively as it changes habits through the seasons and depends on other species. Paulsen's Wil is attracted instinctively to the lake island that teaches him so much about himself and life's infinite mysteries: "He realized he could sit and write and draw and dance the heron, just the heron, for all the pages of all the rest of his life and not understand it."[11] Both Wil and Abel are unusual Crusoes because they discover their own artistic talents through intense experience with nature. Abel moves from mastering the practical skill of making clay pots like Robinson Crusoe to creating sculptures and drawings with natural materials. For Abel and Wil, gradually accepting the island as home and discovering deep connections with the natural environment inspire artistic interests they plan to pursue when they return to society.

Modern Crusoes' complex experiences with other animals range from predatory confrontations to close friendships. Companions such as Julie's bird, Karana's wild dogs, Billie Wind's young otter, and Sam's falcon teach the humans who care for them about the fragile boundaries between living as a wild or tame creature. Taming dogs and birds gives Karana insights quite different from Crusoe's paternalistic attitude toward pets and servants. When fear gives way to wonder at nature's mysteries, Karana decides not to interfere in the dogs' fights, realizing their howls represent "the sound of many things that I did not understand."[12] As characters learn to respect natural instincts of both threatening and tame animals, recognizing that they must sometimes set beloved pets free to live and reproduce in the wild, these books reflect the views of environmentalists who warn us to stop promoting human dominance and to study the diversity and interdependence of species, so that we can adapt to environmental changes as effectively as other animals and preserve complex natural ecosystems for the benefit of all species.[13]

Just as these contemporary Crusoes find that living off the land and beginning to understand the intricacies of nature do not make life simpler, the endings of these books do not provide easy answers to the problem of how individuals can maintain positive relationships with both the natural environment and human society, as these characters all wish to do. Within the framework of the Robinsonnade, and the general traditions of children's literature, these novels all have positive endings; the main characters are rescued or reunited with their families. All are stronger and more mature, proud of their ability to endure hardships independently in the wilderness and identify with other animals. *Abel's Island*, an illustrated chapter book for younger children, presents the most idyllic vision of the mouse's ecstatic celebration of spring after a hard winter. In *The Island Keeper*, the most adult novel in this group, grim deprivations are depicted as Cleo faces fears of death and the necessity of killing animals to save herself, but she knows her suffering strengthens her physically and psychologically. The other novels fall in between on the scale from idyllic to soberly realistic, all demonstrating the value of rational thought and emotional responses as humans develop deep attachments to the natural environments where they make homes for themselves.[14] Matt in *The Sign of the Beaver* realizes that he prefers his rugged frontier home to Robinson Crusoe's "paradise."[15]

The reality that they must leave or accept other humans into their wilderness habitats leads to unanswered questions about the fate of the main characters and the future of the world. Rather than celebrating the possession of new land or the bringing of civilization to the wilderness, as we see at the end of *Robinson Crusoe* and especially *The Swiss Family Robinson*, these novels reflect contemporary uncertainty about how to integrate the needs of individuals, society and the natural environment. The main characters are transformed, but can they share their new perspectives with others? In about half of these books, we know there are parents who simply do not understand the new attitudes of the children with whom they are reunited. In *The Talking Earth,* just as Billie Wind recognizes her kinship with the earth, she sees construction workers bulldozing the Florida island where she has survived a brush fire and discovered an ancestral burial cave. *My Side of the Mountain* illustrates a similar environmental dilemma on a smaller scale. Sam enjoys his very basic lifestyle dwelling in a tree trunk and his sympathetic visitors, yet even one guest requires more living space and resources, upsetting the careful balance of his wilderness life. He is glad to see his family at the end but his mother wants to build a house in the woods. So Sam's life must change (as it does in the sequel when his rural settlement grows), and it seems that we cannot have human society without encroaching on the natural environment. Although these novels offer no solutions to such complex dilemmas, presenting the desire to build a house as an environmental problem brings us a long way from the anthropocentric and colonialist views of the older Crusoe stories.

Recent scholars have studied the use of the Robinsonnade through history to instill society's values in child readers, but Crusoe's modern descendants often do not conform to the mainstream of society. In a book focusing on adult Robinsonnades, the literary critic Lieve Spaas describes *Robinson Crusoe* as "an inexhaustible literary myth," which "provides a prototype for rethinking existing customs and ethical codes and for examining the social and political underpinnings of Western culture." North American writers of novels for children and young adults demonstrate Spaas's belief that "the fictional paradigm of creating society anew is fruitful."[16] They use the intertextuality of the Robinsonnade to create young protagonists of varied backgrounds who survive as successfully as Robinson Crusoe, but unlike the older Crusoes, they learn that past generations made many mistakes in their constructions of human society on this earth. Their isolated initiation experiences encourage these characters to consider new ways of living and to grapple with our unsolved problems about how to live in harmony with the natural environment and other people.

NOTES

1. Carol Ryrie Brink, *Baby Island* (New York: Macmillan, 1937), p. 9.

2. Diane L. Gunstra, "The Island Pattern," *Children's Literature Association Quarterly* 10 (1985), p. 57.

3. John Stephens, "Not by Words Alone: Language, Intertextuality, Society," in *Language and Ideology in Children's Literature* (New York: Longman, 1992), p. 116.

4. Some of these ideas were developed through participation in an American interdisciplinary environmental education project sponsored by the Council on Independent Colleges. I am particularly grateful for insights shared by my colleague at Ferrum College, Professor of Environmental Science Carolyn Thomas.

5. See, for example, Martin Green, *The Robinson Crusoe Story* (University Park: Pennsylvania State University Press, 1990).

6. Diana Loxley, *Problematic Shores: The Literature of the Islands* (London: Macmillan, 1992).

7. Virginia S. Wolf, "Paradise Lost? The Displacement of Myth in Children's Novels Set on Islands," *Studies in the Literary Imagination* 18 (1985), pp. 55–56.

8. Carolyn Sigler, "Wonderland to Wasteland: Toward Historicizing Environmental Activism in Children's Literature," *Children's Literature Association Quarterly* 19 (1994–95), p. 148.

9. See Elaine G. Schwartz's summary of David Orr's goals for ecological literacy in "Thinking Globally, Acting Locally: Fostering Ecological Literacy through Children's Picture-Books," *Journal of Children's Literature* 21 (1995), pp. 49–56.

10. Joseph Meeker, *The Comedy of Survival: In Search of an Environmental Ethic*, 2nd ed. (Los Angeles: Guild of Tutors Press, 1980), pp. 49, 45.

11. Gary Paulsen, *The Island* (New York: Dell, 1988), pp. 49–50.

12. Scott O'Dell, *Island of the Blue Dolphins* (New York: Dell, 1960), p. 118.

13. See also Schwartz's critique of modern picture books that accept human possession and exploitation of the environment, which she contrasts with books that promote "a deep understanding of humankind's interdependence with the other forms of life on earth," in "Thinking Globally," p. 54.

14. Virginia S. Wolf argues that "novels set on islands . . . mostly . . . occupy a middle territory. Arranged in terms of their increasing displacement of the myth of earthly paradise, they reflect the formal characteristics of the children's novel as it ranges from a novel appropriate for the young child to one appropriate for the adolescent," in "Paradise Lost?" p. 49.

15. Elizabeth George Speare, *The Sign of the Beaver* (New York: Dell Yearling, 1983), p. 20.

16. "Conclusion," in *Robinson Crusoe: Myths and Metamorphoses*, ed. Lieve Spaas and Brian Stimpson (New York: St. Martin's, 1996), p. 320.

REFERENCES

Ballantyne, R. M. *The Coral Island: A Tale of the Pacific Ocean*. London: T. Nelson, 1858.

Craighead George, Jean. *Julie of the Wolves*. New York: Harper, 1972.

———. *My Side of the Mountain*. New York: Puffin, 1959.

———. *On the Far Side of the Mountain*. New York: Puffin, 1990.

———. *The Talking Earth*. New York: Harper Trophy, 1983.

Defoe, Daniel. *Robinson Crusoe*. New York: Signet, 1960 [1719].

George Speare, Elizabeth. *The Sign of the Beaver*. New York: Dell Yearling, 1983.

Green, Martin. *The Robinson Crusoe Story*. University Park: Pennsylvania State University Press, 1990.

Gunstra, Diane L. "The Island Pattern." *Children's Literature Association Quarterly* 10 (1985): 55–57.

Loxley, Diana. *Problematic Shores: The Literature of the Islands*. London: Macmillan, 1992.

Mazer, Harry. *The Island Keeper*. New York: Dell, 1981.

Meeker, Joseph. *The Comedy of Survival: In Search of an Environmental Ethic.* 2nd ed. Los Angeles: Guild of Tutors Press, 1980.

O'Dell, Scott. *Island of the Blue Dolphins.* New York: Dell, 1960.

Parrish, Anne. *Floating Island.* New York: Harper and Row, 1930.

Paulsen, Gary. *Hatchet.* New York: Simon and Schuster, 1987.

———. *The Island.* New York: Dell, 1988.

Ryrie Brink, Carol. *Baby Island.* New York: Macmillan, 1937.

Schwartz, Elaine G. "Thinking Globally, Acting Locally: Fostering Ecological Literacy through Children's Picture-Books." *Journal of Children's Literature* 21 (1995): 49–56.

Sigler, Carolyn. "Wonderland to Wasteland: Toward Historicizing Environmental Activism in Children's Literature." *Children's Literature Association Quarterly* 19 (1994-95): 148–53.

Spaas, Lieve. "Conclusion." In *Robinson Crusoe: Myths and Metamorphoses.* Ed. Lieve Spaas and Brian Stimpson. New York: St. Martin's, 1996.

Steig, William. *Abel's Island.* New York: Farrar, Strauss, Giroux, 1976.

Stephens, John. "Not by Words Alone: Language, Intertextuality, Society." In *Language and Ideology in Children's Literature.* New York: Longman, 1992.

Taylor, Theodore. *The Cay.* New York: Avon, 1969.

Thoreau, Henry David. *Walden.* New York: Oxford University Press, 1997.

Traill, Catherine Parr. *Canadian Crusoes: A Tale of the Rice Lake Plains.* Don Mills, Ontario: Carleton University Press, 1986.

Wolf, Virginia S. "Paradise Lost? The Displacement of Myth in Children's Novels Set on Islands." *Studies in the Literary Imagination* 18 (1985): 47–63.

Wyss, Johann. *The Swiss Family Robinson.* 1812–13. New York: Bantam, 1982.

Part III

Adventures in History

8

Constructions of History in Victorian and Edwardian Children's Books

Thomas Kullmann

Historiography, as Hayden White, the literary and cultural critic, has shown, resembles fictional texts in that it invents plots, which are used to connect and give meaning to incidents from the past.[1] While history in general seems to call for a form of representation that resembles forms of literature, I would argue that in Victorian England historiographic discourses show a particular affinity with various forms of fictional writing, most particularly with the fairy tale and with chivalric romance. Historiographic interest at that time focused on the romantic fortunes of kings and queens and the landed aristocracy. The lives of famous historical characters were put into a meaningful shape, often a tragic one, with a lot of circumstantial detail, and then connected to the "life" of a nation which in some ways is treated as a person. Famous examples are the description of the death of Charles II in Macaulay's *History of England* (vol. I, ch. 4) and of the Siege of the Bastille in Carlyle's *French Revolution* (vol. I, bk. 5, ch. 6). In addition to old narrative patterns provided by folktale and medieval romance, historiographers used the techniques of characterization found in eighteenth- and early nineteenth-century prose fiction. Walter Scott's "historical romances," of course, made use of techniques of "emplotment" similar to those of the historiographers.[2] It was fictional works such as Scott's novels that created a new awareness of historical development.[3] This romanticized concept of history, which can perhaps first be traced in Edmund Burke's *Reflections on the Revolution in France* (1790), provided a means of defining personal, political and national identity, an *identité narrative*, to use a term coined by the French critic Paul Ricoeur.[4]

National monuments such as Hampton Court, which was opened to the public in 1838, contributed to this fairy-tale concept of the historical past. Apart from viewing Tudor times as an ensemble of seemingly irregular redbrick architecture, magnificent costumes and extensive interior decoration, the visitor to Hampton Court was regaled with modern, but old-fashioned, glass windows which represented Henry VIII in full array, surrounded by numerous coats of arms.[5] History was not glorified but idealized in a playful way. This playful attitude also manifested itself in the celebration of Guy Fawkes Night, which was particularly popular with Victorian children.[6] The original function of this ritual, which consisted in a ritual killing of popery and its black arts, had largely been forgotten. The Guy Fawkes folk customs no longer functioned as a "reminder of Protestant rage against Roman Catholic misdoings" as they might have done in the seventeenth century.[7] In the Victorian age, and even afterwards, the Gunpowder Plot and its failure appear rather as just another romantic episode in the fairy tale of English history which came to be regarded as a cultural possession.

This concept of history naturally lends itself to the exigencies of children's literature. From the vast body of children's narratives with plots taken from history I should like to discuss—among others—two outstanding examples, Captain Frederick Marryat's *Children of the New Forest* (1847) and Edith Nesbit's *The House of Arden* (1908). In Marryat's *Children of the New Forest*, four children of a noble family take shelter in the famous New Forest when attacked by Cromwell's Parliamentary army in the Civil War. Their father, Colonel Beverley, is described as a staunch supporter of the King: "This Colonel Beverley, as we must call him, for he rose to that rank in the King's army, was a valued friend and companion of Prince Rupert's, and commanded several troops of cavalry. He was ever at his side in the brilliant charges made by his gallant prince, and at last fell in his arms at the battle of Naseby" (p. 6).

Before he joined the King's troops Colonel Beverley requested Jacob Armitage, an old and devoted gamekeeper, to watch over his family. When hunting in the forest to provide the Beverley family with venison, he comes across Parliamentary soldiers: "Jacob had never yet seen the Parliamentary troops . . . but their iron skull-caps, their buff accoutrements, and dark habiliments, assured him that such these must be; so very different were they from the gaily-equipped Cavalier cavalry commanded by Prince Rupert" (p. 8). Jacob then overhears a conversation of the soldiers with a young man of his acquaintance who had been a "verderer" in the forest. This young man has gone over to the Parliamentarians and advises them as to the chances of finding King Charles, who had escaped from confinement. Jacob is "pained . . . to perceive that one who had always been considered a frank, true-hearted young man, and who left the forest to fight in defence of his king, was now turned a traitor" (p. 9). He warns the four Beverley children of the imminent Parliamentary attack on their house and takes them to his cottage; the following night the house is indeed burned down.

The events of the Civil War are thus seen from the Cavalier perspective; sympathies are firmly on the Royalist side. Chivalric, and royalist, virtues such as personal loyalty are emphasized. There also seems to be some connection between primitive innocence and loyalty to the king, as opposed to the corruption of civilization which is associated with disloyalty.

In the forest Edward, the eldest of the children and heir to his father's title and estate, learns to hunt; it is through this old aristocratic pursuit that he and his brother and sisters survive the Civil War and the first years of Cromwell's rule. The political order with the aristocracy as its mainstay is shown to have developed harmoniously from the natural order; for this reason it proves to be stronger than revolutionary upheaval.

After some time in the forest, Edward, who pretends to be the grandson of Jacob Armitage, makes the acquaintance of Patience Heatherstone, whose father has been appointed Intendant of the New Forest by Parliament. Mr. Heatherstone belonged to the Parliamentary party, and the Christian name of his daughter testifies to his Puritan persuasion; however, it soon turns out that he is opposed to King Charles' execution and other excesses of Cromwell and his associates. Speaking to Edward he justifies his commitment:

I considered that our cause was just; and had the power been left in the hands of those who would have exercised it with discretion and moderation, the King would even now have been on the throne, and the liberties of his subjects sacred; but it is easier to put a vast and powerful engine into motion than to stop it, and such has been the case in this unfortunate civil war. (p. 175)

From the point of view of the Royalist side, the narrator invites the reader to accord some sympathies to their opponents as well. The characterization of Mr. Heatherstone as an upright and principled person will be confirmed when he acquires the Beverley property, which had been confiscated by Parliament, only to restore it to Edward Beverley later. The marriage of Edward Beverley to Patience Heatherstone is indeed symbolic of the reconciliation of the parties opposed to one another in the Civil War.

The Civil War is also treated in George Alfred Henty's novel *When London Burned* (1895), which is set in the years 1664 to 1667. Cyril, the young hero, is the orphaned son of a Cavalier gentleman who at the Restoration fails to recover his estates previously seized by Parliament, and dies in poverty and bitterness. This Cavalier is described in ambivalent terms:

Beyond the virtues of loyalty and courage, he possessed few others. He had fought, as a young man, for Charles, and even among the Cavaliers who rode behind Prince Rupert was noted for reckless bravery. . . . Sir Aubrey had been one of the wild, reckless spirits whose conduct did much towards setting the people of England against the cause of Charles. He gambled and drank, interlarded his conversation with oaths, and despised as well as hated the Puritans against whom he fought. (p. 11)

Cyril, his son, enters the service of a ship's chandler as a clerk, and soon distinguishes himself as a valued member of the household. He sets the accounts in order, discovers a robbery, and saves his employer's daughter from dishonor and infamy. When he comes to the rescue of the daughters of a nobleman whose house is on fire, he makes the acquaintance of Prince Rupert, with whom his father had served. While his identity as a gentleman's son is now discovered it takes another turn of his fortunes before he regains his paternal estates. His father's estates had been given to Mr. Ebenezer Harvey, a Puritan whose conscience induces him to seek out their rightful owner. During the plague, Cyril manages to save the lives of Mr. and Mrs. Harvey. After taking part in the sea-battles against the Dutch, he finally takes possession of his family estates. As   in *The Children of the New Forest,* country estates seized under Cromwell are restored to their rightful inheritor by honest Puritans, this inheritor having proved himself worthy of his inheritance. Henty's novel, however, goes further than Marryat's in denouncing the vices of the Cavaliers and attributing virtues to their opponents. Nevertheless, the justice of Cyril's inheritance is not questioned; the novel is told from the Royalist point of view and celebrates the ultimate victory of the Royalist party.

Another Civil War story, Walter Ambrose Bettesworth's *Two Little Cavaliers* (1907), is obviously addressed to younger readers; the two heroes are a twelve-year-old and an eleven-year-old boy, who disguise themselves to get beyond the Parliamentarian lines to notify the King of the danger to Basing House, a besieged Cavalier stronghold. Later on, the two boys meet Oliver Cromwell, who is impressed by their fearlessness and promises to do them a good turn later. When Basing House is finally taken and overrun by Cromwell's troops, Cromwell personally invites the two boys to place themselves under his protection.

The two boys are described as "fine specimens of English boyhood" (p. 13); their tutor teaches them "to be manly, truthful, and straighforward; to fear God and honour the King—to be gentlemen" (p. 15). With less reserve than Marryat and Henty, the author presents the Cavalier side of the conflict as the correct one, and the little Cavaliers as models for identification. As in the other two books, however, this position is offset by a portrayal of an individual from the opposite party which is at least partly sympathetic.

The Royalist point of view enables the authors of the books discussed to provide their fictional versions of history with archetypal romance elements, including the survival of children in a wilderness, the loss and restitution of home, and the eventual discovery of a noble hero's true identity. This emplotment of history illustrates the fairy-tale view of the past initiated by Edmund Burke who, when writing about the French Revolution, lamented the loss of the "pleasing illusions" provided by the chivalric code of honor.[8] The present is seen as the result of the past; by preserving the outward forms of the age of chivalry, historic change loses its threatening and inhuman aspects. In being invited to identify with characters who in moments of historical crisis preserved these traditions, the nineteenth-century British reader was provided with a concept of himself or herself as a participant in the fairy tale of a glorious national history. This fictional formula, however, also allows for the integration or "containment" of systems of value which differ from the dominant conservative discourse. The straightforward and self-denying honesty of Cromwell and his Puritan followers is also given its due; the Restoration period is seen as a paradigm for national reconciliation.

A text which reveals, and in a way deconstructs, the fictionalized and narrative character of English historiography is Edith Nesbit's *The House of Arden*, published in 1908. In this book, twelve-year-old Elfrida travels into the past, together with her ten-year-old brother Edred, to witness various moments of historical crisis. Nesbit here follows the formula established by Rudyard Kipling's *Puck of Pook's Hill* (1906). In one of the episodes Elfrida meets with aristocratic relatives of her family. She does not know what year she has arrived in, but she is told that the date is the fifth of November. Elfrida is immediately reminded of Guy Fawkes Day and begins to hum the famous rhyme:

> Please to remember
> The Fifth of November —
> The gunpowder treason and plot.
> I see no reason
> Why gunpowder treason
> Should ever be forgot. (p. 148)

"Cousin Richard," Elfrida's new companion, has objections against this rhyme: "'Tis not a merry song, cousin," said Cousin Richard, "nor a safe one. 'Tis best not to sing of treason.'" Elfrida has arrived in a time during which treason was not just a literary motif but an ever-present danger. Elfrida's reply, however, emphasizes the narrative and seemingly fictional character of this story: "'But it didn't come off, you know, and he's always burnt in the end.'" If Guy Fawkes is *always* burned, he belongs to a repeated game which is not directly connected to reality.

Elfrida therefore proceeds to tell the story as she had learned it: "The King hadn't been fair to the Catholics, you know," said Elfrida, full of importance, "so a lot of them decided to kill him and the Houses of Parliament. They made a plot—there were a whole lot of them in it" (p. 149). Incidentally, we may notice the ostentatious impartiality of the nineteenth-century history book from which Elfrida obviously quotes; the conspirators are said to have had a reason for their dissatisfaction with King James, even though this may not have justified the actual plot.

Cousin Richard then admits to never having heard this tale from his tutor. Elfrida therefore proceeds:

"Well, Mr Piercy took a house next the Parliament House, and they dug a secret passage to the vaults under the Parliament Houses; and they put three dozen casks of gunpowder there and covered them with faggots. And they would have been all blown up, only Mr Tresham wrote to his relation, Lord Monteagle, that they were going to blow up the King, and—"

"What King?" said Cousin Richard.

"King James the First," said Elfrida. "Why—what—" for Cousin Richard had sprung to his feet, and old Parrot-nose [the tutor] had Elfrida by the wrist. (p. 149)

As it happens, Elfrida in her journey through time has arrived exactly in the year 1605, on the very day of the discovery of the plot. Elfrida now has to realize that the fact of knowing the names of the conspirators has quite another relevance in the aristocratic circles of 1605 than it has in the schoolroom of 1905 where knowing history usually means good marks and the teacher's praise. The stories Elfrida had learned in her history lessons had been secreted in her memory with other, fictional stories; Elfrida had not been aware of their special significance as stories which had actually happened.

"Parrot-nose," Richard's tutor, who now urges Elfrida to name all the conspi- rators, also refers to Elfrida's account as a fictional narrative, calling it a "romance," and a "pretty story," no doubt to cover the reasons for his own interest in this account. Richard then refers to the supposed fictionality of Elfrida's story to exonerate her from the charge of being party to a conspiracy: "'Come, sir,' said Cousin Richard, 'you frighten my cousin. It is but a tale she told. She is always merry, and full of many inventions'" (p. 150). Richard, however, is unable to remove his tutor's suspicion that Elfrida is a party to the secret of the conspiracy; neither does her assertion that she is only repeating "history" and "books" preserve her from being imprisoned in the Tower.

Elfrida does, of course, get back into her own age, together with her brother Edred. At the end of the book, news arrives that, because of the death of a distant relation, Edred has succeeded to the title of Lord Arden and is the rightful owner of that ruinous castle in which he and his sister had played and come across the "Mouldiwarp" (or mole) which had provided the means for time-travelling. The romance is thus shown to continue in the real world. While Nesbit does expose the fairy-tale character of history, this is not done to denounce historiography as unreliable storytelling. On the contrary: she rather seems to suggest to the community of her young British readers that they are all inheritors of a wonderful sequence of stories, and that, because of what happened in history, there is a fairy-tale layer to daily existence.

Thus, an analysis of the treatment of history in Victorian and Edwardian children's books has shown how British history was constructed as a "grand narrative" or fictional romance in a way which can certainly be considered to be characteristic of the Victorian historical and cultural consciousness in general. Young readers are invited to be proud of their national heritage and of the age of their nation's institutions. This patriotic pride naturally seems to encourage a conservative view of history and politics, and is certainly conducive to a sense of British superiority. The fairy-tale "emplotment" given to history, however, also encourages tolerance and respect for differing systems of values, and thus undercuts the imperialist discourse prevalent in other texts of the age. Only by establishing harmony can we hope to live happily ever after.

NOTES
    1. See, for example, Hayden White, *Tropics of Discourse: Essays in Cultural Criticism* (Baltimore: Johns Hopkins University Press, 1978), pp. 58–61 *et passim*.

2. For this term, see White, *Tropics of Discourse*, p. 66.

3. This historical interest was not confined to prose fiction. For a discussion of "Locksley Hall" as a poem about historical identity, see my article "Tennysons 'Locksley Hall' und die Konstruktion von Geschichte im viktorianischen England" in Ahrens and Neumann, eds., *Fiktion und Geschichte in der anglo-amerikanischen Literatur*, Heidelberg: Winter, 1998.

4. Paul Ricoeur, *Temps et Récit*, 3 vols. (Paris: Seuil, 1983–85), 3, pp. 355–359.

5. June Osborne, *Hampton Court Palace* (Kingswood: Kaye and Ward, 1984), p. 186.

6. On 5 November 1605, the Gunpowder Plot, a Roman Catholic conspiracy to blow up King James I and Parliament, was discovered and Guy Fawkes, a principal conspirator, was arrested. In 1606 Parliament established 5 November as a day of public thanksgiving.

7. Laurence Whistler, *The English Festivals* (London: Heinemann, 1947), pp. 202–212: 211.

8. Edmund Burke, *Reflections on the Revolution in France* (Harmondsworth: Penguin, 1986), p. 171.

REFERENCES

Bettesworth, Walter Ambrose. *Two Little Cavaliers.* London: Nelson, n.d.

Burke, Edmund. *Reflections on the Revolution in France.* 1790. Harmondsworth: Penguin, 1986.

Henty, George Alfred. *When London Burned: A Story of Restoration Times and the Great Fire.* London: Blackie, 1895.

Kullmann, Thomas. "Tennysons 'Locksley Hall' und die Konstruktion von Geschichte im viktorianischen England." In Rüdiger Ahrens and Fritz-Wilhelm Neumann, eds., *Fiktion und Geschichte in der anglo-amerikanischen Literatur.* [Fiction and History in English and American Literature]. Heidelberg: Winter, 1998: 219–238.

Marryat, Captain [Frederick]. *The Children of the New Forest.* 1847. Harmondsworth: Penguin, 1948.

Nesbit, E. *The House of Arden: A Story for Children.* 1908. Harmondsworth: Penguin, 1986.

Osborne, June. *Hampton Court Palace.* Kingswood: Kaye and Ward, 1984.

Ricoeur, Paul. *Temps et Récit.* [Time and Narrative]. 3 vols. Paris: Seuil, 1983–85.

Whistler, Laurence. *The English Festivals.* London: Heinemann, 1947.

White, Hayden. *Tropics of Discourse: Essays in Cultural Criticism.* Baltimore: Johns Hopkins University Press, 1978.

9

'Tis a Hundred Years Since: G. A. Henty's *With Clive in India* and Philip Pullman's *The Tin Princess*

Dennis Butts

If the rise of the historical novel for children owes most to the achievements of Sir Walter Scott, whose adult novels, such as *Waverley, or, 'Tis Sixty Years Since* (1814) were enjoyed by many juvenile readers, other writers of tales set in the past were not slow to follow. Harriet Martineau's tale of eighteenth-century pirates *Feats on the Fiord* (1841) and Captain Marryat's English Civil War novel *The Children of the New Forest* (1847) are just two early examples. From the middle of the nineteenth century, in fact, as the thirst for boys' adventure stories grew, so did the production of historical tales. R. M. Ballantyne published *Erling the Bold: A Tale of the Norse Sea-Kings* in 1869, H. Rider Haggard his tale of Ancient Egypt, *Cleopatra,* in 1887, while R. L. Stevenson presented historical fiction in such novels as *Treasure Island* (1883) and *Kidnapped* (1886).

The most prolific and one of the most popular of all Victorian writers of historical tales for children was G. A. Henty (1832–1902). Although he wrote a dozen adult novels, he is best remembered for his boys' stories, over eighty of which are historical, ranging in period from Ancient Egypt in *The Cat of Bubastes* (1889) to the contemporary history of the Boer War in *With Roberts to Pretoria* in 1902. Henty has been credited with sales of 150,000 copies a year at the peak of his popularity, and with total world sales of over 25 million copies.[1]

Most of Henty's historical novels follow the romance-structure typical of so many nineteenth-century adventure stories. The youthful hero, usually a normal teenage boy, as the result of a domestic crisis leaves home to seek his fortune elsewhere. Often accompanied by a faithful companion, the young hero struggles on his journey against various complications—shipwreck, attacks by cannibals, treachery—and the story gradually rises to a great climax, from which the hero emerges triumphant to return home laden with riches.

But Henty's fictions are saturated with facts. Whether his story is set in Roman times, as in *Beric the Briton* (1893), or in the period of Napoleon's retreat from Moscow, as in *Through Russian Snows* (1896), Henty's books are full of historical, geographical and cultural information about the era, the countries and especially the battles the hero lives through. Indeed the books often contain carefully-drawn black-and-white maps and battle-plans, while Henty's prefaces usually contain an account of the historical sources on which his books are based. Today much of this reads like very dull history, such as this account of Russia's preparations to defeat Napoleon:

To oppose the threatening storm Alexander had gathered three armies. The first, stationed in and around Wilna under General Barclay de Tolly comprised 129,050 men; the second, posted at Wolkowich, and commanded by Prince Bagration, numbered 48,000; the third had its headquarters at Lutsk, and was commanded by Count Tormanssow, while the reserve, which was widely scattered, contained 34,000 men.[2]

So successful was Henty that his biographer G. M. Fenn claimed that he "taught more lasting history to boys than all the schoolmasters of his generation."[3]

Henty's historical tales were, however, not value-free, but reflected the ideology of a late-Victorian British imperialist. This is not surprising. Henty was writing when Britain was dramatically expanding her Empire overseas, taking control of the whole of India after the Mutiny of 1857, annexing Burma, and adding vast parts of Africa to the existing colonies in Australia, Canada and New Zealand. Henty's literary career coincided with the high tide of Imperialism, when Britain, under such prime ministers as Disraeli, Salisbury and Rosebery, strongly believed in the legitimacy of British territorial possessions overseas, and endorsed the assumption that the British Empire was an unrivalled instrument for harmony and justice.

Although the religious didacticism present in Captain Marryat's works was not so apparent in adventure stories produced in the second half of the nineteenth century, Henty and his fellow authors took their moral responsibilities just as seriously, guiding their young readers towards the social and political values of imperialism and empire-building, usually by advocating such virtues as courage (or "pluck"), loyalty and honesty within the ideological framework of Victorian *laissez-faire* capitalism and a hierarchical view of society. In the prefaces to his books, Henty emphasizes the importance of various episodes of imperial history and draws attention to the moral virtues which enabled their successes to be achieved. The heroic feats in Henty's tales are, of course, accomplished by young males. Women occasionally appear as patient mothers, girls as gentle sisters, and the pretty girl next-door often survives to marry the hero at the end of the story. But G. A. Henty's books are dominated by male values.

His novel *With Clive in India: Or, the Beginnings of Empire*, produced just over a hundred years ago in 1884, is a typical example. Using the characteristic romance-structure, it tells the story of sixteeen-year-old Charlie Marryat who leaves home in Yarmouth after the death of his father to obtain employment as a civilian writer for the East India Company in Madras. On the journey out he distinguishes himself in action against privateers and then, on reaching India, volunteers for military service against the French with Captain Clive, the authentic historical figure. Acquiring a comic Irishman, Tim Kelly, as his servant and faithful companion, Charlie performs with great distinction over the next ten years, seeing action in such battles as Arcot (1751), Plassey (1757) and Pondicherry (1761). He rises from the rank of ensign to that of colonel, and returns home to England to become a country gentleman and Member of Parliament.

There is little doubt that the main emphasis of Henty's tale is on Britain's imperial history, as the preface makes clear; the preface also gives the reader the sources Henty has drawn on for the story and information about the orthography of Indian place-names. A map of India precedes the first chapter, and there are five battle-plans to show military operations accurately. Though Charlie and his companions experience personal and fictitious adventures, the emphasis of the book is essentially documentary, not least near the beginning of the story when a senior Indian resident devotes much of chapters 5 and 6 to an exposition for Charlie's benefit of the early history of British rule. The accounts of battles are similarly detailed.

And all this is to demonstrate not just the reality but the superiority of British rule, of course. Yet Henty was not an uncritical imperialist. While praising Clive's military genius, for example, he is not afraid to attack him for want of principles or for taking bribes.[4] But this is always within the context of general approval, as if by demonstrating fair-mindedness over minor matters, Henty's objectivity can be trusted over the larger question of imperialism in general.

The action of *With Clive in India* is completely dominated by men. Though Charlie's widowed mother and his sisters appear at the beginning and end of the tale, they are shadowy figures. The other female in the story is Ada, a merchant's young daughter, a passive figure whom Charlie rescues from the "Black Hole of Calcutta," after which she returns home to England to wait for Charlie to marry her at the end of the book. Although many girls may have read *With Clive in India* a hundred years ago, the female roles are peripheral and traditional.

The events of the First and Second World Wars profoundly affected the character of historical adventure stories, however. Not only did they introduce aspects of the new technology, such as wireless, aviation and tanks, but the massive loss of life eclipsing anything experienced in the nineteenth century clearly affected society's attitudes towards wars in general. After the shocks of the Somme and British disasters at Gallipoli, Dunkirk and Singapore, many found it difficult to believe in the unwavering superiority of British might. The growth of international bodies such as the United Nations, and television's revelation of the world as a global village, together with the steady dismantling of the British Empire, beginning with India's independence in 1947, removed the imperial basis of many enterprises. The ideology of an expanding and self-confident British Empire, which had underpinned *With Clive in India*, was gradually eroded, and a new generation of historical novelists, such as Hester Burton, Leon Garfield, Cynthia Harnett, Robert Leeson, Jan Needle and Rosemary Sutcliff, grew up from the 1950s onwards, inspired by a more troubled, multiracial and democratic humanism.

As Western society moved into that stage of capitalism variously defined as the post-industrial or consumer society, adult literature moved from modernism to post-modernism; the production of novels sometimes defined as "metafiction" has, in recent decades, begun to affect children's literature and the character of some historical tales.[5]

Metafiction, according to one of its interpreters, Elizabeth Dipple, "takes the reader's sophistication and complete absorption of genres from the past for granted, so that as a mode it builds ironically on top of the experienced literature of the past." As well as using parody or even pastiche as playful elements, metafiction is also likely to be full of overt references to other literature, and to be witty and sometimes anti-representational.[6]

The recent children's books of Philip Pullman reveal many of the characteristics of metafiction. Not only has he produced a graphic novel, *Springheeled Jack* (1989), a comic-strip story combining prose narrative with marginal jokes and references to other books, but he has also written a remarkable series of historical novels employing metafiction: *The Ruby in the Smoke* (1985), *The Shadow in the North* (1986), *The Tiger in the Well* (1991) and *The Tin Princess* (1994).

All these historical novels are set in the second half of the nineteenth century, and focus on a teenage heroine, Sally Lockhart. In *The Ruby in the Smoke*, set in the backstreets of the London Docks in 1872, Sally discovers that her dead father was mixed up with a mysterious trade in the Far East involving a Chinese triad, before she defeats the criminals all trying to regain a priceless ruby. In *The Shadow in the North*, set in 1878, Sally works as a financial adviser, investigating the activities of Axel Bellman, a Swedish businessman, and discovers that he is a weapons manufacturer with political ambitions, whom she has to defeat before the story ends. *The Tiger in the Well* begins with Sally, who is unmarried, receiving a letter from a complete stranger suing her for divorce and, since the novel is set in 1881 (before Gladstone passed the "Married Women's Property Act" of 1882), this means that her child and almost everything Sally owns actually belong to her alleged husband. Almost every step Sally takes seems to confirm that she is indeed married to this stranger, and the labyrinthine plot takes many twists and turns before the mystery is solved. Finally, *The Tin Princess* focuses upon a friend of Sally's, Becky Winter, who is a language-teacher. One of Becky's pupils, Adelaide Bevan, is married to the Crown Prince of Raskavia, a small state sandwiched between Germany and the Austro-Hungarian Empire, and when Adelaide goes to Raskavia with her husband to help resist the threats of Prussia, Becky goes with them. All sorts of intrigues and assassination attempts follow before Becky returns home to tell Sally about her adventures.

Remnants of the traditional adventure plot survive with the use of a teenage hero(ine), journeys and homecomings and, though based more on imaginary events than Henty's, Pullman's historical stories also contain detailed and accurate descriptions of aspects of Victorian life. They do, however, concentrate more on social than on military history with a particular interest in such issues as crime, immigration and the marriage laws. But all these tales also contain formal aspects of metafiction. They are, for instance, deeply influenced by such novelists as Charles Dickens and Wilkie Collins. Although it is going too far to call *The Ruby in the Smoke* a parody, its plot of Chinese triads, opium-smoking and murder will remind many readers of Collins's *The Moonstone* (1868) and Dickens's last novel, *The Mystery of Edwin Drood* (1870), while the influence of Dickens's sociological detective story *Bleak House* (1851) lies not far below the surface of the melodramatic mystery of Philip Pullman's *The Shadow in the North*.

Like most post-modernists Philip Pullman often gently reminds his reader that he or she is reading a story, not simply looking at a mirror of the world. He does this by drawing attention to the artificiality of his ingenious and multi-plotted structures, when he switches from one thread of his narrative to another, with such expressions as "At the same time . . ." or "Mr Parish, by contrast, had just been having a highly satisfactory meeting with his lawyer."[7] Authorial comments also remind us that we are still reading fiction when, for example, the narrator breaks off from describing the plight of thousands of immigrants to say that "each of them had a story to tell; but we're concerned with the story of Sally Lockhart." He even comments, when a character speaks with an unfamiliar accent: "If it belonged anywhere, it belonged to the future; a hundred years from then, voices like Mr. Brown's would be common, though Mr. Windlesham could hardly be expected to know that."[8] (In this way, Pullman reminds us that historiographic metafiction poses, as the Australian academic Robyn McCallum says, "questions about the relationship between fiction, history and reality."[9]) Finally, Pullman plays games with intertextuality, referring us by name in his story about financial corruption to Anthony Trollope's great Victorian novel about corruption, *The Way We Live Now* (1875): "An amusing book about a financial speculator," says one of his characters.[10] Equally suggestive and witty is the way the heroine's innocent young daughter, Harriet, swears at the end of *The Tiger in the Well* in a surely deliberate 'anticipation' of Shaw's Eliza Dolittle in *Pygmalion* (1912): "Not bloody likely."[11]

Although Pullman does not expect us to mistake his fiction for real life, he does want us to take it seriously, and in his racy but elaborately-plotted historical tales, he deals with major themes such as racism, poverty and the treatment of women. Thus his books offer an extraordinary mixture of almost light-hearted entertainment, combined with subtexts of anger and sadness and admiration. With heroines like Sally Lockhart, these stories are addressed to girls as well as boys.

The Tin Princess is perhaps the best example. Telling the story of sixteen-year-old Becky Winter's adventures when she accompanies Adelaide and her husband to the tiny—but invented—European kingdom of Raskavia, it contains many features similar to Henty's historical tales. Set in 1882, it presents a teenage hero(ine), a faithful companion, and a long journey to foreign parts. The Penguin edition of *The Tin Princess* also contains a Henty-like map of Raskavia and its royal capital Eschtenburg. But its account of intrigues in castles and plots to regain a throne are almost a pastiche of such Ruritanian romances as Anthony Hope's *The Prisoner of Zenda* (1894) and John Buchan's *The House of the Four Winds* (1935). In the end, whereas Henty's heroes are always triumphant, Pullman's romantic adventurers are foiled: Adelaide's husband, King Rudolph, is assassinated; Raskavia is annexed by the German Empire; the heroine and her lover are defeated.

What the story ultimately reveals, in other words, is almost the opposite of Henty's historical novels. Using the stuff of the traditional tale, young heroes, travel, intrigues and battles, *The Tin Princess* shows the grim *realpolitik* of Bismarck and commercial interests and betrayal. Raskavia is not annexed for its romantic castles but for its nickel mines. "You and Adelaide and Jim gave it the best chance it could have had," says Becky at the end of the story, "You did everything that courage and wit and imagination could, but force wins. Enough force always does."[12]

G. A. Henty often depicted corruption and defeat in the course of his historical novels, too, though it is always within the context of the ideology of a triumphant British imperialism. But the events of the twentieth century have seen the end of such one-sided optimism. Whatever era he wrote about, Henty's historical tales—self-confident, imperialistic, male-oriented and hierarchical—reflect the nature and stability of Victorian England, and, paradoxically, they do so by a kind of historical realism. By contrast, Philip Pullman's tales of nineteenth-century Britain, display a version of post-modernist metafiction in their literary technique while, in their values, they reflect the gains, uncertainties, ambiguities and ironies of European society a century later.

NOTES

1. W. G. Blackie (1952), quoted by R. L. Dartt, *G. A. Henty: A Bibliography* (New Jersey: Cedar Grove, 1971), p. v.

2. G. A. Henty, *Through Russian Snows: A Story of Napoleon's Retreat from Moscow* (London: Blackie, 1896), p. 184.

3. G. Manville Fenn, *George Alfred Henty: The Story of an Active Life* (London: Blackie, 1907), p. 320.

4. G. A. Henty, *With Clive in India; Or, The Beginnings of Empire* (London: Blackie, n.d.), pp. 273, 280.

5. See Fredric Jameson, "The politics of theory; ideological positions in the postmodernism debate," and Terry Eagleton, "Capitalism, modernism and postmodernism," both quoted in David Lodge, ed., *Modern Criticism and Theory: A Reader* (London: Longman, 1988), pp. 385–398.

6. Elizabeth Dipple, *The Unresolvable Plot: Reading contemporary fiction* (London: Routledge, 1988), p. 9.

7. Philip Pullman, *The Shadow in the North* (Harmondsworth: Penguin-Puffin, 1973), p. 74; *The Tiger in the Well* (Harmondsworth: Penguin, 1992), p. 81.

8. Pullman, *The Tiger in the Well*, p. 19; *The Shadow in the North*, p.155.

9. Robyn McCallum, "Metafictions and Experimental Work," in Peter Hunt, ed., *International Companion Encyclopedia of Children's Literature* (London: Routledge, 1996), p. 407.

10. Pullman, *The Shadow in the North*, p. 155.

11. Pullman, *The Tiger in the Well*, p. 392.

12. Pullman, *The Tin Princess* (Harmondsworth: Penguin-Puffin, 1994), p. 285.

Part IV

Colonial, Postcolonial

10

Doctor Dolittle and the Empire:
Hugh Lofting's Response to British
Colonialism

David Steege

In his influential work *Culture and Imperialism* (1993), Edward Said focuses on the relationship between narrative fiction and Western imperialism in the nineteenth and early twentieth centuries. He demonstrates how fiction reflected and strengthened the imperial system in which one political entity dominated several others, and asks us as readers and critics to further the work he starts by connecting texts with "the imperial process of which they were manifestly a part."[1] He wishes us to see how novels in particular reproduce imperial ideology, and to understand how many of them reflect a society in which the deeper values of imperialism, such as the superiority of the dominant culture over that of the colonized peoples, are unquestioned.

While Said did not focus on children's literature and its connections to imperialism, it is a logical place to look. Given the need of an empire, such as the British Empire, to sell itself to its people—to win hearts, minds and bodies to the colonial struggle—it is not surprising to find that fiction intended for children drew on and contributed to attitudes toward British colonies and their indigenous peoples. It is also not surprising that some of these books presented the history of British colonialism in as favorable a light as possible. As Said puts it, "stories are at the heart of what explorers and novelists say about strange regions of the world . . . who owned the land, who had the right to settle and work on it, who kept it going—these issues were reflected, contested . . . in narratives."[2]

Hugh Lofting's Doctor Dolittle series makes a useful case study of how history, politics and children's literature connect and interpenetrate. Most adult readers in Great Britain and the United States have a passing familiarity with Doctor Dolittle, the man who could talk to the animals. In Lofting's *The Story of Doctor Dolittle* (1920), the title character is a people doctor in an English West Country village, until one day his parrot Polynesia tells him that animals have languages of their own. After she gives him an example of animal speech, his naturalist's curiosity is awakened: "'Tell me some more,' said the Doctor, all excited; and he rushed over to the dresser-drawer and came back with the butcher's book and a pencil. 'Now don't go too fast—and I'll write it down. This is interesting—very interesting—something quite new. Give me the Birds' A.B.C. first—slowly now.'"[3] Dolittle becomes an animal doctor exclusively, and is soon famous in the animal kingdom.

Lofting's second book, *The Voyages of Doctor Dolittle* (1922), won the Newberry award in 1923, and he went on to write ten more Dolittle books, which, according to his son Christopher, have sold millions of copies worldwide and been translated into a dozen languages.[4] However, ever since the 1960s, one is as likely to be familiar with criticism of the racism in the books as with the books themselves. Critics have cited numerous problems, from Polynesia's use of the word "nigger" to offensively caricatured illustrations of Africans drawn by Lofting himself. At least partly as a result of this criticism, the series began to fall out of favor, especially in the United States, where the books were first published.

However, in 1988, the publishers Delacorte and Dell, with the blessing of Christopher Lofting, eliminated the more obviously offensive language and pictures and reissued eight of the twelve books in the series in the United States. The expurgation of the most blatantly insensitive material has made it easier to see a feature of the series intimately connected but not confined to race: namely, how several of the books reveal Lofting's struggle with colonialism. Lofting's ambivalence toward imperialism led him in his Dolittle books to re-invent and revise British colonialism, from its beginnings and development to its possible future.

Almost every piece on Lofting quotes the same account of Dolittle's origin, in which Lofting relates that *The Story of Doctor Dolittle* began as a series of letters to his children during World War I, after he was dismayed by the lack of veterinary care for horses wounded in battle. He felt that he could not write about the terrible war to his children; instead, he sent them letters about an eccentric, roly-poly British doctor living in the first half of the nineteenth century, a man whose attributes are kindness, defense of the weak, love of animals and impatience with the narrow-mindedness of humanity. In the Dolittle books, the English past is more or less pastoral, slow-paced and distant from the chaos of Lofting's own age. Given their nature, these letters were probably written not just to satisfy his children but also to escape from the reality of his own situation. Lofting was retreating to a largely idealized early nineteenth century as a reaction to World War I.

At the same time, critics have made almost nothing of the connection between the settings of several Dolittle books and Lofting's life before the war. From 1910 through 1911, Lofting worked as a civil engineer for the Lagos Railway in West Africa. There he was able to observe firsthand a region profoundly affected by the imperial dreams of Europeans. The time spent in Africa clearly helped shape the Dolittle series: West Africa is the setting for many of the Doctor's adventures, including the first volume and, later, *Doctor Dolittle's Post Office* and *Doctor Dolittle and the Secret Lake*.

He wrote later that he had become an engineer in order to see the world, but that he was a bad engineer and "hated every minute of it."[5] His experiences, combined with World War I, led him to formulate a belief in internationalism. In 1924, he spoke of "two big empires striving for economic mastery of the world" prior to World War I, and of the war itself as "the death throes of two ugly giants, the epochs of Competitive Industrialism and Armed Imperialism." He feared the two giants might "come back to life and have their ugly fight all over again," and advocated "a campaign for the right of Peace Preparedness" beginning with children.[6] In other words, Lofting was a self-proclaimed anti-imperialist and anti-nationalist who believed in cooperation, not competition, between nations and peoples.

Certainly these notions are evident in the Dolittle series. We see his stress on cooperation between nations in the first volume, when Dolittle manages to get the Lion Kingdom and other predatory animals to come to the aid of plague-stricken monkeys. Then, in *The Voyages of Doctor Dolittle*, the doctor defends a small tribe of "Indians" (as Lofting calls them) against a larger tribe, yet Dolittle chooses not to punish the aggressor but to forge a peace pact in which the two tribes promise to help one another. This inclusion of a generous and just peace treaty may even have been a veiled criticism of the recently concluded Treaty of Versailles. It was certainly a positive re-invention of the actual history of relations between indigenous peoples and colonial governments.

Despite his strongly stated anti-imperialist and anti-war views, he rarely directly criticizes in his Dolittle books the country of his birth or his adopted country, the United States. In the first book is a passage in which an African king explains why he distrusts all whites. He tells the Doctor that "Many years ago a white man came to these shores; and I was very kind to him. But after he had dug holes in the ground to get the gold, and killed all the elephants to get their ivory tusks, he went away secretly in his ship."[7] Here Lofting comes close to blaming Europeans for their past actions in Africa—yet he dilutes it by making the king superstitious, gullible and a poor judge of character for not recognizing Dolittle as a better kind of white man. Note, too, that a child could read the king's words and assume the unnamed white man was an exceptional type of visitor to Africa rather than a frequent one; this single reference hardly reflects the true scope of Britain's colonial history.

Again, it is important to note that Lofting chose to set the Dolittle books in the first half of the nineteenth century. This was the period, he reminds us at the beginning of *Doctor Dolittle's Post Office*, when Britain and most other European governments had officially forbidden the transatlantic slave trade and the British navy was attempting to blockade West Africa to prevent its illegal continuance. When the Doctor sets out to help rescue a West African from a slave-trader, he is delighted to stumble upon the H.M.S. Violet. He cries, "It's a man-o'-war—a navy vessel. The very thing we want to deal with slave traders."[8] By choosing that historical period, Lofting can emphasize the best side of Britain's intervention in African affairs, and ignore the imperial scramble for Africa that Britain participated in after 1876. He does not have to deal with the military, political or economic realities of the British Empire in the Africa of his own day, either.

Lofting does not simply throw out the idea of British civilization dominating others; instead of portraying British colonialism as it really began and developed, he creates his own version of imperialism through Doctor Dolittle himself. When we put aside Lofting's statements in his writings for adults and simply look at the Dolittle series, he seems rather in favor of some kind of imperialism, if not of a military or economic kind. The character of Doctor Dolittle is Lofting's attempt to soften, re-shape and humanize the face of colonialism while maintaining a sense of the white British male's key place in creating and maintaining civilization.

One of the clearest places to find Lofting working out his brand of imperialism is in *The Voyages of Doctor Dolittle*. After the good Doctor wins the war of the weaker, smaller tribe against their larger, more aggressive neighbors, the smaller tribe elects him their chief, and the larger tribe, recognizing his greatness, unites its lands to the smaller tribe's so it can be ruled by the Doctor as well. Dolittle protests—he doesn't want the responsibility—he won't be able to do his own scientific work—but is finally persuaded that he, now called "King Thinkalot" and "The Kindly One," must stay and help these people. His coronation takes place in a huge natural amphitheater, where he sits on a raised throne in the very center. During the coronation, an ancient prophecy is fulfilled when a great hanging stone falls into the island's extinct volcano as the crowd roars out Dolittle's name; it is only supposed to fall when the "King of Kings" is crowned. Dolittle, predictably, is a wise and beloved leader who builds a new town and introduces sewers, garbage service, dams, iron and copper mines, and schools. When he leaves, he fears that his "children," as he calls them, will "go back to their old habits and customs: wars, superstitions, devil-worship and what not; and many of the new things we have taught them might be put to improper use."[9]

Dolittle's experiences as King Thinkalot are really imperialism without military conquest, mercantile interests, or patriotic rhetoric, and with the full cooperation of all the indigenous peoples. It is the image of the kindly, paternalistic Great White Father, without whom the natives would be lost, carrying his burden gamely if reluctantly. Instead of being presented the history of British colonialism as a scramble for power and position, children are encouraged to think of it as the kind-hearted actions of a lovable English eccentric who would rather be catching butterflies and classifying plants. In *Voyages*, a British white male sits on a throne in the literal center of the tribe and outperforms all their previous, native leaders. The island they live on is a floating island—the only one of its kind—and when that hanging rock falls into the volcano, it causes the island to stop floating forever: the white man has given the island a fixed identity, a definite place in the scheme of things.

In *Doctor Dolittle's Post Office*, Dolittle brings prosperity and civilization—this time to a fictional West African kingdom, Fantippo—in much the same way he did in *Voyages*. Here the African king is left in place, and the Doctor becomes instead of a monarch a kind of idealized colonial civil administrator, instituting a post office and a weather bureau as well as improved medical care. These kind of projects, instead of reminding us of the colonial situation in Africa during the setting of the series, instead most closely resemble the more attractive side of British colonialism in West Africa during the time Lofting wrote his books. The 1920s were indeed a period when, as the historian Lawrence James recounts, there was a stated desire by many British leaders to develop colonies for the benefit of everyone, not just Europeans. During this time, in addition to developing trade, the colonial administration focused on education, health care and other social services.[10] In other words, Lofting is re-inventing the early nineteenth century to mirror his own age in order to highlight the most positive aspects of contemporary colonialism.

It is also notable that Nigeria is often seen by historians as one of the less strife-torn examples of British imperialism in Africa. John Iliffe, the historian of Africa, has pointed out that, in southern Nigeria, "occupation was relatively peaceful and foreign trade extensive," and thus government was financed by customs duties, not by direct taxation; furthermore, "administration could be confined to a handful of white officials seeking to guide African rulers gradually towards European notions of good government."[11] This indirect rule reminds one of Dolittle in his floating post office, going onshore to have tea with the King and engage him in, as the King puts it, "instructive conversation."[12]

In this rather rosy picture of British/African relations, however, at no time does the Doctor (or Hugh Lofting) show any interest in learning about or maintaining the cultural traditions of the indigenous peoples. The cultures and societies are there to be moved toward British notions of civilization. There is no discomfort in creating Europeanized Africans in Lofting's work, only occasional humor at the ways they misinterpret or misuse what is introduced to them, as when the king of Fantippo builds a post office thinking that letters will magically deliver themselves if one simply drops them in the mailbox. Lofting's books demonstrate surprisingly little interest in other cultures, except to show off the Doctor's superiority to them. The tribal culture on the islands seems to have nothing to teach the doctor; only he can teach them.

One might respond to this by citing Lofting's general distrust of humanity; he did not appear to think much of human culture in general. This is where turning to Lofting's portrayal of animals helps show how fully Lofting believed, at heart, in the values of his own culture and civilization. The Doctor's relationships with animals are very similar to his relationship with the island tribes. The animal kingdom, because he can cure their illnesses, loves him intensely and calls him "The Great Man." In *The Story of Doctor Dolittle*, the Doctor is given the two-headed Pushmi-Pullyu by the grateful African monkeys so that he can display it at a circus to pay off his debts. It does not seem an exaggeration to see this as another facet of Lofting's transformation of the development of imperialism in the nineteenth century into something gentler: it's as if the treasures of Africa, if the British had been kind enough, would have been given to them freely.

Finally, Lofting shows his ambivalence about the British Empire in the manner in which the Doctor ends his involvement with the indigenous people. In the early 1920s, the dissolution of the Empire was seen as necessary by some, as inevitable by others and as intolerable by many. In other words, the issue was very much in doubt. But leave-taking is a major element in all three of the 1920s books about Dolittle overseas. And in all three cases the Doctor, always reluctant to be the hero-king, longs for dear old England, decides to leave, and is barely able to get away because those he had helped desperately want him to stay.

In *The Voyages of Doctor Dolittle*, for instance, Dolittle leaves the island not because of the tribes' wishes but despite them. As England began to face the twilight of empire in the real world, Lofting in Dolittle's world finds a way to have colonialism end happily: with regret more on the part of the colonized than the colonizers. The Doctor is now able to pursue his work as a naturalist; in fact, he is lured away from his throne by a voyage of discovery to the bottom of the ocean inside the shell of a giant sea-snail. From gentle mastery over people, this kindly imperialist now seeks out knowledge of realms hitherto hidden from human eyes, an impulse historically often allied with imperialism. Lofting's Dolittle is a late imperialist's fantasy; the colonizer is beloved and withdraws from his colony with no loss of honor or affection among the subject peoples.

Lofting's emphasis on the end of British domination is another example of the author focusing on the least exploitative phases of the empire. He emphasized the early, pre-imperial days when Britain championed anti-slavery; he also makes use of the positive development of educational and medical institutions in his own day; lastly he looks ahead to a time when a tired and successful Britain gracefully lays down the White Man's Burden .

Edward Said sees Joseph Conrad as "both anti-imperialist and imperialist," one engaged at the same time in "criticizing and reproducing the imperial ideology of his time," a writer whose works "argue that the source of the world's significant action and life is in the West," and deeply doubtful that "Africa or South America could ever have had an independent history or culture."[13] In many ways, Lofting is similar, an author who did not perceive himself as deeply centered in the West and its ideology. It is amusing to note that Dolittle takes a trip into the heart of Africa—as Marlowe does in *Heart of Darkness*—at the end of *Doctor Dolittle's Post Office*, when he journeys upriver to find the Secret Lake and Mudface, the turtle who lived through the Flood and who tells the Doctor all about it, including the story of Noah's Ark. So at the Doctor's heart of darkness is not horror, but confirmation of the Judeo-Christian version of ancient times. The secret of the Secret Lake, therefore, is that the Bible was right all along. Africa is there to confirm the West's view of itself, not to disturb it.

And Doctor Dolittle, while certainly a nicer, much less grasping imperialist, is not really a radical alternative to Lofting's twin ugly giants, "Competitive Industrialism and Armed Imperialism," but rather a more acceptable, ethical version of them. Lofting creates this version by avoiding certain eras in British colonial history and by substituting a past that includes a jolly, kindhearted Great White Father. Dolittle, then, allowed Lofting not only to escape the horrors of war, but to escape having to give up the notion of the British male as indispensable to those under his power.

NOTES

1. Edward Said, *Culture and Imperialism* (New York: Knopf, 1993), p. xiv.
2. Ibid., pp. xii–xiii.
3. Hugh Lofting, *The Story of Doctor Dolittle* (New York: Dell, 1988), pp. 9–10.
4. Christopher Lofting, Afterword to *The Story of Doctor Dolittle*, by H. Lofting (New York: Dell, 1988), p. 151.
5. Humphrey Carpenter and Mari Pritchard, eds., *The Oxford Companion to Children's Literature* (Oxford: Oxford University Press, 1984), p. 324.
6. Anne Commine, "Lofting, Hugh," in *Something About the Author*, Vol. 15 (Detroit: Gale Research, 1979), pp. 181–82.
7. Lofting, *Story*, p. 48.
8. Hugh Lofting, *Doctor Dolittle's Post Office* (New York: J. B. Lippincott, 1923), p. 11.
9. Hugh Lofting, *The Voyages of Doctor Dolittle* (New York: J. B. Lippincott, 1922), p. 325.
10. Lawrence James, *The Rise and Fall of the British Empire* (New York: St. Martin's, 1994), p. 430.
11. John Iliffe, *Africans: The History of a Continent* (Cambridge: Cambridge University Press, 1995), p. 199.
12. Lofting, *Post Office*, p. 38.
13. Said, *Culture*, pp. xviii–xx.

REFERENCES

Carpenter, Humphrey and Prichard, Mari, eds. *The Oxford Companion to Children's Literature*. Oxford: Oxford University Press, 1984.

Commine, Anne. "Lofting, Hugh." *Something About the Author*. Vol. 15. Detroit: Gale Research, 1979.

Iliffe, John. *Africans: The History of a Continent*. Cambridge: Cambridge University Press, 1995.

James, Lawrence. *The Rise and Fall of the British Empire*. New York: St. Martin's, 1994.

Lofting, Christopher. Afterword to *The Story of Doctor Dolittle*, by Hugh Lofting. Centenary ed. New York: Dell, 1988.

Lofting, Hugh. *Doctor Dolittle's Post Office*. New York: J. B. Lippincott, 1923.

———. *The Story of Doctor Dolittle*. New York: J.B. Lippincott, 1920.

———. *The Voyages of Doctor Dolittle*. New York: J. B. Lippincott, 1922.

Said, Edward. *Culture and Imperialism*. New York: Knopf, 1993.

Photo 11.1
Front cover, from Eve Pownall and Margaret Senior, *The Australia Book*, Sydney: John Sands, 1951.

11

Picturing Australian History:
Visual Texts in Nonfiction for Children

Clare Bradford

Visual texts work on their readers in a visceral and immediate way, and because of this their capacity to inscribe ideologies is especially powerful. In this chapter I consider visual texts in nonfiction for children published in the 1940s and 1950s on the subject of Australian history. The artworks, maps, charts and photographs which feature as illustrative materials in nonfiction texts of this period are themselves texts of the past, and construct narratives about the past; but they are as much about a projected future, because in them the past constitutes an array of exemplary narratives, promoting in their child readers behaviors and beliefs appropriate to Australian citizens. In the interests of uncovering some of the discursive strategies through which these visual texts position their child readers, I have a two-fold focus: the ways in which the selected visual texts manifest the ideologies and preoccupations of their time and place, and the strategies through which they seek to persuade their child readers of the lessons of history.

On the front cover of a canonical Australian children's text, *The Australia Book* by Eve Pownall and Margaret Senior, published in 1951 (Photo 11.1), chronology is offered as teleology; the procession of people and animals striding purposefully from past to present enacts a timeline which begins with Captain Cook and identifies Australian history with progress, so that the prosperity of the 1950s, encoded on the bottom row by products of the land (wheat, milk and wool), is seen to derive from the endeavors of convicts, soldiers, settlers and farmers, in an unbroken line of cause and effect. This is also a view of history as pageant, as a display of types differentiated as to class and occupation but unified by their positioning within a metanarrative around the development of national identity.

There are, in this procession, three transgressive figures. All three feature in the top row, in the years immediately following white settlement; all face towards the left of the picture instead of the right, that is, towards stasis and not change;[1] all are motionless, and all are Aborigines, two children and an adult. It is impossible to consider texts thematizing the Australian past without encountering what the art historian Bernard Smith has called "the locked cupboard of our history,"[2] the presence, frequently encoded in absence, of those whose invasion and dispossession was the necessary ground for colonization. The three Aboriginal figures in this picture metonymically represent a people disengaged from history; the fixed gaze of the adult, the stereotypical posture of the child on the left and the waving hand of the child on the right signify a paradoxical combination of inertia and wilfulness, as though the three passively choose to remain in a realm located, as it were, outside the book and so outside both history and modernity.

History as manifested in these images is his-story, not hers. Men are represented here in two ways: in relation to their occupations and as fathers (mainly to sons), but—as in the masculine images of the bottom row—they can straddle the private and public spheres. Women, however, can only be mothers— or, as in the top row, ladies—defined as they are in relation to the maternal; for in the ideological formations which produced this picture, maternity *naturally* restricts women to the private sphere of home and family.

The boy walking behind the sheaf of wheat on the bottom row and before the bus labelled "To-day" is carrying a copy of the *Australia Book* and reading it as he walks, a reflexive move which provides him with a multivalent significance, as the reader of the book and as a character experiencing the past as heritage and the present as history in the making, being himself the subject of the historical narrative. This ideological load on the figure of the focalized child seeks to persuade child readers of the linearity of Australian history, its steady progressivism and, in particular, the dynamism of what is constructed as a young country, rich in resources and possibilities.

The final picture from *The Australia Book* incorporates Australian history into a larger cultural narrative. Captain Cook and his companion stand on a clifftop, and their focalizing gaze looks towards an expansive scene which represents the new Australia. In this scene, an aeroplane represents the brave new world of air travel, but the land below is also made new by technology, for the picture shows a modernist townscape in which the allusions to industry serve to modify the rural mythology of the book's cover. The land itself is tamed and controlled, a neat patchwork of cultivated farmland and vegetation hemmed in by road and fences. Child readers are invited to align their subjectivities with those of a group of children viewed proceeding up a hill and towards the reader, and to join in their triumphalistic march onwards and upwards.

The narrative strategies of selection, shaping and focalization evident in these pictures from nonfiction books are strikingly similar to those which characterize much historical fiction for children.³ In addition, these pictures offer visual equivalents of the focalizing characters of historical fiction, for while the verbal text of *The Australia Book* does nothing so postmodern as to interpolate invented child characters into its accounts of historical events, such child figures can be introduced through the visual texts alone, where they serve to invite identification on the part of child readers.

Similar narratalogical and ideological moves are evident in a mass-market text of 1946, Margaret Pearson's *The Story of Australia*, the front and back endpapers of which are of particular interest because of the absences they encode. The front endpapers offer a stylized view of a grassy shore from which is seen a sailing ship, framed by a Union Jack and by the figures of two eighteenth-century children (a midshipman and a servant girl) planting a gum tree. The back endpapers show two 1940s children admiring the tree, which is now very large. Again, Australian history begins with white settlement; more than this, white settlement effects an ontological leap, since Australia, signified by the gum tree, exists only when touched by white hands. The two children on the back endpapers offer child readers subject positions appropriate to history-makers of the future. The two sets of children (the colonial children on the front endpapers and the contemporary children on the back) are framed in the same way, so inviting a reader alignment that reinforces the similarities between present and past, denying the past its alterity and constructing children of the past as "Us in funny clothes."⁴

Two other forms of visual representation appear in postwar histories of Australia for children: re-presentations of colonial artworks; and drawings, maps, charts and photographs which purport to work as conceptual pictures, explaining history in a realist or scientific mode. Val Biro's illustrations in P. R. Smith's *The Story of Australia* (1959), published in London by Ernest Benn, provide examples of reworkings of colonial artworks. The artworks that constitute Biro's pre-texts for his versions of Australian history were produced by artists in the first years of the colony, and embody not simply what was seen, but how the people, topography, plants and animals of the new land were viewed by European eyes, and what significances were attributed to them. That is, these works speak of the ways in which the unfamiliar was incorporated into existing conceptual models, and of the collisions and gaps which were made manifest when "appropriate words, images, symbols and ideas" had to be found to encode the new.⁵

John Hunter, a naval officer, created a seminal first-fleet drawing later reproduced as an engraving. Reading the land through his knowledge of European landscapes and texts, Hunter writes as follows about his first impressions of Sydney:

Near, and at the head of the harbour, there is a very considerable extent of tolerable land, and which may be cultivated without waiting for its being cleared of wood; for the trees stand very wide of each other, and have no underwood: in short, the woods on the spot I am speaking of resemble a deer park, as much as if they had been intended for such a purpose.⁶

Hunter's drawing displays a similar blend of idealism and nostalgia, representing Sydney Cove as an idyllic space, the Union Jack fluttering in a neatly-fenced enclosure, Australian trees transmogrified to suit a setting somewhat reminiscent of Capability Brown's elegantly controlled landscapes. But Hunter and his companions soon discovered that the climate and soil of Sydney Cove had very little in common with those of English deer parks; few of the settlers' seeds grew, and their animals died. Thus, by the time it was published in Hunter's *Journal* in 1793, the drawing signified another set of meanings common in discourse of the early colonial period, that of the Australian landscape as a *locus* of illusions, "an enchanted park in which things were not what they seemed."[7]

Hunter's drawing is introduced into an entirely different set of cultural and reading practices in Biro's reinterpretation in *The Story of Australia*. With its caption "Sydney Cove in 1788," this picture claims to represent how Sydney Cove *was*, not how it *seemed*. Biro's technique, with its reliance on pen-and-ink line, hints at the striations of engraving and so claims both a link with artistic production of the past, through what Jane Doonan, the writer on children's book illustration, describes as "a certain gravitas," and an authoritative historicity.[8] Perhaps this illustration is best seen in the light of the sycophantic foreword, by Robert Menzies (then Australia's Prime Minister), which introduces *The Story of Australia,* and which proclaims what a splendid thing it is that "a famous publishing house in London" should publish "what are some of the greatest and most romantic stories of the growth and bestowal of the British inheritance."[9] In drawing on a colonial text, Biro seeks the authority of the "British inheritance" which produced it, but in retaining the features of Hunter's reading of the land, he naturalizes the colonial significances of Hunter's drawing, which are of course impenetrable to child readers with no experience of the illustration's pre-text. A further effect in Biro's version results from the foreshortening of the scene, which confers on it a certain coziness, so that the huts and tents of the first-fleeters appear more like a holiday camp than a colony.

Another reinterpretation of a colonial text in the same 1959 history shows a scene entitled "Crossing the Blue Mountains."[10] Here, two men are located on an outcrop, framed by rock formations and twisted tree-trunks and looking out to a scene of cliffs and gullies. The two explorers are placed in a patch of white at the center of the picture, and are constructed as heroic figures battling enormous odds. The artwork on which this scene is based is an anonymous drawing which had appeared as an engraving in an 1888 publication entitled *Australia the First Hundred Years: The Picturesque Atlas of Australasia*. In the *Picturesque Atlas* this picture is called simply "Govett's Leap," and like others in the atlas it offers the armchair reader scenes observed through picturesque travel. The two men are not of central significance to the scene, being placed off-center and in the shadows; the man standing looks down to the gulf below, not (as in Biro's re-presentation) out to the new lands to be conquered. In the *Atlas* version there appears a fence at the top of a lookout, against which stand a woman and a child, a detail which domesticates a view otherwise encoding the grandeur and sublimity valued in picturesque art. The vertical hatching of Biro's version recuperates something of the picturesque delight in the Gothic, but the most interesting feature of his treatment of the colonial pre-text lies in the way in which the land is transmuted from spectacle to obstacle, its human figures from aesthetes to conquerors.

The third category of visual texts in Australian histories of the mid twentieth century locates history within frameworks represented as objective and scientific. An illustration featuring Aboriginal artefacts (Photo 11.2) appears in a 1940 school text, the eighth Victorian Reader, in an historical piece entitled "The Old Inhabitants." It presents its collection of items frontally, against a neutral, flat background, as generic objects used by an objectified and homogenized group ("the Australian Aborigines"). The two sub-categories, "Offensive Weapons" and "Message Stick" are implicitly located within a common "overarching category;"[11] the strangeness of the latter's taxonomy becomes clear if one considers equivalent western artefacts: say, guns (for offensive weapons) and the telephone which, like message sticks, is a means of communication. The implied overarching category, therefore, may be seen as that of Aboriginal technology, which is implicitly compared with "western technology." The dominant ideological effect of the illustration, concealed by its façade of analytical description, thus lies in the implicit contrast between the poverty and simplicity of these artefacts and the artefacts of a "developed" or "advanced" culture, a reading supported by the verbal text; its conclusion demonstrates the lasting influence of Social Darwinism well into the twentieth century:

Whether the blacks could have developed much further without communication with the rest of the world is rather hard to decide. It is not clear, either, what animal in Australia they could have tamed for food purposes, if they had wanted to do so; and, without herds of some sort, they could not have attained to a pastoral stage.[12]

The slippage between tenses (present tense in the illustration and past in the narrative) quarantines Aborigines contemporaneous with the production of this text in the ahistorical past occupied by the Aboriginal figures on the cover of *The Australia Book*. While both visual and verbal texts imply white children as readers, the school readers were so widely used that Aboriginal children must also have read these narratives, positioned through textuality as objects of colonial discourse.

Narratives of exploration loom large in Australian children's histories of the 1940s and 1950s, generally in conjunction with maps, which plot not only the journeys of explorers but also epistemologies of space and distance. In these maps, explorers are always constructed as the conquerors of virgin territory, and the maps incorporate discovery with the naming by which rivers and mountains are known and possessed. What counts as knowledge is precisely what is encoded in these maps; what does not count is present as absence, for these maps elide Aboriginal knowledge and knowledge systems of the land, distance and significant places. The organizing metanarrative into which the maps of discovery fit is of an Australia known only when it becomes the object of the explorer's gaze; in the twelve frames of a table from Eve Pownall's *Exploring*

Australia (1958), the country comes into being in exactly this way: the outline of Australia is gradually mapped, from non-existence before the seventeenth-century Dutch explorers to the final completed frame, where Australia exists "after 196 years exploration."[13]

At the time these texts were published, black and white Australians were producing oppositional readings of history, gender, indigenousness and landscape; the historian John Mulvaney, for example, was conducting research which was to result in his groundbreaking 1969 work, *The Prehistory of Australia*, which begins with the statement "The discoverers, explorers and colonists of . . . Australia, were its Aborigines."[14] But such oppositional readings did not find their way into children's histories and school texts of this period, which are socially conservative and uniformly ethnocentric.

The visual texts on which I have focused construct powerful ideologies by way of their representations of history and of Australia. Many of them, especially those presented as conceptual pictures, seem at first glance to be innocent of ideologies, but it is their very covertness which gives them potency. The child readers of these texts are positioned to believe that the only past that counts is the colonial past constructed through narratives about white male heroes, and that they themselves are the subjects of new narratives sustaining and continuing the colonial past in a new, technological world. Finally, I return to Bernard Smith's phrase, "the locked cupboard of our history,"[15] which reminds me of a Pandora's box or a Bluebeard's room upon which is placed an interdiction bound to be broken. The cupboard containing Aboriginal narratives is, in many of these texts of the 1940s and 1950s, not so much locked as concealed, denying child readers even the knowledge that it exists. This is, of course, itself a discursive strategy, one which has found various forms of representation in Australian cultural practice from 1788 until and including the present. In the texts discussed, strategies of silence and concealment concerning Aboriginality position child readers to see Australian history as beginning with white settlement, and to view Aboriginal people as locked in a mystical and mythical past which precludes them from modernity.

NOTES

1. See Gunther Kress and Theo van Leeuwen, *Reading Images* (Melbourne: Deakin University Press, 1990), p. 108.

2. Bernard Smith, *The Spectre of Truganini* (Sydney: Australian Broadcasting Commission, 1980), p. 10.

3. See John Stephens, *Language and Ideology in Children's Fiction* (London and New York: Longman), pp. 202–40.

4. Greg Dening, "Ethnography on My Mind," in *Boundaries of the Past*, comp. Bain Attwood (Melbourne: The History Institute, Melbourne University, 1990), p. 16.

5. Bernard Smith, *European Vision and the South Pacific* (Oxford: Oxford University Press, 1960, rev. ed. 1989), p. vii.

6. Ibid., p. 179.

7. Ibid., p. 180.

8. Jane Doonan, *Looking at Pictures in Picture Books* (Stroud: Thimble Press, 1993), p. 83.

9. R. Menzies, foreword to *The Story of Australia*, by P. R. Smith and B. Biro (London: Ernest Benn, 1959), p. 4.

10. Smith and Biro, *The Story of Australia*, pp. 20–21.

11. Kress and van Leeuwen, *Reading Images*, p. 20.

12. *The Victorian Readers: Eighth Book* (Melbourne: Government Printer, 1940), p. 9.

13. Eve Pownall, *Exploring Australia* (London: Methuen, 1958), p. 9.

14. John Mulvaney, *The Prehistory of Australia*. (London: Methuen, 1969), p. 12.

15. Smith, *The Spectre of Truganini*, p. 10.

REFERENCES

Bradford, Clare. *Reading Race. Aboriginality in Australian Children's Literature.* Melbourne: Melbourne University Press, 2001.

Dening, Greg. "Ethnography on My Mind." In *Boundaries of the Past.* Comp. Bain Attwood. Melbourne: The History Institute, Melbourne University, 1990.

Doonan, Jane. *Looking at Pictures in Picture Books.* Stroud: Thimble Press, 1993.

Kress, Gunter, and van Leeuwen, Theo. *Reading Images.* Melbourne: Deakin University Press, 1990.

Mulvaney, John. *The Prehistory of Australia.* London: Methuen, 1969.

Pearson, Margaret Mary. *The Story of Australia.* Sydney: Australasian Publishing Company, 1946.

Pownall, Eve, and Senior, Margaret. *The Australia Book.* Sydney: John Sands, 1951.

Pownall, Eve. *Exploring Australia.* London: Methuen, 1958.

Smith, Bernard. *The Spectre of Truganini.* Sydney: Australian Broadcasting Commission, 1980.

———. *European Vision and the South Pacific.* Oxford: Oxford University Press, 1960, rev. ed. 1989.

Smith, P. R. and Biro, B. *The Story of Australia.* London: Ernest Benn, 1959.

Stephens, John. *Language and Ideology in Children's Fiction.* London and New York: Longman, 1992.

The Victorian Readers: Eighth Book. Melbourne: Government Printer, 1940.

Watson, Don. *The Story of Australia.* Melbourne: Thomas Nelson Australia, 1984.

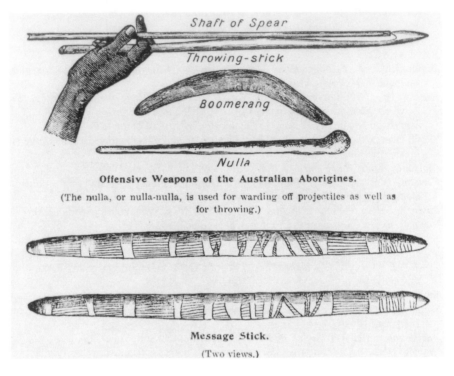

Photo 11.2
Unattributed drawing, "Message Stick" and "Offensive Weapons of the Australian
Aborigenes," from *The Victorian Readers: Eighth Book*, Melbourne: Government Printer,
1940, p. 10.

12

Narrative Tensions:
Telling Slavery, Showing Violence

Paula T. Connolly

The depiction of violence, particularly in books for the very young, has been a matter of constant debate. That debate becomes even more problematic when representing historical atrocities. While a range of fiction books about American slavery has been published in the United States for older children, until fairly recently the absence of picture books on the same topic has been marked. A few examples were produced in the past—such as Jacob Lawrence's *Harriet and the Promised Land* (about Harriet Tubman) in 1968—but it has been especially within the last decade that authors and illustrators have begun grappling with this topic. Clearly the problem in publishing picture books about such issues derives from the specific age range of the books' intended audience: to erase the violence of such events would be to mitigate the atrocity itself, yet including violence could easily alienate or terrify very young children. For example, in retelling U.S. slavery, how does one portray—in pictures and for such a young audience—scenes of whippings, murders, rapes, and the forcible separation of families? In short, how does one tell the truth?

Picture books are a sophisticated literary and art form. The sometimes jarring juxtapositions of visual and verbal texts, the use of white space to set narrative pace, and the presence of both literary and artistic symbol all heighten the variety of ways the form can be used. Indeed, in their exploration of such issues as slave communities, identity, coded language, rebellion, and even physical violence and oppression, many of the authors and illustrators of these recent texts have successfully navigated daunting minefields. Further, these authors and illustrators have engaged intriguing and complex blends of words and pictures that provide narrative tensions all their own. I argue that it is in these narrative tensions that one sees the depiction of violence, the presentation of atrocity.

While there are, of course, many issues that could be discussed about the "retelling" of this part of American history, here I focus on three specific elements that identify techniques used to balance concerns of accuracy and audience; they can be broadly stated as narrative focus, the interplay of word and picture, and reader placement. In this regard, three general types of picture book about slavery are examined, namely those which recount successful escape, non-escape, and failed escape stories.

Most picture books about slavery—such as Jeanette Winter's *Follow the Drinking Gourd* (1988), Faith Ringgold's *Aunt Harriet's Underground Railroad in the Sky* (1992), and Deborah Hopkinson and James Ransome's *Sweet Clara and the Freedom Quilt* (1993)—tell the fictional stories of escaping slaves. Escape tales are inherently hopeful. They are, ultimately, journeys out of slavery, and that provides comfort to the young reader who follows the plight of the protagonist at first trapped in slavery. The focus of such stories also provides a narrative tension between the threat of harm and the solace of a successful bid for freedom. In *Follow the Drinking Gourd* the escaping family is shown framed by trees; on one tree is a reward poster for their capture, on another, a sign leading them along the Underground Railroad:[1] they are depicted as literally caught between the symbols of capture and freedom.

The central issue and focus in these stories is often the re-establishment of family; in *Follow the Drinking Gourd* the escape attempt is motivated by the fact that the father "would be taken away, / their family torn apart."[2] In *Aunt Harriet's Underground Railroad in the Sky* and *Sweet Clara and the Freedom Quilt*, young Cassie and Clara, respectively, struggle to be reunited with their families. It is not only the focus on family and the fear of its dissolution that make the stories relevant to young children; so too does the position of the child within a community. Indeed this is crucial, for it is with the young protagonist that reader identification is established. In these texts, the initially enslaved protagonists are young children, and these children not only escape, but are often shown to be protected and cared for by others. In *Follow the Drinking Gourd* the very young child is depicted being held or touched by his parents and is even shown to be asleep during frightening scenes, as if no matter how terrible the situation becomes, the child will be protected.

Although these books clearly do not illustrate the same level of physical violence or sexual exploitation included in books for older children, the threat of violence is an inherent part of these escape stories so images of violence are often conveyed symbolically. In *Follow the Drinking Gourd*, this is shown when the escaping slaves stand on a mountain top, looking toward the North Star; behind them a predatory wolf bares its teeth to a defenseless sheep.

Further, the illustrations and words often provide a balance of their own; as verbal texts describe danger and violence, pictures often alleviate that violence (and vice versa). In *Sweet Clara and the Freedom Quilt*, for example, the text reads: "Me and Jack left Home Plantation in a dark thunderstorm. The day after, it was too stormy to work in the fields, so Jack wasn't missed. . . . We went north. . . . There was the old tree struck down by lightning." Despite the description of a storm, the illustration shows a near idyllic scene of Clara and Jack walking across a clear grassy area, the sky washed in soft yellow. In this way it is the juxtaposition of word and picture that illustrates the tension of the danger and the hope of escaping to freedom. In *Follow the Drinking Gourd*, we also see such a juxtaposition. Here it is the illustration that depicts imminent threat as a mother huddles with her child inside the hollow trunk of a tree while pursuing dogs are shown on the other side of a nearby river. The setting is dark but the anxiety of this scene is countered by the verbal text: "But the dogs lost the runaways' scent at the stream, and [they] . . . were not found." While one might argue that such balancing lessens the communication of violence, it also keeps the narrative possibility of violence omnipresent and the reader in a state of constant tension between simultaneous fear and relief.

If the story does not focus on escape but the protagonist is a slave, as in Courtni Wright and Gershom Griffith's *Jumping the Broom* (1994) or the McKissacks' book, *Christmas in the Big House, Christmas in the Quarters* (1994), the depiction of violence is inversely proportional to the possibility of escape. That is, in these stories, the child reader is relieved of the trauma of seeing/reading characters who never escape either by a fairly idealized depiction of slavery (as in the case of Wright) or the promise that slavery will soon end (McKissack). *Jumping the Broom* describes a wedding celebration in the slave quarters. Although young Lettie notes how her father visits them from another plantation and that her brother will not be at the celebration because "Master sold him away last year," Lettie is more concerned with the preparations for her sister's wedding and this results in slavery (apparently) doing little to hamper their joy; yet in reality slave marriages were not legally recognized. Moreover, while actual marriage celebrations between slaves often carried the promise "Till death or distance do us part" as a terrifying acknowledgment of their susceptibility to separation,[3] there is no acknowledgment—in either written or picture text—that this marriage could ever be threatened by the conditions of slavery. Indeed, the celebration seems idyllic and an opportunity for Lettie's mother to promise, as they sew the bride's dress, that the sewing Lettie learns can be passed on to her daughter in later years. Not merely the celebration, but slavery itself is described in continuous and even hopeful terms. Illustrations show scenes of beautiful clothes and an abundance of food at a celebration which includes "roasted chickens, pig, squirrels, venison, . . . rabbits . . . yams and biscuits."

The final page shows Lettie smiling gently as she lies securely wrapped beneath a brightly colorful patchwork quilt; she feels "lonely, knowing that Tillie will never sleep next to [her] again. . . . At the same time, [she's] glad because this was a special day. . . . [She] can hardly wait until the next jumping the broom!" Ironically, here it is marriage—not slavery—that causes the dissolution of the immediate family.

Christmas in the Big House, Christmas in the Quarters contrasts the lives of the slaves' and master's families during the holiday. Although the two groups are ostensibly amicable toward one another, clear tensions are defined and the politics of oppression articulated. In one scene, the Master is shown giving his fiddle to a slave so that it can be used for holiday dances. The illustration freezes that moment of exchange, Master and "music-maker" smiling. Yet an underlying unease is evident. The Master adds a "subtle warning . . . that the borrowed violin had better be 'returned in the same good repair'" (p. 32). In the illustration, the slave standing furthest to the right is cast in shadow, his expression at the exchange betraying some concern. As the slaves leave, they reveal that they, too, have felt the implicit tension of the meeting: "'Thank goodness!' they whisper to each other on the way back to the Quarters. 'That is over'" (p. 32).

The tension within a single scene between apparent amicability and underlying anxiety is furthered in the juxtaposition of entire scenes. On the first day of the new year the Master gathers together those same slaves with whom he had just recently shared his fiddle and eggnog. Shown standing on the step of his porch, and hence above the surrounding group of slaves who stand in poses of both expectation and sorrow, the "Massa calls the names of those who have been sold or hired out. His voice shows no emotion." Indeed, he tells a woman, "'No sense in screaming, mother. Your daughter is twelve years old. ... You'll get to see her next Christmas.' Begging, crying, pleading changes nothing. Massa's decisions are final!" (p. 54). This scene clearly sets up the marked distance between the two groups, as well as redefines the mood of Christmas, and makes explicit the anxiety of the slaves that had underpinned their earlier interactions with the seemingly friendly Master.

Although *Christmas in the Big House, Christmas in the Quarters* ends with the reality of enslavement, it also ends with the promise of coming freedom. The final entry describing life in the big house has the Master's daughter asking when she can have her own slave. Her father reassures her that although she is too young now, on the Christmas of her sixteenth birthday, in December 1865, "'There'll be plenty of slaves for you to choose from'" (p. 58). That promise, which denotes the year that would mark the end of the Civil War and the passage of the 13th Amendment to the American Constitution outlawing slavery, is one that will not be fulfilled. Further, the final voice is left to a "slave mother . . . [and] her son." He vows to run to freedom, and the mother tells him that "'I got a feeling, we aine gon' need to run away. One day, soon, we gon' celebrate the Big Times in freedom" (p. 58). The final illustration shows the mother holding and looking at her son, who stands tall, and looks outward, past the confinement of the page and clearly past the confinement of slavery.

The fact is, of course, that most slaves were never able to escape, and Ann Turner and Ronald Himler's *Nettie's Trip South* (1987) and Patricia Polacco's *Pink and Say* (1994) tell of people who never reach physical freedom. Unlike the other stories, however, these are told by white protagonists. Although these narrators cannot fully show the slave community (because, especially by virtue of their race, they stand outside of that), what this perspective does provide is a narrative tension that allows horrifying truths to be told while achieving reader placement through a white character.

Establishing reader identification through the white narrator creates distance and moderates the reader's trauma when the escape is not effected. That perspective speaks clearly to the differences in race, expressing the irony that it is one who is white who talks about slavery because those keenly affected by it are silenced. In *Nettie's Trip South*, for example, while Nettie travels from North to South and is sickened by slavery, the slaves are often not individualized and generally appear *en masse*. One double-page illustration shows three women—two of them holding children—who have individualized and distinct features; however, on the same pages, a group of young men standing behind a white slave-trader, as well as a group of women sitting in a wagon partially covered by an oversized advertisement for a slave auction, have no individualizing features. The depiction of those groups as undifferentiated people evokes the central politics of slavery, namely that it denies one's individuality and personhood.

Although Nettie wonders what it would be like to be a slave, crude psychological appropriation is avoided as Turner and Himler show the clear distinctions between Nettie and the slaves she sees. This is evident in the illustration of Nettie once she returns to the North and is sitting with a friend in their treehouse. There, separated from the ground, they are shaded from the sun by lush trees, wearing fine dresses, and refreshed by a waiting pitcher of water. Nettie realizes the differences between her life and that of slaves, a realization pictorially punctuated by the illustrations before and after this scene which show slaves working in the fields and waiting at slave auctions. Nettie has understood that the politics of race is the politics of power, and tells her friend,

I can't get this out of my thoughts: If we slipped into a black skin . . . everything would change. No one would call us by our last names, for we would not have them.... When someone called, we'd jump! We could not read in the apple tree with the sun coming through the leaves, for no one would teach us to read and no one would give us a book. And . . . at any time we could be sold . . . and we'd have to go, just like that.

Patricia Polacco does personalize slavery in *Pink and Say*, the true story of Pinkus Aylee (Pink) who saved the life of Sheldon Curtis (Say). Pinkus has been a slave and Say is a white boy from the North; both are young and fighting for the Union Army. The two become brothers in many ways, but race remains the ultimate marker between the two, at least to others. When they are both captured by Confederate soldiers, they are immediately separated and the double-page illustration shows the arms of two white men trying to pull Say away from Pink. Although Say's profile and part of his upper torso remain in the picture on the left-hand page, only Pink's wrist and the hand that still grasps Say's hand can be seen on the far right side. It is as if, with the blank space surrounding their grasp and only Pink's hand showing, he has already been expunged from the picture itself, as he is surely to be expunged from the scene at Andersonville prison.

Indeed, although both are Union soldiers and are brought to the same prison, Polacco clearly shows that racial bigotry is the motivation for their different treatment. The final illustration of both men follows their separation and shows them in uniform and saluting while facing the reader; behind them is a large United States flag, which covers three-quarters of the two-page spread. The red of the flag is diffuse as if blood, and the text reads:

Sheldon . . . Curtis was released from Andersonville prison some months later. . . . [He] returned to his home and recovered. . . . Pinkus Aylee never returned home. . . . It was told that he was hanged within hours after he was taken in to Andersonville. His body was thrown into a lime pit.

The story, Polacco tells us, is meant to serve as a "written memory" of Pinkus, who was an actual person, and the story, of course, could be told only because Sheldon was *not* killed and returned home, events clearly based on his race.

Current concerns about the realistic presentation of history have cultivated a public more receptive to picture books about horrific historical events, yet authors and illustrators still have the added burden of considering their young audience and the extreme violence of the histories they seek to tell. In the case of recent picture books about American slavery, the texts have been intricately interwoven with a sophisticated and often subtle blend of focus, form, and reader positioning. It is there, in the narrative tensions created by these techniques, where one can find representations of the *actual* tensions between the violence of oppression and the acute desire for freedom that defined slave-owning society.

NOTES
1. "Underground Railroad" is a common term in the United States indicating the networks that abolitionists set up to help fleeing slaves escape the South and reach Canada or the Northern US.

2. Page references cannot be provided since most picture books for young children have no page numbers; the McKissacks' *Christmas in the Big House, Christmas in the Quarters* is the only exception among the books discussed.

3. The historical use of the expression "Till death or distance do us part" in slave marriages featured in Kenneth Burns' television documentary on the Civil War, broadcast in 1990.

REFERENCES
Burns, Kenneth, dir. *The Civil War*. Public Broadcasting System, 1990.
Hopkinson, Deborah. *Sweet Clara and the Freedom Quilt*. Illus. by James Ransome. New York: Knopf, 1993.
Lawrence, Jacob. *Harriet and the Promised Land*. New York: Aladdin-Simon and Schuster, 1993 [1968].
McKissack, Patricia C. and McKissack, Frederick L.. *Christmas in the Big House, Christmas in the Quarters*. Illus. by John Thompson. New York: Scholastic, 1994.
Polacco, Patricia. *Pink and Say*. New York: Philomel Books-Putnam and Grosset, 1994.
Ringgold, Faith. *Aunt Harriet's Underground Railroad in the Sky*. New York: Crown-Random House, 1992.
Turner, Ann. *Nettie's Trip South*. Illus. by Ronald Himler. New York: Macmillan, 1987.
Winter, Jeanette. *Follow the Drinking Gourd*. New York: Dragonfly-Knopf, 1998.
Wright, Courtni. *Jumping the Broom*. Illus. by Gershom Griffith. New York: Holiday House, 1994.

13

Narrative Challenges:
The Great Irish Famine in Recent Stories for Children

Celia Keenan

The story of the Great Irish Famine of the 1840s is one of the most problematic episodes in Irish history. It is such an emotive story that efforts to commemorate the 150th anniversary of "Black '47" aroused passionate debate in Ireland. *The Irish Times* printed an angry series of letters arguing that a concert of popular music was not a suitable way to remember the deaths of a million people.

A letter from the British Prime Minister, Tony Blair, on the subject was deeply appreciated in Ireland for observations such as these: "that one million people should have died in what was then part of one of the richest and most powerful nations in the world is something that causes pain as we reflect on it today" and "those who governed in London at the time failed their people through standing by while a crop failure turned into a massive human tragedy." However, his comments were not universally welcomed in Britain, where *The Times* accused him of pandering to the Irish tendency to engage in self-pity (*Irish Times*, 5 June 1997).

Given the level of unease with the memory of the Famine and that its history has been written only recently (notably by women historians), it is not surprising that efforts to tell the story to children should prove difficult for British and Irish writers alike.[1] The subject is intrinsically difficult to shape into narratives for children. It lacks some of the ingredients of a good children's tale, and the most important of these is the potential for action. The Great Famine is a story of mass suffering. The children's writer must do justice to that without the relief that adventures or conflict provide, and without over-indulging in suffering and despair in the manner of a horror story. The second and related missing ingredient is that of an agreed villain. Only in the most extreme nationalist history can it be suggested that the Famine was simple genocide by the British. Only in the most extreme Unionist version of the story can the lazy Irish peasants or the greedy Irish landlords be solely blamed.[2] People writing for children like to use strong plots, clear characterization, and simple explanations for events. Even characterization becomes difficult in Famine narrative. There is a tendency for the hungry to become indistinguishable from each other, mere objects of pity and horror.

Three writers—Walter Macken, David Rees and Michael Mullen—who were interested in the Famine and who wrote historical novels for children chose not to write about the Famine for children, but did so for adults. The fact that these three writers avoided telling their Famine story to children may be indicative of an awareness of problems inherent in the notion of Famine as a subject for children's books.

Children's writers in recent years have begun to set their stories in the Famine period. An opportunistic element may have had some part to play in the fact that in 1997 in Ireland no fewer than four children's novels about the Famine were published, one of which seems to me to be an exploitative, poorly written novel that insults Irish Famine victims, and the Choctaw people of America, who contributed $470 for Irish Famine relief in a time of great tribulation for themselves.[3]

Writers resort to a variety of expedients to make the Famine in some way tellable to children. One device used by several novelists is to abandon the Famine quite early in the novel, so that the narrative becomes an emigration story, usually to North America. This transforms a tale of suffering into one of adventure, travel to exciting places, chance encounters and the opportunity to make fortunes. This is the pattern in Michael Morpurgo's *Twist of Gold* (1983), Arthur McKeown's *Famine* (1997), Michael Smith's *Boston! Boston!* (1997) and Colette McCormack's *Mary Anne's Famine* (1995). In a number of novels with this pattern a family survives intact, or is re-united in North America. This is the structure most likely to offer a happy ending, which often includes love, marriage and prosperity. The most explicit expression of this comes at the end of McKeown's story *Famine* where the elderly father (in West Virginia) says, "'It's a long way from Ballymore, Maggie. I'm glad we made the decision to come here all those years ago.' 'Yes, I'm glad we came too,' Maggie replied. 'It was a hard journey but we have a good life here'" (p. 42). One novel, Soinbhe Lally's *The Hungry Wind* (1997), uses the emigration plot in an unusual way. The destination is Australia, not North America, and the long journey comes quite late in the novel. The bulk of the novel is an account of the experiences of two sisters in the workhouse, an institution avoided as a location for action in all the other novels. Issues of pubertal sexuality and sexual exploitation by the master of the workhouse are confronted. There is a note of hope in the end, but not a happy ending. A significant absence in Irish Famine novels is that not a single one of them gives an account of emigration to Britain, yet during the period of the Great Famine Britain was the destination of the vast majority of refugees. Between 1841 and 1851 the number of people born in Ireland and taking up residence in Britain doubled. These people provided a sizeable proportion of the workforce in the industrial areas of Yorkshire and Lancashire and had a profound effect on the culture of the towns they found refuge in.[4] My suspicion is that these English stories of migration are not being told because they do not conform to the national myth of freedom. Freedom can be found in America or in Australia, but not in the bosom of the ancient oppressor. The Irish relationship with England has been too problematic to tell this story yet. Until very recently there was a particular sense of failure or shame about Irish emigration to England.

If there are omissions in the stories that Irish writers tell about the Famine, there are difficulties for British writers too. A particular difficulty seems to be created by the role of British soldiers in Ireland during the Famine. Soldiers would have been the most obvious manifestation of English power in Ireland. They were Englishmen, not Irish. In Irish accounts they figure in two ways: assisting at evictions and protecting stocks of food from hordes of starving people. In two novels by British writers, Morpurgo's *Twist of Gold* and Elizabeth Lutzeier's *The Coldest Winter* (1996), an individual soldier behaves in a way that would be frankly unthinkable in a novel by an Irish writer. In both novels a kind soldier is appalled at the role he is forced to play in Ireland and gives food, money in the form of a gold coin, and physical protection to starving children. In both cases his intervention is pivotal to the narrative. Morpurgo's soldier even includes fishing lessons in his benevolence: "'One day I'll not be here to feed you, and you must learn to live from the land. There's people dying in this country because they don't know where to look for their food. They've dug the potatoes for so long they've forgotten. Eels are there in plenty if you can only catch them, and I shall teach you'" (p. 23). An unconscious colonial condescension here assumes that the natives need to be taught how to exploit their own land by a representative of the colonizing power. The assumption that country boys would not know how to fish is absurd, and the historical fact that fishing rights belonged to landlords is ignored. Elizabeth Lutzeier's novel is much more nuanced, but her soldier gives a gold coin to the hero Eamonn saying, "'Here buy yourself something to eat'" (p. 19). The soldier does not seem to know the value of the coin. We later discover it is enough to pay rent for almost a year. Lutzeier recognizes that the device of the soldier giving the boy so much money is an unusual one; later in the novel another character is surprised at the soldier's altruistic gesture: "the baker's wife had never heard of any soldier giving away money before" (p. 36).

Lutzeier's novel is very fine; her initial focus is on the peasant boy Eamonn's family—poor, hungry, and evicted from their home. She succeeds where many other Famine novelists fail, giving an intelligent consciousness to her characters, so that we can identify with them. They are not mere victims and objects. Hence it was a real disappointment that although she avoided using emigration as a way of escaping from the implications of Famine, she resorted to a related device. In chapter five she shifts the center of interest from hungry, Catholic, peasant Eamonn, to the middle-class, Protestant and altruistic Kate, and her and her family's efforts to alleviate Famine misery. In a sense Lutzeier retreats from her central story to tell a different story of how the Irish were saved by charity, and Eamonn Kennedy and his family, who were so well drawn in the earlier part of the novel, become victims and objects of charity. Of course what is really happening is that the political implications of the Famine are avoided .

One novel that is more explicitly political in its intentions is Eve Bunting's Famine adventure novel, *The Haunting of Kildoran Abbey* (1978), originally published in the USA. The perspective is clearly northern Unionist. In the beginning the hungry children blame England for their misery and threaten revenge. However, they are proved wrong. England turns out to be Ireland's savior, symbolized by the presence of an English boy, Christopher, and the all-benevolent Lord Lieutenant of Ireland, Lord Bessborough, who says, "'I have always found the Irish to be a simple people but not stupid. It's difficult to believe that if you have been a good landlord all these years they would turn against you for no reason'" (p. 139). In this novel the villains are unscrupulous Irish landlords, whom England would no doubt punish, if only she knew: "'It's hard for him [the Lord Lieutenant] to know when something needs remedying when it looks alright on the surface,'" one of the characters says and Colum, the reformed rebel, says, "'It's hard for us to understand that there can be justice if we look for it'" (p. 153). The problem is that the simple Enid-Blyton-like adventure story sits a little uneasily alongside the colonial polemics.

There is a number of points to be made about the treatment of religion in almost all of these novels. The most striking point is that they all avoid the most common motif of traditional Famine lore, the proselytizing dimension of the soup kitchens, or "soupers" as they were known. If people converted from Catholicism to Protestantism the phrase used was "they took the soup."[5] (The charity of the Quakers was the one strong exception in this myth for their charity was seen as being disinterested.) There is no hint of this sectarian tension to be found in any of the contemporary novels for children. Another point about the depiction of religion in contemporary novels for children is the unflattering way that Catholic priests are frequently depicted: plump with smooth hands, eating cheese, eating fried bacon, taking money from desperate people, giving clichéd sermons about sin and self-indulgence to the starving. This may be a reflection of modern Irish anti-clericalism, for there is no evidence of it in Famine folklore, where the priest is often as poor as the people and is often their only comfort. Yeats' poem, "The Ballad of Father Gilligan," comes closer to the traditional image of the Famine priest as one who exhausts himself through devoted care for the sick.[6]

It is only in very recent books that the depiction of Protestant victims of the Famine occurs. In McKeown's 1997 book *Famine,* Joe and his daughter are Protestant, County Antrim farmers who live in comfort on the fruits of their farming and linen-weaving until the Famine strikes. They leave their farm and sell their loom and emigrate to America with their savings and their Bible and are able to buy a farm in West Virginia. They hear stories about the Famine from other less fortunate people on their journey to America, an example of a very obvious distancing device. In a sense they conform to stereotypes of Protestant prosperity and the Unionist myth that the famine spared Ulster, a myth recently exposed by Christine Kinealy.[7] Only in Lally's *The Hungry Wind* do we find Protestant victims of destitution and exploitation—Hannah and Rachel in the workhouse—who can speak Irish, and who find comfort in their Bible, particularly in the story of Jonah in the belly of the whale.

Perhaps the greatest cultural effect of the Great Famine was the near destruction of the Irish language; many of the writers are aware of this and it occasionally causes problems in their narratives. Sometimes we are told that families speak only Irish, and then find that they have learned very good English in a matter of months. Sometimes they tell each other to speak quietly so that soldiers will not hear what they are saying. Lally is the only writer who integrates the language issue into her plot and characterization in a creative way; thus, when her Irish-speaking heroine wants to explain about the sexual abuse of another girl by the workhouse master, she is overwhelmed by the fluency of her interrogator's English, loses her confidence in her own ability to speak English, and so justice fails.

One of the strangest references to the Irish language occurs in Ann Pilling's novel *Black Harvest* (1983) in which three modern English children holidaying in Ireland are possessed by the ghosts of a family which died in the Famine. When the English children hear an old man talking, "the voice was shrill and harsh. They couldn't tell whether he was speaking Irish or just making horrible noises . . . he was letting out a stream of foul Irish . . . spitting the words out, slavering" (p. 22). The English family suffers all the pangs of hunger. The baby almost dies and the dog pines away, until the Famine grave is found and the original victims are given a proper burial. It is a ghost story, indeed a horror story, that is redolent of a post-colonial sense of guilt and a desire to atone for past wrongs. The suffering is internalized and in a sense becomes "ours" rather than "theirs." It finds an interesting solution to a narrative problem by setting its story in the contemporary world.

Marita Conlon-McKenna's *Under the Hawthorn Tree* (1990) is one of the best known Irish Famine stories for children and it too finds ways around some of the problems of this kind of narrative. Her narrative is simple, third person, and stays with the Famine from beginning to end. It has no unbelievable adventures, no great gifts, no magic, no soldiers with money. Three children set out in search of their great-aunts after they are evicted from their home. In order to make their suffering tolerable Conlon-McKenna emphasizes the beauty of nature, the changes of the seasons, and the colors of the sky, gorse, hawthorn and bluebells. Famine narratives usually assume that all nature, not just the potato, has failed. Here, like the vision of nature, women's story-telling is a device used to relieve suffering. The mother tells tales of her grandmother and aunts, and her daughter Eily repeats these tales. Women's domestic skills function as emblems of hope. The tragedy of the baby's death is framed by the fact that she is buried in a little white robe which had been made by her grandmother for her mother's christening and that she is buried under a hawthorn tree which protected the living children at play and will now protect the dead child. The hawthorn is where people traditionally buried infants who died before they were christened, a fairy burial place, a sacred place where memories are kept. Myth, legend, storytelling, and religious tradition are all used to humanize a nightmare world. Conlon-McKenna's characters are always allowed to speak for themselves; loyalty and resourcefulness are what save them. This is a deceptively simple narrative in which the courage of ordinary people triumphs.

A recent picture book extends the parameters of Famine literature for children. Starkly beautiful black and white illustrations and a simple elegiac text bring the suffering of the Choctaw and Irish nations together in *The Long March* (1998) by Marie-Louise Fitzpatrick. The effect is to universalize pain without diminishing it. The fact that both nations are called "Potato People" highlights their common humanity.[8]

Famine stories for children in Ireland reverse a tendency that is prevalent in other forms of Irish fiction for children which reject urban life and its values in favour of a romantic rural ideal. Famine narratives end with rural children finding refuge in the comfort of large towns and cities whether in Ireland or in America. The horrors of the Irish Famine are an antidote to the fashionable notion that most human problems are caused by urban living.

In summary, the challenge of writing stories about the Famine for children has created some difficulties common to all writers who have chosen to write about it; related to the nature of the material, these derive from the lack of conflict or of action and the passivity of the victims. As a subject it also poses problems specific to writers from particular cultures or traditions. In the present very largely post-colonial culture of Ireland and the post-imperial culture of Britain, it is not surprising that a process of revision should continue. Post-colonial angst is not experienced solely by the colonized nation. British writers also feel the need to re-examine their colonial history in the light of dramatically changed relationships with the larger world. Children's writers are conscious of the burden of the past in a particularly acute way because they believe that their books may influence the values and even the actions of young people. It is therefore not surprising that the truth is sometimes somewhat approximate. For a British writer of children's fiction it is difficult to depict a world in which a British soldier is merely an oppressor. For an Irish writer it is difficult to depict Britain as a refuge from the Famine. In both cases cherished national narratives are challenged.

NOTES

An earlier version of this chapter was published in: Valerie Coghlan and Celia Keenan, eds., *The Big Guide 2: Irish Children's Books* (Dublin: Children's Books Ireland, 2000). Permission to publish the work in the present volume is gratefully acknowledged. The author wishes to acknowledge with gratitude the assistance of Valerie Coghlan, librarian at the Church of Ireland College of Education, Dublin; Robert Dunbar, CICE, Dublin; Rosemary Hetherington, librarian Dublin Public Libraries; Dr. Margaret Kelleher, English Department, St. Patrick's College, Maynooth; and Martin Maguire, Department of History, St. Patrick's College, Maynooth. She would also like to thank participants at the York IRSCL Congress, 1997, for their comments on an earlier version of this paper.

1. Cecil Woodham-Smith, *The Great Hunger: Ireland 1845–1849* (London, 1962); Mary Daly, *The Famine in Ireland* (Dundalk, 1986); Christine Kinealy, *This Great Calamity: The Irish Famine 1845–52* (Dublin: Gill and Macmillan, 1994); Margaret Kelleher, *The Feminization of Famine: Expressions of the Inexpressible?* (Cork: Cork University Press, 1997).

2. *Unionist* is the term used to denote that political view which supports the union of Great Britain and Northern Ireland.

3. The Choctaw, mentioned in Colin Vard, *Trail of Tears* (Dublin: Mentor Press, 1997), were forced to march to distant territories on the confiscation of their homelands at this time, many dying on the journey.

4. Frank Neal, *Sectarian Violence: The Liverpool Experience 1819–1914, An Aspect of Anglo-Irish History* (Manchester, 1988), chapter 3.

5. Desmond Bowen, *Souperism: Myth or Reality: A Study in Souperism* (Cork, 1970).

6. Cathal Poirtéar, *Famine Echoes* (Dublin: Mercier Press, 1995).

7. Christine Kinealy and Trevor Parkhill, *The Famine in Ulster* (Belfast: Ulster Historical Foundation, 1997).

8. Marie-Louise Fitzpatrick, *The Long March* (Dublin: Wolfhound Press, 1998).

REFERENCES

Bunting, Eve. *The Haunting of Kildoran Abbey*. New York: Frederick Warne, 1978.

Coghlan, Valerie, and Keenan, Celia. *The Big Guide to Irish Children's Books*. Dublin: Irish Children's Book Trust, 1996.

Conlon-McKenna, Marita. *Under the Hawthorn Tree*. Dublin: The O'Brien Press, 1990.

Fitzpatrick, Marie-Louise. *The Long March: A Famine Gift for Ireland*. Dublin: Wolfhound Press, 1998.

Hunt, Peter. *Criticism, Theory and Children's Literature*. Oxford: Basil Blackwell, 1991.

Keenan, Celia. "Because There Is a Lot of It." *Children's Books in Ireland* 14 (1996): 11.

Kelleher, Margaret. *The Feminization of Famine: Expressions of the Inexpressible?* Cork: Cork University Press, 1997.

Kinealy, Christine. *This Great Calamity: The Irish Famine 1845–52*. Dublin: Gill and Macmillan, 1994.

Kinealy, Christine, and Parkhill, Trevor. *The Famine in Ulster*. Belfast: Ulster Historical Foundation, 1997.

Lake, Wendy. "A Question of Identity: Some Aspects of Historical Fiction for Children Set in Ireland." *Children's Literature in Education* 18, 1 (1987): 13–19.

Lally, Soinbhe. *The Hungry Wind*. Dublin: Poolbeg Press, 1997.

Langton, Jane. "Time Thirst." In *Travellers in Time Past, Present and to Come*. Cambridge: Green Bay Publications, 1990: 131–136.

Lukacs, Georg. *The Historical Novel*. London: Merlin Press, 1962.

Lutzeier, Elizabeth. *The Coldest Winter*. Oxford: Oxford University Press, 1991; Dublin: Wolfhound Press, 1996.

Lysaght, Patricia. "Perspectives on Women During the Great Irish Famine from the Oral Tradition." *Béaloideas* Iml (1996–97): 64–65.

McCormack, Colette. *Mary-Anne's Famine*. Dublin: Attic Press, 1995.

McKeown, Arthur. *Famine*. Dublin: Poolbeg Press, 1997.

Morpurgo, Michael. *Twist of Gold*. London: Kaye and Ward, 1983.

O'Sullivan, Emer. "The Development of Modern Children's Literature in Late Twentieth-Century Ireland." *Signal* 81 (1996): 189–211.

Pilling, Anne. *Black Harvest*. London: Collins, 1983.

Smith, Michael. *Boston! Boston!* Dublin: Poolbeg Press, 1997.

West, Máire. "Kings, Heroes and Warriors: Aspects of Children's Literature in Ireland in the Era of Emergent Nationalism." *Bulletin of the John Rylands Library, University of Manchester*. 76, 3 (1994): 104–24.

Part V

War, Postwar

14

On the Use of Books for Children in Creating the German National Myth

Zohar Shavit

T he following is a rough outline of what a German child is likely to learn about the Third Reich and the Holocaust from reading a range of German historical novels for children, both original and translated from other languages:

There was a terrible war in Germany, in which the Germans suffered dreadfully. People had no food and were often forced to flee their homes. Hitler alone was responsible for this war, since the German people themselves had no desire for it. The Germans were not Nazis and the Nazis were not Germans. In fact, the German people were victimized by Hitler. Under the Third Reich the Germans assisted the Jews, resisted Hitler, and some even risked their lives to oppose him by joining the Resistance movement. The Nazis oppressed the German people, who are the main victim of the Third Reich. It is true that the Jews, in most cases the German Jews (Jews of other countries hardly ever receive attention), were also oppressed by the Nazis, but nevertheless they are to be blamed for their own fate.

So what? one may ask. What is the significance of this shared historical narrative in books for children? After all, these texts are read mostly, often exclusively, by children; more often than not they have no great literary value, nor are they, as children's books, particularly well positioned in the culture.

Despite the low cultural status of children's literature, books for children play a fundamental role in the construction of a national past. This is because they often serve as the leading, at times the only, mediator between their readers and history. The unequivocal view of these books as a central socializing agent implies that at an early stage they are actively involved in the creation of a national past. Understanding the past as it is manifested in books for children simultaneously creates images of the past and provides a paradigm for interpreting the nation's present and future.

Every national children's literature produces both direct and less direct historical narratives which seek to shape the child's view of his/her nation through a certain understanding of the past. The historical narratives created by the various texts for children have pretensions to historical accuracy and strive to be historically credible. At the same time, they aim through subjective retellings of the national myths, to be sources of national pride and identity, to provide the underpinnings for children's sense of belonging.

The issue raised in this chapter concerns the mechanism of constructing distorted historical narratives as manifested in German narratives for children. How can "reality" be depicted in a manner that is so distorted and yet still retain historical relevance? How, indeed, is it possible to create this kind of historical narrative? The answer, it seems, is simple, almost trivial: German books for children, like most other national narratives, represent a wishful image of their history. As in the case of other historical narratives, the German historical narrative for children is also the result of constructing and reconstructing available historical material. The ways in which this material is modified and altered, as well as the subsequent version(s) of a community's history, are determined by the given community's or nation's cultural and political needs at a specific point in time.

Although it is commonly believed that historical novels enjoy more freedom than other historical narratives, in principle they are devised according to the same methodology. Like other historical narratives, their construction entails the selection and organization of a given body of historical matter. In terms of organizing events and protagonists, the narrative of German books for children is constructed primarily from the following constituents:

> Fictive borders of time and space;
> Anti- and philo-semitic descriptions of the Jews;
> An opposition between the Germans and the Jews;
> An opposition between Nazis and pseudo-Nazis;
> An analogy between the Nazis and the Jews;
> Foregrounding the Underground;
> Presenting the Germans as victims and depicting their mourning;

> Rejection of the burden of guilt;
> Misplaced elements.

My book, *A Past without a Shadow* (1999, published in Hebrew), addressed in some detail the ways in which the German narrative is organized. Here, however, I can only allude briefly to some of them, so I will address the representation of the Germans, the Nazis and the Jews, and the portrayal of German victimization. My findings are based on a careful and thorough reading of books for children published after 1945 in the former West German Republic. *A Past without a Shadow* deals primarily with 74 titles that have been awarded prizes in Germany. The prize-winning books were selected for analysis because they represent what is regarded by "people-in-culture" as the best mainstream literature; in other words, my analysis concerns books that were well received and institutionally recommended as culturally the most valuable. Moreover, they are perceived as representing the most "fitting" and preferred version of the German past. At the same time, in order to establish a control sample, I also analyzed several books that did not win awards; the results yielded by these analyses are similar to those of the prize-winning books.

THE REPRESENTATION OF GERMANS, NAZIS AND JEWS

The texts establish a polar opposition between the Nazis and the German people, according to which the Germans are not perceived as Nazis and the Nazis are not perceived as German. In order to draw an even sharper distinction between Germans and Nazis, an analogy is drawn between Nazis and Jews. Absurd though it may sound, this construction has a logic of its own: The depiction of both Jews and Nazis is drawn from a reservoir of alien attributes which has long-since provided the range of physical, mental, individual and national features attributed to Jews. Since it is not only the Jews, but the Nazis as well, who are contrasted with the "real" Germans, the symmetry constructed between the Jews and the Nazis as "non-Germans" is almost unavoidable. As a result, Nazis and Jews share many traits. Whereas Germans are hardly ever ascribed physical descriptions, both Jews and Nazis always are. For instance, in Hans Peter Richter's *Damals war es Friedrich* [Then it was Frederick] (1961), Herr and Frau Schneider, Herr Rosenthal and the Rabbi, as well as the "real" Nazis, Herr Resch and Special Delegate Gelko from the District Office, are introduced in the text by way of direct or indirect physical descriptions. Moreover, Jews and "real" Nazis always resemble each other: they are physically small, if not diminutive, and dark. Little Cohn in Christine Nöstlinger's *Maikäfer flieg* [Fly away, ladybird!] (1973) who has curly black hair and pointed ears, Abiram in *Die Webers* [The Weber family] (Noack, 1980), Frau Schneider in *Damals war es Friedrich* (1961), Ruth in *Nie wieder ein Wort davon?* [Not one word ever again?] (Gehrts, 1975), Dr. Jokesch, Lajos and the American commander of the camp in *Geh heim und vergiß alles* [Go home and forget everything] (Recheis, 1964), Sofie in *Im roten Hinterhaus* [In the red annexe] (Berger, 1966), and the Jewish grandmother in *Emma oder Die unruhige Zeit* [Emma, or The troubled time] (Fuchs, 1979) are all described as small and dark.

Like the Jews, the Nazis are depicted as small and black-haired, mirroring, needless to say, the image of Hitler himself as a type of super-Nazi. For example, there is the parade commander who welcomes the Führer in *Wir waren dabei* [We were there] (Richter, 1962), the Nazi Siegbert in *Wann blüht der Zuckertütenbaum?* [When does the sugar-cone tree bloom?] (Hartig, 1986), and the hunchback in *Damals war es Friedrich* (Richter, 1961), all of whom are either dark or small, or both.

A further analogy between the Jews and the Nazis is constructed by showing members of both as active participants in strange or bizarre ceremonies and rituals. In addition, the Jews and the Nazis are both ascribed national credos, while the Germans are hardly ever represented through shared national or cultural affiliations, particularly those which might be perceived as "peculiar." In presenting the Jews and the Nazis, the texts are replete with detailed descriptions of seemingly strange ceremonies, such as the Friday night ceremony before *Shabbat* (Saturday, the seventh day of the week, considered as the Jewish day of rest), a *Bar Mitzvah* (the initiation ceremony for 13-year-old Jewish boys), and the consecration of the Nazi *Jugendvolk* (youth movement) organization.

Another similarity involves the tendency of both Jews and Nazis to give orders, which is juxtaposed to the German trait of simply obeying orders. The grandfather in *Damals war es Friedrich* is a tyrant who abuses his family, and his behavior is likened to that of a Jew named Cohn who was once his supervisor. His conduct is also said to resemble that of Herr Schneider, who obviously enjoys ordering his workers about.

While the Nazis and Jews never seem to want for food, the Germans are always either starving or have extremely little to eat. Furthermore, the Nazis and the Jews are described as working in tandem to feed the starving German people: both in *Damals war es Friedrich* and in *Als Hitler das rosa Kaninchen stahl* (1973, translated from Judith Kerr's *When Hitler Stole Pink Rabbit*), the unemployed Germans are "nourished," as it were, by Jews until the Nazis replace them as providers. What's more, these texts suggest that had they been given the chance, the Jews themselves would readily have joined the Nazi Party. *Damals war es Friedrich* presents the Jewish protagonists as being prepared to join either the *Jugendvolk* or the Nazi Party. When a neighbor tells Friedrich's father that he has joined the Party, the father expresses his understanding and adds that he, too, might have joined the Nazi Party had he not been Jewish. This notion resonates elsewhere: earlier in the story, Friedrich enthusiastically tries to join the *Jugendvolk*. Seemingly ultra-Catholic, he is the only young child in possession of a swastika ring. Later, when Friedrich takes his friend to the department store, he greets the man outside the district council building with a rousing "Heil Hitler."[1] Despite the alleged proneness by the Jews to join the Nazis, there are very few Nazis to be found in Germany. Notwithstanding their alleged numerical marginality, the Nazis do manage to oppress their victims, namely the Germans of the Third Reich.

VICTIMIZATION

The books in question present the "German People" as the ultimate victims. Their tale of woe begins with the first World War, continues through the years between the wars, and ends with the rise of the Third Reich, when they too are subjected to Hitler's tyrannical ruthlessness. In corroboration, the texts emphasize the pre-war conditions which gave rise to the Third Reich: unemployment and its deprivations, postwar devastation and ruin, disease, mourning, family disintegration, and the tragic displacement of individuals. The texts are saturated with densely detailed descriptions of German suffering; it would appear that the greater the evidence provided of German suffering, the more forcefully persuasive the narratives are thought to be. *Damals war es Friedrich* portrays a German family in the 1920s which experiences various kinds of hardship. The father is unemployed, and he and his family are financially dependent on the tyrannical grandfather. Noack's *Die Webers* (1980) begins by describing masses of people queuing in the 1930s for their unemployment allowance, which is scarcely enough to keep them alive. Highlighting hunger in the wake of unemployment, brutally harsh weather conditions, and the loss of all civil rights, the text implies that the German people became victims and that the circumstances were beyond human control.

Klaus Kordon's *Mit dem Rücken zur Wand* [With your back to the wall] (1990) gives a comprehensive description of unemployment in the 1920s and 1930s and of the appalling misery and disastrous social consequences it entailed. Accounting for the rise of the Nazis to power, the book stresses, over and above the political situation, the unbearable living conditions of the working- and lower-middle classes. Large families raise cramped and undernourished children in tiny, foul-smelling flats, and only a few were lucky enough to be employed. All the Germans, even the high-ranking ones, endure hunger to some degree. In *Nie wieder ein Wort davon?* (Gehrts, 1975), the family of Anna, daughter of a high-ranking officer in the *Wehrmacht* (armed forces), is short of food. From time to time, however, thanks to her father's position, the family does manage to procure an extra supply of food, although her mother still has to queue for it.

Not only were the Germans hungry before the war, it seems; during and after the war they were again humiliated by hunger. In *Sonderappell* [Special Roll-Call] (Schönfeldt, 1979), we are told that while serving in the RAD (*Reichs Arbeits Dienst*),[2] the girls were forced to eat worm-infested food: Charlotte was so hungry that, disgusting as it was, she ate fruit soup which had worms in it. *Heute Nacht ist viel passiert* [A lot happened last night] (Klare, 1989) describes the prevalence of hunger after the war. The two children, Hilde and her friend Franz, walk for miles to find a bit of bread, and are not always lucky. If it were not for their aunt's connections through which they manage to obtain a little bread, people in their street, especially the elderly, would surely have died of hunger. The hunger suffered by the Germans is underscored by juxtaposing them to the Nazis, who never want for food. The social scale is clear and unvarying: the Nazis always eat royally, while the Germans go hungry. *Wir waren dabei* (Richter, 1962) describes the grand meals served in the home of Heinz's Nazi family alongside the hunger in Günther's Communist family, where the father is unemployed.

German suffering does not end with hunger and starvation. *Stern ohne Himmel* [A star with no heaven] (Ossowski, 1978) describes the torment undergone by Kimmich, a political prisoner in a concentration camp. He is just one of many good Germans who experienced suffering and hardship under the Nazi regime. *Sonderappell* describes a girls' RAD camp located not far from Auschwitz (of which little is said); on the other hand, the suffering undergone by the girls in their own camp is described in detail. Misery, pain, and the horror of death are foregrounded, described repeatedly and in considerable detail, in all the books, including *Maikäfer flieg* (Nöstlinger, 1973), in which Gerald's father and Auntie Hanni are killed, *Stern ohne Himmel*, in which numerous civilians are killed at the end of the war, *Damals war es Friedrich*, the final scene of which recounts the destruction of Germany, *Wir waren dabei* where Günther and Heinz die on the battle-field, and *Die Webers* which contains a long list of dead soldiers, including Mrs. Krüger's twins, both killed in battle on the same day. In *Das Jahr der Wölfe* [The year of the wolves] (Fährman, 1962), so many soldiers lose their lives that the local priest can no longer mention them all as he used to in his Christmas sermon.[3] *Nacht über dem Tal* [Night over the valley] (Staden, 1979) highlights the great number of German casualties, both dead soldiers and civilian victims, felled by the occupying armies and the bombing raids.

These texts provide detailed descriptions of encounters with the dead and the wounded, never sparing the reader. In *Sonderappell*, Charlotte gives a graphic description of the circumstances of her uncle's injury. "Als der Bahnhof brannte," by Käthe Recheis, published in the collection *Damals war ich vierzehn* [I was fourteen at the time] (Bruckner, 1978), describes the destruction of an entire city, where a man's headless body is discovered by children in the ruins. *Sonderappell* vividly describes Charlotte's horrible encounter with death when she comes across a mother carrying her dead baby and fleeing for her life.

Not all these deaths are attributed to German responsibility, or to Nazi Germany or Hitler. Many are ascribed to bombing raids carried out by the Allies. The texts hardly refer at all to the countless victims of other nationalities and religions, and seem to imply that it was indeed the Germans who suffered the greatest losses. The war is regarded as the result of a clash of cosmic powers, while the presence of German soldiers all over Europe is not explained. The texts emphasize the distress and hardship brought about by the war, but hardly say anything about the circumstances which led to the war, or about its consequences for non-Germans. In fact, the texts seem to suggest that virtually all the Germans who died in this war, whether young or old, soldiers or civilians, lost their lives for no good reason. In no way were they responsible for the war, nor for the rise to power of the Nazis, nor for any of the other events which led to the war.

The recurrent descriptions of countless German victims seem to suggest that Germany was in fact guiltless: an innocent nation suddenly confronted with a monstrous war that inflicted a terrible toll. Cities and villages, whole families and individual parents, all mourn those who died—as it appears—in vain. The story of the Third Reich, as well as that of the First and the Second World Wars, is transformed, so to speak, into a narrative about how the Germans were victimized. It is hardly surprising that when asked in 1995 whether the exile of the Germans from the East was as much a crime against humanity as the Holocaust, 36 percent of Germans answered affirmatively, 40 percent of these being people aged over 65.[4]

CONCLUSIONS

It may well be asked how Germany—as I believe—managed to create a historical narrative which absolves the Germans and enables them genuinely to believe that they were blameless during the Third Reich. The answer seems to lie, at least partially, in the historical narrative provided by German books for children. In all the books examined, except a few such as Clara Asscher-Pinkhof's *Sternkinder* [Children of the star] (1961), Winfried Bruckner's *Die toten Engel* [The dead angels] (1963) and Gudrun Pausewang's *Reise im August* [A journey in August] (1992), the horror of the Third Reich is systematically screened and filtered, concealing the darker, most oppressive aspects of German history.

The books examined are sanctioned by the cultural establishment of modern Germany, and sell in great numbers; as already mentioned, most have received glowing reviews and have been awarded prestigious literary prizes. Their success can be attributed to the way they respond to the tacit demands of present-day German society. In fact, it may be assumed that most attempts to violate the national consensus on German history would be rejected.

Metahistorical, sociological, philosophical and psychological discussions, including a number of recent studies, address the creation, recreation and denial of the various phases of communal and national past images (Bond and Gilliam, 1994; Diner, 1990; Friedlander, 1993; Hobsbawm, 1983; Kaes, 1989; Lewis, 1975; White, 1992). All these studies seem to agree that images of the past are subject to manipulation favoring national, political and social interests. Rather than reiterate the shared arguments embodied in this rich corpus, I have preferred to use them as a point of departure for determining the ways in which texts for children serve as an effective means for creating, disseminating and internalizing past (self-)images, and crystallizing past (self-)perceptions. In the case of the German past, the prevailing narrative for children fails to acknowledge German responsibility for the suffering caused by the German people during the Third Reich and the Holocaust; this means it cannot come to terms with the existence of German guilt. German books for children create a wishful picture of the German past with which the German people can live comfortably, and which they can, without question, pass on to their children. Whether their children and grandchildren will choose to adopt this image of the past still remains to be seen.

NOTES

This chapter is based on a comprehensive research project which discusses the "story" created by German historical novels for children. The author wishes to thank the Bertelsmann *Stiftung* for the generous support provided for the research.

1. H. P. Richter, *Damals war es Friedrich* (Nürnberg: Sebaldus, 1961), p. 55.
2. The RAD was the state work agency of the Third Reich.
3. W. Fährmann, *Das Jahr der Wölfe* (Würzburg: Arena, 1962), p. 52.
4. Robert G. Moeller, "War Stories: The Search for a Usable Past in the Federal Republic of Germany," *American Historical Review* (October 1996), p. 1009.

REFERENCES

Children's Literature

Asscher-Pinkhof, Clara. *Sternkinder*. Berlin: Dressler, 1961. Hamburg: Oetinger, 1986.

Berger, Peter. *Im roten Hinterhaus: Die Geschichte einer Familie in verworrener Zeit*. Stuttgart: Schwaben, 1966. Würzburg: Arena, 1995 (10th ed.).

Bruckner, Winfried. *Damals war ich vierzehn. Berichte und Erinnerungen*. Wien: Jugend und Volk, 1978. Ravensburg: Ravensburger Maier, 1981, 1994 (9th ed.).

———. *Die toten Engel*. Wien: Jungbrunnen, 1963. Ravensburg: Ravensburger Maier, 1996 (16th ed.).

Fährmann, Willi. *Das Jahr der Wölfe. Die Geschichte einer Flucht*. Würzburg, Arena, 1962, 1995 (11th ed.).

Fuchs, Ursula. *Emma oder Die unruhige Zeit*. Kevelaer: Anrich, 1979. München: DTV, 1983, 1993 (10th ed.).

Gehrts, Barbara. *Nie wieder ein Wort davon?* Stuttgart: Union, 1975. München: DTV, 1978, 1995 (15th ed.).

Hartig, Monika. *Wann blüht der Zuckertütenbaum?* Würzburg: Arena, 1986. Würzburg: Arena-Taschenbuch, 1990, 1993 (2nd ed.).

Härtling, Peter. *Krücke*. Weinheim: Beltz and Gelberg, 1986, 1992 (7th ed.). Weinheim: Beltz and Gelberg, Gulliver Taschenbuch, 1994, 1995 (2nd ed.).

Kerr, Judith. *When Hitler Stole Pink Rabbit*. London: William Collins, 1971. Translated as *Als Hitler das rosa Kaninchen stahl*. Ravensburg: Ravensburger Maier, 1973. Ravensburg: Ravensburger Taschenbuch, 1995 (24th ed.), 1997.

Klare, Margaret. *Heute Nacht ist viel passiert. Geschichten einer Kindheit*. Weinheim: Beltz and Gelberg, 1989. Weinheim: Beltz and Gelberg, Gulliver Taschenbuch, 1993, 1995 (2nd ed.).

Kordon, Klaus. *Der erste Frühling*. "Wendepunkte" trilogy, Vol. 3. Weinheim and Basel: Beltz and Gelberg, 1993, 1995 (4th ed.).

———. *Mit dem Rücken zur Wand*. "Wendepunkte" trilogy, Vol. 2. Weinheim and Basel: Beltz and Gelberg, 1990, 1995 (4th ed.).

Luft, Gerda. *Heimkehr ins Unbekannte*. Wuppertal: Peter Hammer Verlag, 1977.

Noack, Hans-Georg. *Die Webers: Eine deutsche Familie. 1932–1945*. Ravensburg: Ravensburger Buchverlag Otto Maier, 1980, 1995 (14th ed.). Originally published as *Stern über der Mauer* (Baden-Baden: Signal, 1962).

Nöstlinger, Christine. *Maikäfer flieg*. Weinheim: Beltz and Gelberg, 1973. München: DTV, 1980, 1993 (15th ed.).

Ossowski, Leonie. *Stern ohne Himmel*. Weinheim: Beltz and Gelberg, 1978. München: Heyne, 1994 (9th ed.).

Pausewang, Gudrun. *Reise im August*. Ravensburg: Ravensburger Maier, 1992. Ravensburg: Ravensburger Taschenbuch, 1995, 1996 (2nd ed.), 1997.

Recheis, Käthe. *Geh heim und vergiß alles*. München: DTV, 1988, 1992. Originally published as *Das Schattennetz* (Freiburg i. Br.: Herder, 1964).

——— *Lena. Unser Dorf und der Krieg*. Freiburg i. Br.: Herder, 1987. Wien: Herder, 1987. München: DTV, 1993, 1994 (3rd ed.).

Reuter, Elisabeth. *Judith und Lisa*. München: Ellermann, 1988, 1993 (2nd ed.).

Richter, Hans Peter. *Damals war es Friedrich*. Nürnberg: Sebaldus, 1961. München: DTV, 1974, 1995 (34th ed.).

———. *Wir waren dabei. Jugendjahre im Dritten Reich*. Freiburg: Herder, 1962. Würzburg: Arena, 1977, 1993 (12th ed.).

Scholl, Inge. *Die weiße Rose*. 1955. Frankfurt am Main: Fischer, 1993, 1996.

Schonfeldt, Sybil Gräfin. *Sonderappell: 1945 – ein Mädchen berichtet*. Wien: Ueberreuter, 1979. München: DTV, 1984, 1996 (10th ed.).

Staden, Wendelgard von. *Nacht über dem Tal: Eine Jugend in Deutschland*. Dusseldorf: Diederichs, 1979. München: DTV, 1982, 1985 (4th ed.). Translated into Hebrew by Yehudit Osterer-Bein as *Afelah al ha-Emek*. Intro. Wendelgard von Staden (Tel Aviv: Massada, 1986).

Tetzner, Lisa. *Die Kinder aus Nr. 67. 1944–49*. München: DTV, 1993–94:

Vols. 1 and 2, *Erwin und Paul; Das Mädchen aus dem Vorderhaus*. Aarau and Frankfurt am Main: Sauerländer, 1947, 1980. München: DTV, 1985, 1994 (10th ed.);

Vols. 3 and 4, *Erwin kommt nach Schweden; Das Schiff ohne Hafen*. Aarau: Sauerländer, 1944, 1981. München: DTV, 1986, 1993 (6th ed.);

Vols. 5 and 6, *Die Kinder auf der Insel; Mirjam in Amerika*. Aarau and Frankfurt am Main: Sauerländer, 1944–46, 1981. München: DTV, 1989, 1994 (4th ed.);

Vols. 7 and 8, *War Paul schuldig? and Als ich wiederkam*. Aarau and Frankfurt am Main: Sauerländer, 1945–46, 1982. Munchen: DTV, 1990, 1993 (3rd ed.);

Vol. 9, *Der neue Bund*. Aarau and Frankfurt am Main: Sauerländer, 1949. Revised ed. 1990. München: DTV, 1990, 1993 (3rd ed.).

Vinke, Hermann. *Das kurze Leben der Sophie Scholl*. Ravensburg: Otto Maier Buchverlag, 1980. Ravensburg: Ravensburger Maier, 1987, 1995 (9th ed.).

Secondary Sources

Angress, Ruth K. "Gibt es ein 'Judenproblem' in der deutschen Nachkriegsliteratur?" *Neue Sammlung, Vierteljahres-Zeitschrift für Erziehung und Gesellschaft* 26,1 (1986): 22–40.

Bond, George Clement and Gilliam, Angela. Introduction, in George Clement Bond and Angela Gilliam, eds., *Social Construction of the Past: Representation as Power*. London and New York: Routledge, 1994: 1–22.

Diner, Dan. "Historical Experience and Cognition: Perspectives on National Socialism." *History and Memory* 2, 1 (1990): 84–110.

Even-Zohar, Itamar. "Reality and Realemes in Narrative." *Poetics Today* special issue 11, 1. Durham, NC: Duke University Press. (1990): 207–218.

Friedlander, Saul. *Memory, History, and the Extermination of the Jews of Europe*. Bloomington and Indianapolis: Indiana University Press, 1993: vii–xiv, 95–101.

Hammerman, Ilana. *National Socialism in the Mirror of Modern German Literature*. [In Hebrew]. Tel-Aviv: Hakibutz-Hameuchad, 1984.

Hobsbawm, Eric. "Inventing Traditions." In Eric Hobsbawm and Terence Ranger, eds. *The Invention of Tradition*. Cambridge: Cambridge University Press, 1983: 1–14.

Kaes, Anton. *From Hitler to* Heimat*: The Return of History as Film*. Cambridge, Mass.: Harvard University Press, 1989.

Lewis, Bernard. "Masada and Cyrus." In *History, Remembered, Recovered, Invented*. Princeton, New Jersey: Princeton University Press, 1975: 3–42.

Lotman, Yuri M. *Universe of the Mind: A Semiotic Theory of Culture*. London and New York: I. B. Tauris, 1990.

Moeller, Robert G. "War Stories: The Search for a Usable Past in the Federal Republic of Germany." *American Historical Review* October (1996): 1008–1048.

Shavit, Zohar. "Aus Kindermund: Historisches Bewußtsein und nationaler Diskurs in Deutschland nach 1945." [Out of the Mouths of Babes and Sucklings: Historical Consciousness and the National Narrative in Germany after 1945]. *Neue Sammlung* 36, 3 (1996): 355–74.

———. *A Past Without a Shadow*. (In Hebrew). Tel Aviv: Am Oved, Ofakim, 1999.

White, Hayden. "Historical Emplotment and the Problem of Truth." In Saul Friedlander, ed. *Probing the Limits of Representation*. London: Harvard University Press, 1992: 37–53.

15

Reverberations of the Anne Frank Diaries in Contemporary German and British Children's Literature

Susan Tebbutt

ANNE FRANK AND HER DIARIES

The internationally famous *Diary of Anne Frank*, first published in 1947, recounting the everyday pleasures and pains of the childhood of a German Jewish girl, forced into hiding in the annex of a canal-side house in Amsterdam, was originally written in Dutch. It has now been translated into over 50 languages, has sold two million copies worldwide, and in a 1996 survey was 26th in a list of the hundred best literary works of the twentieth century.[1] The *Diary of Anne Frank* is arguably the world's best-known work of children's writing, while Anne herself is perhaps the best-known female autobiographer, and is seen by many as an icon, a symbol of the Holocaust and of Jewishness.

Questions about the authenticity of the diaries have diminished since the publication of the authorized new version, in which material originally censored by Otto Frank, Anne's father, has been included.[2] Although considered by some to be a historical source, as a document of the period, it is important to remember that the diary was conceived as comprising both fact and fiction, evident not least in Anne's inclusion of a number of fictional stories in the diary.[3] She does not merely reflect the world around her, but sets out deliberately to revise her own work to make it more accessible. Readers can now see Anne's three separate versions, emphasizing the narrative, creative nature of her work, which is not a naive spontaneous account. Anne Frank the person is almost indivisible from the *Diary of Anne Frank*; however, she is not primarily intent on providing an authoritative study of life in hiding, but is interested in exploring her own soul, in writing as a therapeutic process. "Paper is more patient than people are," she writes on 20 June 1942.

The varied reverberations of the Anne Frank diaries in different countries in the 1980s and 1990s, including those transmitted in picture books, a biography, and creative writing inspired by or based on the diaries, offer insights into the complex interrelationship between history and fiction and into the development of the genre of children's literature itself. How do the history of the period, the personal history of Anne, and the diary make an important contribution to the developing history of children's literature? Are the works inspired by Anne significant, or do the nonfiction historical works appear as a pale shadow of the original events and the subsequent writings a pale shadow of the original diary?

THE DIFFICULTIES OF REPRESENTING THE HOLOCAUST IN CHILDREN'S LITERATURE

For many people Anne Frank is synonymous with the Holocaust. Although hers is the best known of all autobiographies of the period, this does not mean that it is the most useful source or the one which conveys the most accurate picture. James Young (1988), in his study of writing and rewriting the Holocaust, refers to Anne as a "two-sided metonymy for both Jewishness and Holocaust."[4] Although Anne acts as a symbol of the innocent who suffered in the Holocaust, she was not the only German Jew in the Netherlands to go into hiding,[5] nor was the Frank family typical of all other Jews,[6] nor were the Jews the only group to suffer.

There have been many lengthy debates about the impossibility of expressing the Holocaust in words, and this is no less true for children's literature; rather the difficulty is exacerbated. Although there have been hundreds of works written since the 1960s that deal with this period of history, the majority stop short of the cataclysmic and tend to present a version of history which glosses over the extremes of suffering. In the majority of cases the young protagonists are not personally involved in suffering and the inhumanity of the concentration camps tends to be relegated to the background. There is a danger of rendering the history too sanitized, too acceptable, and there is often little to distinguish children's adventures in this context from other adventure stories. Taboo topics such as death, sterilization, the tattooing of numbers on bodies, or mass gassing are rarely described in children's literature, and even in the factual works to be examined here there is a very real danger that the uniqueness of the Holocaust will be lost.

Representations of History in Children's Literature

History can be conveyed in a variety of forms, from the historical adventure, to the historical biography, to factual, educational historiography for young people.

Table 15.1
Characteristics of Children's Books Inspired by the Anne Frank Diaries

	Derivative	*Innovative*
Presentation of history:	Emphasizes personal and family elements	Emphasizes the wider social context
Characterization:	Focus on Anne	Wide range of characters
Presentation of Anne Frank:	Seen as an individual, in a family context	Seen as representative of many and as a catalyst
Register:	Homely, cozy	Uncompromising tone in treatment of death and inhumanity
Narrative stance:	Tries to remain objective	Includes a personal response

History may be used as an indirect way of writing about the present, and a historical work of literature may in its turn inspire and influence the form of a new work, the content of which concerns the present day. In *Language and Ideology in Children's Fiction* (1992), John Stephens highlights the ways in which language can be used to interrogate official culture. Table 15.1 offers a model that I suggest can act as a framework for discussion of the representation of history in works written in the 1980s and 1990s based on the Anne Frank diaries. Using a variant of Stephens' categorization of interrogative texts, and taking into account the perspective from which history is viewed, the characterization, the presentation of Anne Frank, the register and the narrative stance, I divide the texts into two main groups, the derivative and the innovative. It is important to stress that the term *derivative* does not automatically mean that a work is weak, nor that all *innovative* texts are superior.

NONFICTION WORKS ABOUT THE
ANNE FRANK STORY

Ruud van der Rol and Rian Verhoeven's *Anne Frank: Beyond the Diary* (1993), a collection of over one hundred photographs with excerpts from the diaries and accessible, explanatory large-print text, won the ALA Notable Book of the Year and many other literary prizes. The Anne Frank Foundation produced the excellent *A History for Today: Anne Frank* (1996), which includes information on the stage version of the diary and its success, and material about continuing anti-Semitism in the postwar period. Photographs of Swedish Neo-Nazis and of a Croatian boy at the funeral of his father stress the link between the past and the present. Fred Rendell's *Into Hiding* (n.d.), produced for primary school work in Scotland, serves a very different purpose, being principally designed for the use of teachers in their exploration of the Anne Frank topic in school; it contains a collection of suggestions for lessons, including discussion themes, group and individual projects and activities, and background stimuli to encourage an interactive approach to history. Johanna Hurwitz' *Anne Frank: A Life in Hiding* (1999) is aimed at a similar age group and is in simple English with a few black-and-white illustrations. It begins with Anne's thirteenth birthday and conveys in some 50 pages the key facts about Anne's background, the family's life in hiding and their capture, and the continuing importance of Anne's diary. Hurwitz gives her young readers insights into the cultural reverberations of the diaries:

Anne has inspired artists who have used many different art forms. Sculptors have created statues and busts of her. Marc Chagall illustrated with lithographs a deluxe edition of Anne's diary. A ballet and several cantatas and requiems are also based on Anne's diary.
The name "Anne Frank" has been given to dozens of schools throughout the world, as well as to youth hostels and homes and clubs for young people. The Montessori School that Anne attended in Amsterdam and was forced to leave when the Germans took control of the city has changed its name to the Anne Frank School. And in Bergen, Germany, the city where Anne died in the concentration camp, there is an elementary school named for her.
A forest of over 10,000 trees has been planted in Anne's name in Israel. In Belgium, a new rose was cultivated and named *Souvenir d'Anne Frank*. And in Anne's adopted homeland, Holland, a country known for its beautiful tulips, a new tulip was named for her, too.[7]

All these nonfiction works fall into the category of wide-ranging, innovative presentations of history with clear links between past and present.

PICTURE BOOKS ABOUT THE
ANNE FRANK STORY

The four picture books considered here were produced independently of the Anne Frank Foundation. Two works entitled *Anne Frank*, by Richard Tames (1989) and Wayne Jackman (1992), both in large print and containing suggestions for further reading, are reasonable introductions to the theme. Jackman relies heavily on color illustrations, with a few small photographs. Tames uses authentic photographs, but chooses rather oddly to include three mediocre color illustrations, one of the house on the Prinsengracht, one of the type of meals Anne ate, and the third of the presents Anne received on her birthday. In both books there is a strange mixture of adult themes with childish language which reads very uncomfortably. Jackman, for example, writes, "Anne's talent for writing and the tragedy of her short life seemed to say everything about the terrible war and the hateful Nazis."[8] The works of Tames and Jackman remain largely derivative. Far from saying everything about the "hateful Nazis," they end by giving a diluted version of one girl's story as if it were an isolated case.

Can simpler picture stories with less information be more enlightening? Harriet Castor's work *Anne Frank* (1996), which forms part of an English series of "Biographies of famous people to support the National Curriculum" is published in large print and has black-and-white line drawings. The "Ladybird"-

book style of narration—"Hitler hated Jews and wanted to kill them all"[9]—seems strangely out of place. The language is frequently so bland as to reduce Hitler and his henchmen to the simplistic role of "baddies." The combination of the authentic sign "No Jews" with the speech-bubble "Go away"[10] is perhaps an attempt to be innovative and make the language relate to the level of the young reader, but the episode dealing with the family's arrest is told in such a way that it is trivialized: "Anne and her family heard shouting downstairs. It was the police. They had come to take everyone in the Annex away."[11] The story falls into the category of a derivative work and does not stand on its own as a significant work of children's literature.

Karen Ritz's illustrations, based on photographic evidence, for David Adler's book, *A Picture Book of Anne Frank* (1993), are more expressive and sensitive. Anne is presented in simple language but seen as a member of a community rather than merely as an individual. There is a sense of the enormity of the crimes being committed in the concentration camps. Whereas Castor stops at the arrest of the Frank family, Adler traces Anne's last steps:

Anne and the others were sent in locked railway cars to Westerbork, a camp in eastern Holland. One month later they were loaded onto another train. . . . After two days and nights of travelling, the doors to the train were opened. They had been taken to Auschwitz, a Nazi death camp in Poland. . . .
When prisoners arrived at Auschwitz, some were "selected" for immediate death. Others, like Anne, were saved for work. But working in the cold with little food or clothing—and suffering beatings—led to death, too.[12]

Adler explains a personal reason for writing about the history of the Holocaust for young people: "For me the Diary is especially poignant. Like Anne, my mother was born in Frankfurt am Main, Germany. My mother's family had also lived there for hundreds of years. My mother, along with her parents, sister, and brother, moved to Amsterdam, Holland, to escape Nazi persecution. Fortunately they left Holland in 1939, before the German invasion." A great strength of Adler's work is his commitment to the depiction of the annihilation of many different social groups, not only the Jews: "The Nazis murdered millions of others, too, including cripples, the mentally ill, beggars, Russian prisoners of war, Romanies, homosexuals, and communists."[13]

A DIFFERENTIATED BIOGRAPHY
FOR GERMAN TEENAGERS

What can a biography bring to the representation of history in children's literature that goes beyond merely retelling the story of Anne Frank and her diary? Mirjam Pressler, herself Jewish, and one of Germany's most successful exponents of socially critical books for teenagers, who has won the prestigious German literature prize for her translation work, has not only translated the definitive new edition of the diary from the original Dutch but, in her biography *Ich sehne mich so* (1992) (translated into English as *Anne Frank: A Hidden Life*, 1999) has introduced a wider range of teenagers to the many issues surrounding Anne Frank.[14] There is clearly a high degree of overt intertextuality in the biography. Starting with the Liberation, Pressler traces the genesis of the diaries, then considers the Frank family, Jews in the Netherlands, and the time before the family went into hiding. Five chapters are devoted to the different people in hiding with the Franks. Pressler then discusses the helpers, the outside world, Anne's development and difficulties as a teenager, and finally the arrest and deportation.

Given the upsurge in right-wing extremism in Germany, Pressler felt it was extremely important to underline and analyze the background and social context against which Anne wrote her diary. The biography is also innovative in its wide variety of characters and in its presentation of Anne as a real person with human failings, rather than as an icon. There is a frankness in the treatment of the Holocaust linked to a deep understanding of the individual. Pressler is extremely sensitive to words and writes both to enlighten and to entertain. Literary historians like Heinrich Wolgast, who pleaded at the turn of the nineteenth century for every work of children's literature to be a "work of art,"[15] would no doubt have approved.

THE CHILD'S VOICE: ORIGINAL RESPONSES
TO THE ANNE FRANK STORY

Whereas there is a strong tendency for the picture books about the diary to be derivative in style and frequently patronizing in tone, however good the intentions, there can be no doubt about the innovative character of *Dear Anne Frank* (1995), where the impact of history and of the diaries can be seen in a selection of reader responses written in the 1990s by British children (aged between 7 and 15) who had been invited to take part in a letter-writing project inspired by the diary.

The young people address the issues squarely, without compromising in language or style. The letters are grouped into seven categories, with "Letters from the Past and the Future," "The World Today," and "Anne's Legacy" taking up over half the work. These sections make overt reference to the passage of time and go beyond direct comments on the Anne Frank story to ideas generated by it. The freshness of the writing is striking and exhilarating, even when the complexities of the situation are not necessarily all appreciated.

Seven-year-old Matthew writes:

Dear Anne,
  I have been looking at the plan of the house where you are hiding. It must be like jail in there. It must have been boring having no friends. It would be horrible having dry bread to eat and porridge and lettuce. I would like to be able to bring you some fresh vegetables and cake and chocolate biscuits.[16]

In one of the fictional letters, in which writers imagine themselves as people associated with Anne's life, 14-year-old Betty Wong imagines she was a girl called Angela who betrayed the family and apologizes for having sent the Franks to a concentration camp:

You might not know who I am, because you have never met me before, but I've met you . . . .

I betrayed you because you were a Jew, I just didn't care who you were. I am sorry that this has happened, it is because Hitler said that he would exchange a Jew for money. At the time, my family needed money desperately.

. . . If I did not feel guilty I would not be writing to you. I know you will never forgive me for this, I am not expecting you to, I just want to tell you I am very sorry.[17]

"Angela" feels that she has "met" Anne, and it is this intersection between the history—and the history of children's literature—with the present which makes the representation of history here so exciting. The elements of the diary that interest different readers are obviously diverse. Daleen (aged 14) from London writes: "Since the time you were alive, many things have changed. Man has landed on the moon, people can now travel faster than sound, there is an underwater train tunnel joining England and France, and also you do not have to be engaged to kiss a boy."[18]

The final letter in the collection is from Beth, aged 13: "Dear Anne, Thank you for being like me and showing that ordinary people can be special." Although it could be argued that this letter shows nothing of the history, the register appeals to a young reader: the message is direct and immediate. Beth is both representing history, in that she is relating to the wartime story of Anne, and is following in Anne's footsteps, albeit on a modest scale, by herself conveying her thoughts to paper and creating a piece of children's literature written by a young person.

The publication *Das sind wir* [This is us] (Dijk et al., 1995), produced by the Anne Frank Foundation, consists of six stories (each recounted by a child but written down by an adult) about young children in Germany who come from Ghana, Kurdistan, Turkey, Russia, Macedonia and Germany itself (the German child has moved from a city to a village); each child, in one way or another, is an outsider as Anne Frank was. Here the history is very recent but it is possible to trace the continuity of experience from that of Anne. These stories, however, can be considered as part of the oral tradition in literature and also—although mediated by adults—as narratives by young people. As in the letters to Anne, it is the relationship of contemporary children to Anne's past which makes history live.

Zlata Filipovic's *Zlata's Diary* (1993), described in Britain by a *Sunday Times* critic as the story of a "girl robbed of her childhood," is in the strict literary tradition of the Anne Frank diaries, and has the effect of stressing the innocence of children who are caught up in war and hostilities. Zlata, a child living in Sarajevo in the 1990s and later evacuated to Paris, started her diary in 1991 before the war came and she, like Anne, writes about her everyday life and concerns as well as the politics and intrigues of the outside world of grown-ups. She actually acknowledges her debt to Anne Frank:

Monday, 30 March 1992
Hey, Diary! You know what I think? Since Anne Frank called her diary Kitty, maybe I could give you a name too. What about

ASFALTINA   PIDZAMETA
SEFIKA   HIKMETA
SEVALA   MIMMY
or something else???
I'm thinking, thinking. . . .
I've decided! I'm going to call you
MIMMY[19]

Not only in details like the naming of the diary, but in the reactions to being locked away and caught in the middle of a war, can the parallels to Anne and her diaries be seen. Unfortunately Anne's horrific experience of history, as well as her need to conceive of writing as therapy, continue to be reactivated.

CONCLUSION

The reverberations of the Anne Frank diaries today are a positive indication of their international appeal and enduring humanitarian message. Studying them reveals many of the problems inherent in writing for children. Nonfiction works can be eminently accessible to the young, but educational texts do not always succeed in combining enlightenment with entertainment, and simplifying a work does not automatically make it more accessible, but tends to debase or distort the truth. Adler's picture book is both derivative and yet innovative within a very small number of pages, and here, as in Mirjam Pressler's biography, with her differentiated rather than idealized picture of Anne, it is the quality of the writing which distinguishes the work from other attempts to present the same history in children's books.

Further research into the legacy of the diary in the children's literature of other countries would ascertain to what extent national culture and historical and political circumstances condition responses to this story, which has not ceased to fascinate readers of all ages. Indeed, it has influenced the path of both children's literature and children's writing. But where precisely is the spirit, if not the letter, of the Anne Frank diaries to be found? Not in derivative documentary works, but in those works that follow directly in the literary-historical tradition of children's writing as a personal record, and which are oblique and innovative in their response to the diaries. Anne was a very idiosyncratic girl, and it is in the personality and individuality of the creators of *Dear Anne Frank, Das sind wir* and *Zlata's Diary* that we see history vividly represented in children's literature.

NOTES

1. The survey was conducted in Britain by the booksellers Waterstones.

2. Some parts were cut because they reflected badly on the relationship between Anne and her mother, others because Otto Frank felt that the more explicit private and sexual comments were not suitable for publication. Some 50 years later the social climate has changed.

3. As Peter Boerner points out in *Tagebuch* (Stuttgart: Metzler, 1969), the genre of the diary and the interrelationship between the diary and history are extremely complex, and there is no longer considered to be a binary opposition between history and fiction.

4. James E. Young, *Writing and Rewriting the Holocaust: Narrative Consequences of Interpretation* (Bloomington: Indiana University Press, 1988), p. 110.

5. Over 4% of the German Jews who fled Germany went to the Netherlands, numerically the fifth most popular destination after the USA, Palestine, Britain and France. See Volker Jakob and Annet van der Voort, *Anne Frank war nicht allein: Lebensgeschichten deutscher Juden in den Niederlanden* (Berlin: Dietz, 1988), who edited the recollections of over 20 German Jews who had sought refuge in the Netherlands.

6. See Bob Moore, *Victims and Survivors: The Nazi Persecution of the Jews in the Netherlands 1940–1945* (London: Arnold, 1997) who points out that few families managed to evade capture by the Germans for a time, and the Franks' case cannot be taken as at all typical particularly since by 1940 the family firm was well established.

7. Johanna Hurwitz, *Anne Frank: A Life in Hiding* (New York: Avon, 1999), pp. 46–47.

8. Wayne Jackman, *Life Stories: Anne Frank* (Hove: Wayland, 1992), p. 27.

9. Harriet Castor, *Anne Frank* (London: Franklin Watts, 1996), p. 3.

10. Ibid., p. 13.

11. Ibid., pp. 38–39.

12. David A. Adler, *A Picture Book of Anne Frank* (London: Macmillan, 1993), no page numbers.

13. Ibid.

14. The work is part of a major series in German teenage literature intended to provide challenging biographies of famous people (and in the case of Anne Frank to disprove the clichéd saying that "geography is about maps, biography about chaps").

15. See Susan Tebbutt, *Gudrun Pausewang in context* (Frankfurt am Main: Peter Lang, 1994), pp. 13–76, for a survey of German socially critical teenage literature.

16. *Dear Anne Frank: A Selection of Letters to Anne Frank Written by Children Today*, (Harmondsworth: Penguin, 1995), p. 16.

17. Ibid., p. 43.

18. Ibid., p. 59.

19. Zlata Filopovic, *Zlata's Diary* (Harmondsworth: Puffin, 1995), p. 27.

REFERENCES

Children's literature

Adler, David A. *A Picture Book of Anne Frank*. 1993. Illus. Karen Ritz. London: Macmillan, 1994.

Anne Frank's Tales from the Secret Annexe. Translated by Ralph Mannheim and Michel Mok. London: Penguin, 1986. Originally published in Dutch (1949).

Anne Frank Stichting. *A History for Today: Anne Frank*. 5th revised ed. Amsterdam: Anne Frank House, 1996.

Anne Frank Stichting. *Anne Frank in the World*. Amsterdam. Anne Frank House, 1993.

Anne Frank Tagebuch, Fassung von Otto H. Frank und Mirjam Pressler. Translated by Mirjam Pressler. Frankfurt am Main: Fischer, 1992.

Castor, Harriet. *Anne Frank*. Illus. Helena Owen. London: Franklin Watts, 1996.

Dear Anne Frank: A Selection of Letters to Anne Frank Written by Children Today. Intro. Eva Schloss. Harmondsworth: Penguin, 1995.

Dijk, Lutz et al., eds. *Das sind wir: Ein Lesebuch mit Geschichten von Olivia, Irfan, Gülcihan, Sadber und Filipp*. Amsterdam: Anne Frank House, 1995.

Filopovic, Zlata. *Zlata's Diary*. Translated by Christina Pribichevich-Zoric. Harmondsworth: Puffin, 1995. Originally published in French (1993).

Hurwitz, Johanna. *Anne Frank: A Life in Hiding.* 1988. Illus. Vera Rosenberry. New York: Avon, 1999.

Jackman, Wayne. *Life Stories: Anne Frank.* Illus. Jon Davis. Hove: Wayland, 1992.

Pressler, Mirjam, *Ich sehne mich so: Die Lebensgeschichte der Anne Frank.* Weinheim, Germany: Beltz and Gelberg, 1992. Translated by Anthea Bell as *Anne Frank: A Hidden Life* (New York: Penguin, 1999).

Rendell, Fred. *Into Hiding.* Glasgow: Jordanhill College of Education, no date.

Rol, Ruud van der, and Verhoeven, Rian. *Anne Frank: Beyond the Diary.* Translated by Tony Langham and Plym Peters. New York: Viking, 1993.

Tames, Richard. *Anne Frank.* London: Watts, 1989.

Secondary Sources

Boerner, Peter. *Tagebuch.* Stuttgart: Metzler, 1969.

Currie, Mark. *Metafiction.* London: Longman, 1995.

Gies, Miep, with Gold, Alison Leslie. *Anne Frank Remembered: The Story of Miep Gies Who Helped to Hide the Frank Family.* London: Bantam, 1987.

Heinemann, Marlene E. *Women Prose Writers of the Nazi Holocaust.* Ph.D. diss., Indiana University, Ann Arbor, 1981.

Jakob, Volker, and van der Voort, Annet. *Anne Frank war nicht allein: Lebensgeschichten deutscher Juden in den Niederlanden.* Berlin, Bonn: Dietz, 1988.

Lindwer, Willy. *Anne Frank: Die letzten sieben Monate: Augenzeuginnen berichten.* Translated by Mirjam Pressler. Frankfurt a. M.: Fischer, 1990. Originally published in Dutch (1988).

Moore, Bob. *Victims and Survivors: The Nazi Persecution of the Jews in the Netherlands 1940–1945.* London: Arnold, 1997.

Müller, Melissa. *Anne Frank: The Biography.* Translated by Rita and Robert Kimber. New York: Henry Holt, 1998.

Nijstad, Jaap, ed. *Westerbork Drawings: The Life and Work of Leo Kok 1923–1945.* Amsterdam: Uitgeverij Balans, 1990.

Schloss, Eva, with Kent, Evelyn Julia. *Eva's Story.* Edgware, UK: Castle-Kent, 1988.

Schnabel, Ernst. *Anne Frank: Spur eines Kindes.* Frankfurt a. M.: Fischer, 1958.

Stephens, John. *Language and Ideology in Children's Fiction.* London: Longman, 1992.

Young, James E. *Writing and Rewriting the Holocaust: Narrative Consequences of Interpretation.* Bloomington: Indiana University Press, 1988.

16

War Boys: The Autobiographical Representation of History in Text and Image in Michael Foreman's *War Boy* and Tomi Ungerer's *Die Gedanken sind frei*

Gillian Lathey

R obert Louis Stevenson's assertion in *Essays on the Road* that, "The future is nothing, but the past is myself, my own history, the seed of my present thoughts, the mould of my present disposition" was chosen by Christabel Bielenberg (1968) as an introductory epigraph to the story of her life in Germany during the Second World War.[1] The appeal that such a self-exploratory approach to the past holds for autobiographers is apparent. Personal history, however, is not lived in isolation; it is conditioned by the wider historical, social and political forces at work both during the writer's earlier life and at the time that the record is made. When the focus of autobiographical writing is a historical turning point such as the Second World War, self-definition and the selective recording of history can hardly be separated.

A wartime childhood was the defining moment in many lives; the recording of it for a young reader is shaped both by the writer's concern with identity and currently privileged views of history at the time of writing. Indeed, relativist views of history are nowhere more apposite than in the appraisal of personal, lived history reviewed after several decades. The New Historicist view outlined by Cox and Reynolds (1993) that history is "an ongoing series of human constructions, each representing the past at particular present moments for particular present purposes" (p. 4), can usefully be applied to the recording of that infinitely adaptable subject, the writer's own past. The present, then, determines the past just as surely as the past determines the present, when childhood is redefined by the knowing—or falsifying—adult. A concern to account for and contextualize childhood behavior and attitudes in the light of the adult's understanding of history can cause tensions within the text. How, for example, is the revisionary process determined by the specific historical situation of the child and the nationally privileged assessment of the Second World War? I address this question by examining the radically different approaches to their wartime childhoods of two picture-book artists: Michael Foreman from Britain and Tomi Ungerer who grew up in German-occupied France. Illustrating his bilingual upbringing, with its political connotations, Ungerer first published his autobiography in French in 1991 (as *À la guerre comme à la guerre: Dessins et souvenirs d'enfance* [Oh what a lovely war! Drawings and memories of childhood]), then wrote a German version with additional material published in 1993 (*Die Gedanken sind frei: Meine Kindheit im Elsass* (meaning literally "Thoughts are free," or more idiomatically, "I think what I like: My childhood in Alsace"); it is the German version which is considered here.[2]

The surface similarities between Foreman's and Ungerer's representations of wartime childhood are clear, particularly in their choice of genre. As artists, they represent visual memories of the war years in a hybrid of the picture book and illustrated information book, forms both usually associated with a child audience. Both supplement their own artwork with historical documentation — the cigarette cards, evacuation notices and other contemporary images never forgotten by two boys particularly sensitive to visual impressions. Moreover, both authors share an ambivalence in the implied audience and the reception of their texts. Foreman's *War Boy* has been enjoyed by children and reminiscing adults, although the written text indicates a young readership. Ungerer's target audience appears to be even more uncertain. The translation into German of a review from *Le Monde* of *Die Gedanken sind frei*, cited on the back cover of the 1993 edition, poses the questions, "Is this a book for adults? Is it a book for children?" The review concludes that it is a book about childhood for all. The self-doubt expressed by Ungerer in *Die Gedanken sind frei* speaks to adults, yet he closes his narrative with a 1905 speech on patriotism and international peace by Ernest Lavisse addressed to children. Such points of contact between Ungerer and Foreman, however, only serve to emphasize a divergence in the nature of retrospective analysis.

Although touched by sadness at the fate of the young men who went to war and never returned, Foreman presents the prevailing ideology of the period uncritically. His retrospective vision of life on the English East coast "front line" in the rural village of Pakenfield near Lowestoft is tinged with national pride and expressed in a mixture of exact technical drawings copied from original sources, humorous vignettes and luminous watercolors. A mood of innocent nostalgia predominates in these scenes, as Foreman's wartime adventures take place in the context of a loving and secure domestic setting. We see the happy faces of Foreman's family and visiting soldiers round the table on Christmas Eve 1942 in the warm, hazy glow of the festively decorated room, who look out of the picture (in the reader's direction) at "the little boy they had just kissed goodnight" (p. 36), which is to say, Foreman himself. The enemy is clearly defined in the separation Foreman establishes between the kindly, brave British soldier and the propaganda-induced image of the evil German enemy. There is no doubt as to who the "goodies" and "baddies" are and Foreman describes how playing "cowboys and Indians" was quickly transposed into games of British versus Germans. Foreman as narrator does not distance himself from this simplistic morality, even where it may cause offence. The book closes on a celebratory note with the burning on bonfires of effigies of Hitler, Himmler and Goebbels on VE day and of stereotypical Japanese figures—"a lot of yellow guys with big teeth and glasses"—on VJ day (p. 92).[3] As well as condemning the enemy, the child seeks identification with powerful members of the social order through play, in the acting out of adult roles or a fascination for military weapons and insignia. There is even a sense of exhilaration in his account of the so-called doodlebug bombs which were usually hit by coastal gunfire. The reader is invited to share young Foreman's delight at the "spectacular show" that local people viewed from the cliff top: "A direct hit would result in a tremendous orange flash, a bang and a shower of shrapnel, hopefully over the sea" (p. 84).

This carnival atmosphere again raises the question of illustrative and narrative perspective. There are references to the unknown fate of the soldiers passing through the town, to local casualties in air raids or to the havoc caused by the doodlebug, yet any fear or distress the child may have experienced has been avoided in an account where child and adult narrator do not appear to diverge in their response to events. Childhood is savored by Foreman, as domestic security parallels a world view conditioned by the ideology of the war years. Foreman's childhood recollections—as reflected in the subtitle "A country childhood"— belong to the romantic "pastoral idyll" tradition of British childhood autobiography, a tradition which can be traced back from the more recent popular evocations of rural childhood by Laurie Lee (*Cider with Rosie*, 1959) or Dirk Bogarde (*Great Meadow*, 1992) to Wordsworth's "The Prelude" (1805). The re-creation of the childhood self is conditioned by what appears to be the adult's current positive and celebratory vision.

The difference in approach to wartime childhood between *War Boy* and Tomi Ungerer's *Die Gedanken sind frei* is immediately apparent in the reference to Auschwitz in Ungerer's preface.[4] Ungerer comments that his anecdotal account "könnte auf den ersten Blick fast beleidigend wirken" (might at first sight seem to be an insult, p. 8). He recognizes that in relation to the misery, violence and torture suffered by others, his childhood view of the war years as a great adventure has to be contextualized, "Aber wenn ich über diese Epoche spreche, als seien es die grossen Ferien gewesen, so deshalb, weil ich als Junge mit der Unbefangenheit des Kindes alles wie ein grosses Schauspiel empfunden habe" (I talk about this period as one long holiday because I experienced everything with the innocence of a child as a great spectacle, p. 8). This preface sets the pattern of an adult narrator's voice which pauses at points throughout the narrative to reflect on the childhood self. Ungerer is a self-conscious narrator who even admits to the falsification of history in earlier accounts of his childhood. Stories that he had been forced to dig trenches on the German front line, Ungerer confesses, were designed to impress and arouse sympathy (p. 115). It is therefore not surprising that Ungerer calls the text itself into question by claiming that he mistrusts "Kindheitserinnerungen" (memoirs of childhood, p. 82), although he asserts his intention in this account to avoid all sentimentality (p. 115). The autobiographical process and its pitfalls are made visible to the reader as Ungerer rewrites history.

Ungerer adopts an implicitly confessional tone in reflecting on the consequences of his own successful—if subversively critical—adaptation to life under the aegis of the Third Reich. He describes being caught up in the Nazification process: "Wir waren im Räderwerk dieser riesigen Uhr gefangen" (We were trapped in the mechanism of this gigantic clock, p. 54). Two of the most striking images in *Die Gedanken sind frei* testify to this process and its emotional aftermath. As a consequence of the introduction of NSDAP ideology into schools,[5] one of Ungerer's first pieces of homework under the new regime was to draw a Jew. He sketched a caricature based on his mother's description, which is reproduced in the book with the adult narrator's ironic commentary on its unreality: "This is an image of which the adult cannot be proud." Ungerer goes on to explain his position as an undoubted opponent of the Germans—as reflected in his satirical portraits of German military types on a set of playing cards (pp. 68–69)—who was nevertheless able to conform to the system: "zu Hause Franzose, in der Schule Deutscher, mit meinen Kameraden Elsässer" (a French boy at home, a German at school and an Alsace lad with my friends, p. 57). Ungerer attributes to this period his chameleon-like qualities, a description which implies a degree of moral flexibility (p. 57). This moral self-examination continues by implication in the closing pages of his account when Ungerer again confronts the issue of the Holocaust in a reference to the concentration camp Struthof in the neighboring Vosges hills. He includes a drawing completed in 1948 of a bleeding and despairing camp inmate with the caption "Dachau Buchenwald Auschwitz," which the reader inevitably compares with the caricature of a Jew drawn seven years earlier. The emotional impact of this act of atonement for the child's lack of awareness is intensified by its juxtaposition with a detail from the Isenheim altarpiece by Mathias Grünewald (itself located in Alsace, at Colmar), a comparison echoed in the text. Ungerer's preoccupation with Struthof has continued; he writes that he often visits the site of the camp, a place which affects him profoundly.[6]

Although Ungerer uses original source material, there is a contrast with Foreman's picture book in the nature and function of the artist's own work. Ungerer's impressively detailed and at times scurrilous drawings, influenced by Disney cartoons and the Alsatian folk artist Hansi—are those he completed at the time, between the ages of nine and fourteen. The child's visual record of the era provides a counterpoint to the adult's reassessment of the period of German occupation; childhood is not reconstructed according to a current idealization of the period as in Foreman's nostalgic watercolors. The ambiguity of the circumstances of Ungerer's wartime experience in an enemy-occupied area—as compared to the national pride evoked by Foreman—is reflected in both childhood drawings and the retrospective written commentary. It is significant that in answer to a question on the relationship between text and image in his work as a whole, Ungerer cited the supremacy of text over images in the earlier French version of *Die Gedanken sind frei*, adding that, "les images sont là pour assaisonner le matériel de base" (the images are there to season the basic content).[7]

Ungerer's view of humanity was indelibly altered by his wartime childhood; even his own memories of the period are suspect. One of the most telling points of contrast between his narrative and Foreman's lies in the final words of both authors. Ungerer closes his account of a turbulent, exciting period of his life with a reference to his sister's wedding in Normandy where he saw the sea for the first time and was overwhelmed by its grandeur and purity: "eine vibrierende, klare Heiterkeit ohne Pflaster und ohne Lügen" (a vibrating, luminous brightness without pavements and without lies, p 140). The immensity and non-humanity of the sea, free of any sign of human existence and therefore free of lies, is described by Ungerer as representing both a visual and spiritual turning point in his life. The adult world has demonstrated its unreliability at all levels of society: even the version of French history delivered in school had changed utterly during the Occupation, much to the young Ungerer's surprise. Reversals in cultural heritage and political ideology during his formative years have made the narrator wary, mistrustful and introspective in his review of wartime adventures. The final paragraphs of Foreman's *War Boy*, on the other hand, epitomize its retrospective glow; there is a poignant reflection on childhood games and the soldiers Foreman met as a child, preceded by a passage which adapts the text of a popular patriotic song ("There'll Be Bluebirds Over the White Cliffs of Dover," sung by Vera Lynn[8]). "So it was true, all the things the grown ups had said during the dark days. Now the war was over everything would be all right, there'll be blue birds over the white cliffs, not barrage balloons. And men with rainbows on their chests would, like my kite, come home" (p. 95). The language of wartime propaganda—of which popular songs form a significant part—has been woven into a pean to the British wartime spirit. The reinforcement of the "truth" spoken by adults contrasts with Ungerer's disillusionment with adult lies arising from the accommodation and complicity of an occupied nation.

Both Foreman's and Ungerer's views of history are inevitably partial. Foreman retains—in the apparently unified vision of child and adult—the positive national perspective on the war years reflected in 1995 in the 50th anniversary commemoration of VE day; by contrast, Ungerer's text, although it reflects a far greater awareness of the moral complexities of the period, is troubled by an underlying personal guilt which is never fully explained in historical terms. Yet such autobiographical picture books do count as historical texts, according to the New Historicist view of texts as "objects and events in the world" (Cox and Reynolds, 1993, p. 4), which in all their contradictory partiality become "part of human life, society, the historical realities of power, authority, and resistance" (p. 4). It is not just the books which are part of the historical process, since their gestation—the thinking behind the selection and redrawing of particular fragments of memory—is endlessly intriguing. Does Ungerer become a self-conscious narrator because, despite the illustrated information book format, he has an adult audience in mind, or is his account underpinned by an implicit didactic purpose? Does Foreman choose to evade ideological questions by writing and illustrating history for the young in a positive tone which, ironically, appeals directly to the adults who are his contemporaries? How pressing is the underlying therapeutic need of both artists to revisit the war years, given that Ungerer has composed accounts both in French and then in German and that the success of Foreman's *War Boy* has generated a sequel (Foreman, 1995)? These are the tantalizing questions raised by overtly personal views of history and the ideology that frames them. "The past is myself," but so are its continual redefinitions in the present, and even a limited point of view can, when appreciated as such, reveal national preoccupations. It is important to recognize not only the personal but also the cultural provenance of these memorable, entertaining and thought-provoking reinterpretations of wartime childhoods.

NOTES

Throughout, unattributed translations are my own.

1. R. L. Stevenson, *Essays on the Road*, cited in C. Bielenberg, *The Past Is Myself* (London: Chatto and Windus, 1968) as an epigraph.

2. Tomi Ungerer, À *la guerre comme à la guerre: Dessins et souvenirs d'enfance* (Paris: La Nuée Bleue, 1991); an idiomatic translation for the original title might be: "Oh what a lovely war! Drawings and memories of childhood." During work on the German edition new material was added, so that a completely new book emerged: *Die Gedanken sind frei: Meine Kindheit im Elsass* (Zürich: Diogenes, 1993).

3. The word "guys" is not an Americanism but a reference to the English tradition of celebrating 5 November with bonfires and fireworks (particularly as a children's festivity). It commemorates the confounding of the "Gunpowder Plot," on 5 November 1605 when, because of increasing religious oppression, a group of Roman Catholics attempted to blow up Parliament and kill King James I; one of the conspirators, Guy Fawkes, is represented annually in the effigies—or "guys"—which are burnt on some bonfires.

4. Ungerer, *Die Gedanken sind frei*, p. 14.

5. The Nationalsozialistische Deutsche Arbeiterpartei (NSDAP, abbreviated to Nazi) was elected to power in Germany in 1933.

6. Ungerer's anger and disgust during a visit to Struthof is visible in the documentary *Fascination*, broadcast on British television, Channel 4, in 1996.

7. Ungerer, "Tomi Ungerer par Tomi Ungerer," *La Revue des livres pour enfants*, Numéro Spécial 171 (1996), p. 50.

8. Vera Lynn, now Dame Vera Lynn, was known in wartime by the sobriquet "The Forces' Sweetheart;" a popular singer who specialized in patriotic and morale-raising songs, she toured the war zones to entertain Allied troops during World War II.

REFERENCES

Bielenberg, Christabel. *The Past Is Myself*. London: Chatto and Windus, 1968.

Bogarde, Dirk. *Great Meadow*. London: Viking, 1992.

Cox, J. N., and Reynolds, L. J. *New Historical Literary Study: Essays on Reproducing Texts, Representing History*. New Jersey: Princeton University Press, 1993.

Foreman, Michael. *War Boy*. London: Pavilion Books, 1989.

———. *After the War Was Over*. London: Pavilion Books, 1995.

Lathey, Gillian. *The Impossible Legacy*. Bern, Switzerland: Peter Lang, 1999.

Lee, Laurie. *Cider with Rosie*. London: The Hogarth Press, 1959.

Ungerer, Tomi. *Das grosse Liederbuch*. Zürich: Diogenes, 1975.

———. *À la guerre comme à la guerre: Dessins et souvenirs d'enfance*. Paris: La Nuée Bleue, 1991.

———. *Die Gedanken sind frei: Meine Kindheit im Elsass*. Revised and enlarged version of *À la guerre comme à la guerre*. Zürich: Diogenes, 1993.

———. "Tomi Ungerer par Tomi Ungerer." *La Revue des livres pour enfants*. Numéro Spécial 171 (1996), pp. 48–57.

Part VI

Modern, Postmodern:
Questions of Time and Place

17

"House and Garden": The Time-Slip Story in the Aftermath of the Second World War

Linda Hall

In *The House of Arden* (1908), E. Nesbit invented the time-slip story as we know it today,[1] reversing Rudyard Kipling's method of time-travel in *Puck of Pook's Hill* (1906), by sending her child characters back into the past. She retained Kipling's Shakespearean emphasis on a quintessentially English pastoral setting,[2] and added another typically English ingredient, an old country house. Despite being a lifelong Socialist and founder member of the Fabian Society, Nesbit liked grand old houses. The critic and biographer Humphrey Carpenter suggests this had something to do with a nostalgic yearning to recapture childhood happiness. In her early teens Nesbit had lived in Halstead Hall in Kent, which was just "the kind of rambling country house and garden she glorified in *The Wouldbegoods*" (1901).[3] Later, with her earnings from juvenile fiction, she bought Well Hall in Eltham, Kent, a substantial Elizabethan manor house.

The house of Arden is both a medieval castle and a dynastic home. The well-brought-up but impoverished children of the story, Edred and Elfrida, even share the castle's name. The continuity of this aristocratic pedigree in that same location, we are told, can be traced back to before the Norman Conquest and clearly reinforces the children's sense of rootedness and belonging. It is this sense of identity and of personal and cultural inheritance that time-slip stories—particularly in the period after the Second World War, 50 years later than

Nesbit's early example—seem concerned to explore. It is noteworthy how many examples of the genre feature an old house and its garden.

Time-slip stories, which may be defined as fiction with its feet in the present but its head and heart in the past, seem far removed from any interest in the future. But if personal and cultural continuity is the shaping theme of the genre, then this implies that the future is inextricably bonded with the present and thereby with the past; thus the present and future are not safe if the past is forgotten or obliterated. In the late 1940s and early 1950s when these novels were being gestated and written, there was a real threat to the past. The war had destroyed much and postwar reconstruction in Britain did not follow the European pattern. Where the Poles and Germans showed a reverence for their respective pasts by replacing their razed cities with faithful replicas, Britain set about sweeping away the bombed remains of architectural gems and medieval city centers. In an epidemic of modernity and apparent hatred of the past, loved landmarks and townscapes succumbed to rebuilding mania. The past was often obliterated by anonymous modern blocks.

It is hardly surprising, then, that these levelling processes, also at work in the social and economic sphere, should be reflected in the work of a number of cultivated, middle-class women writers of time-slip stories and historical novels; they nowhere overtly address contemporary national change, yet haunted by a sense of loss, these writers attempt to recapture and preserve in an inhospitable present a past that seems to be as much under threat as the present.

Nesbit's prototype, written before the First World War, obviously had different origins. The seriousness with which Nesbit presents the old house and its garden is particularly noteworthy, for her preferred narratorial voice in *The House of Arden*, as in her earlier novels, is ironic. The irony lapses only when the house and its garden reappear in the story. The ruined castle of Edred and Elfrida's own time is described in elegiac terms. The Elizabethan garden, which is associated with earlier children's innocent games, is described in terms that stress its formal beauty. For all her radicalism, Nesbit presents the feudal heyday of the Arden family with respect and even gravitas. In the novel's present, the Arden lands have passed into the hands of an industrialist, whom Nesbit derides as "The Tallow King." Her clear preference for feudalism over urban industrialism no doubt reflects a romanticized view of the feudal system, as well as an attachment to the rural world. It may also derive from a liking for feudalism's requirement that individuals be linked in an interconnected web of duties and responsibilities, a social and moral cohesiveness that industrialism had damaged.

Since a house and its garden seem to provide the ideal focus for exploring a feeling for the past, this readily suggests a desire to preserve; indeed the major postwar examples of time-slip narratives are essentially conservative, in the best sense of that word, meaning—as Peter Hollindale puts it in relation to Lucy Boston—conservationist, both historically and environmentally.[4] Environment and history in fact unite in that sense of place on which the structure of feeling in these stories is so often focused. This is manifested in a concern with the fate of a particular house and is most memorable in Lucy Boston's *The Children of Green*

Knowe (1954) and in Philippa Pearce's *Tom's Midnight Garden* (1958). The house which is both the setting and the subject of Boston's novels seems almost more important than the people who have lived within its walls, if only because it outlasts their individual mortality and so can become the symbol as well as the receptacle of that continuity without which all human effort seems purposeless. The significance of this durability is acknowledged too by Penelope Lively in *The House in Norham Gardens* (1974) when Clare, the central character, considers that,

Houses like this have stood and watched the processes of change. People swept by the current, go with it; they grow, learn, forget, laugh and cry, replace their skin every seven years, lose teeth, form opinions, become bald, love, hate, argue and reflect. Bricks, roofs, windows and doors are immutable. (p. 5)

In *The Children of Charlecote* (1989),[5] Philippa Pearce puts it more simply: "it's the house that remembers" (p. 176), an idea echoed by Lively's Clare: "it seemed to her that the house itself, silent round her, was a huge head, packed with events and experiences and conversations. And she was part of them, something the house was storing up" (p. 38). Lively has said that "children need to sense that we live in a permanent world that reaches away behind and ahead of us."[6] The houses in these novels enclose layers of past lives that are accessible to us if we are sufficiently attuned.

The living nature of the building itself seems to have the power to put the imaginative child in touch with its peopled past. But these children—like Clare and Tom and Tolly—must be solitary, whether in enforced isolation like Tom Long in *Tom's Midnight Garden*, or as an only child, like Tolly and Clare. They must also be lonely and longing for company. The reiterated "Green grow the rushes Oh / One is one and all alone / And ever more shall be so" (p. 28) in *The Children of Green Knowe* is not just a refrain from an old folksong. It also indicates a psychological state, the necessary precondition for access to the spiritual plane that can put someone in touch with the family's and the culture's past. In *The Children of Green Knowe* the past is invested with a living presence. It carries the same spiritual charge for Tolly and Mrs. Oldknow as for the people of New Guinea whom Clare's great-grandfather had studied on his anthropological expeditions.

Not all houses have the power to withstand change, as Pearce makes plain in *Tom's Midnight Garden*. There the old house in which Tom spends his quarantine from measles has been subdivided into small flats, in keeping with a more democratic age. It no longer resembles the grand Victorian family house of Tom's dreams and Mrs. Bartholomew's memories, while its magical garden has disappeared altogether, eaten up by encroaching development. All that is left of the garden is a hard, paved backyard as a space for dustbins.

It is significant that when Pearce wrote *Tom's Midnight Garden* in the 1950s, the transformation of her own family home, the inspiration for Tom's temporary residence, had not actually taken place. However, the future, as envisaged by her, involved the inevitable destruction of the continuity of the house in which her father had been born in 1876: "I set the story slightly in the future—say, the nineteen sixties. This was because, in the fifties, I thought the house and garden—hardly changed from my father's childhood—was under threat, and I wanted to imagine that threat executed—the house split into flats, the garden built over" (p. 72).[7]

She enacts the future threat herself, perhaps to keep the destruction within bounds, while at the same time her story resurrects the house and garden as it was, not in her own time but in her father's childhood—a period when the threat did not exist. Perhaps her sense that the changelessness of the house and garden could not last was a response to the levelling ideology of the time. At all events, her form of the time-slip story is innovative in simultaneously bringing to life the past and the probable future, in narrating two different time-frames both of which are imagined.

To revive the past, make it live again, and trace its links of kinship with the present, is Lucy Boston's narratological method as well as her spiritual purpose in *The Children of Green Knowe*. The setting is the early 1950s. A boy of seven goes to stay with his great-grandmother because (after the death of the child's mother) his father has remarried and, in true fairy-tale fashion, his stepmother wants him out of her way. The story, such as it is, of Tolly, Mrs. Oldknow's great grandson, is delayed by stories of the children who lived in the house three hundred years earlier. Though they make only fleeting appearances in Tolly's life, their presence is all around him, in toys, a doll's house, a birdcage, even in the natural world, and especially in the stories told of them. Tolly's own story concerns making contact with the past by, gradually, seeing the ghostly children of the house—Alexander, Toby and Linnet—which occurs only after sensing them. Eventually, in one of the most moving episodes of the story, Tolly becomes aware of Feste, the phantom horse that once belonged to Toby and that Mrs. Oldknow herself has never seen. The whole movement of the story is towards this "realization" of the past, not in any normal sense, but by poetically apprehending it through the senses, and by developing an openness to, and a feeling for, the past. In the end—a sensitive refinement by the writer—Tolly does not actually see Feste; in all the fullness of a realized experience (but one which the rationalizing mind can explain as "a waking dream"), he hears him and then touches him and feels his breath upon his skin.

What this episode seems to convey is that the past cannot come fully back to life: it may be apprehended by contact with its petrified remains, as in the sight of old buildings, the touch of old stones, the handling of old possessions. These are necessary to activate the imagination. The novel encourages this delicate and sensitive perception of the pervasiveness, the ever-presentness of the past, if one can only detect it: Boston makes visible and palpable the vanished presences of times gone by.

The Green Knowe story enshrines innocence and makes that state concrete in an evocation of both the children's cultivated lives—their world is filled with music, art and literature, access to which is clearly contingent on their privileged status as gentry—and their harmonious relations with the natural world. Contributing to the picture of their innocence is their richly fulfilling respect for the animal and bird life at Green Knowe, a loving attitude towards nature which is not confined to their social position. The scene which expresses most fully Boston's proto-conservationist ideology and underscores the children's oneness with the natural world occurs when, under the yew tree in the snow, they manifest themselves to Tolly's sight for the first time:

In the centre, leaning against the bole of the tree, were Toby and Alexander, with Linnet sitting on the dry yew needle carpet at their feet. It was Alexander of course who was playing [a flute], while a red squirrel ran up and down him, searching in his pockets for nuts. Toby was feeding the deer, the red deer, the beautiful dappled deer with black ears and white breast. It wagged its tail like a lamb as it ate from his hand. Linnet was playing with the lanky hare, making it stand up and dance to music. (p. 88)

The inheritance and continuity that the novel celebrates belongs to more than just the house and its human inhabitants. The natural world is also involved in this process of transmission. Before the magical moment when the dead children manifest themselves to him, Tolly has already made contact with the descendants of the creatures the children had tamed, who carry the memory of that previous close relationship. Chaffinches fly to his window and join him in his room when he inadvertently sings an old folk song of which Alexander was fond. Mrs. Oldknow only has to play Alexander's (clearly magic) flute for a hare to appear and for the air to become "as full of birds as of snow" (p. 65). Even the roses in the garden are seen as belonging to this rich pattern of transmission, having first been brought to this country and this garden by the children's sea-captain father. For all our sense of Mrs Boston's patrician sympathies, it is a democratic vision of heritage, for the natural world recognizes no social hierarchies.

It has been noted that a feeling for the past and for nature, combined with the spirit of place, belongs to a conservative ideology.[8] But in the modern world, it also confronts capitalist and corporate despoliation of ancient and beloved townscapes and landscapes and substitutes an organicist view of social relations built up over time, involving individuals in duties and responsibilities, not just rights. Lucy Boston and Philippa Pearce clearly demonstrate that it is the duty of Mrs. Oldknow and Mrs. Bartholomew to pass on their memories of the past to the younger generation to ensure both the survival of the past and the development of the child's sense of its own identity.

For all that Nesbit, the Socialist, welcomed change, she depicted the house and garden in *The House of Arden* as a symbol of a better, albeit feudal, past. Her hatred is reserved for the world spawned by urban industrialism. For all three writers discussed in this chapter, the house and garden represent a golden age, which, despite social inequalities, enshrined certain values proper to the good society—courtesy and beauty, a sense of duty and of responsibility—values that they fear the modern world would discard or discredit and without which civilized life is impossible. Boston and Pearce are keenly aware of the threat to their sense of English cultural identity that the transformations in the postwar world would foster. Inevitably, their "poetic" form of time-slip story is a cultural challenge to both the materialist aspect of historical fiction and to the materialist forms of political thinking whether of Left or Right. In a consumer-driven world their challenge is still pertinent.

NOTES

1. Gillian Avery and Julia Briggs, eds., *Children and Their Books: A Celebration of the Work of Iona and Peter Opie* (Oxford: Oxford University Press, 1989).

2. Kipling derived Puck from *A Midsummer Night's Dream*, ostensibly set in Greece, but suggestive of rural England.

3. Humphrey Carpenter, *Secret Gardens: The Golden Age of Children's Literature* (Boston: Houghton Mifflin, 1985).

4. Peter Hollindale, "The Darkening of the Green," *Signal* 61 (Jan. 1990), pp. 3–19.

5. Philippa Pearce's *The Children of Charlecote* was originally published in 1968 as *The Children of the House*.

6. Penelope Lively, quoted by Humphrey Carpenter and Mari Prichard in *The Oxford Companion to Children's Literature* (Oxford: Oxford University Press, 1984), p. 322.

7. Philippa Pearce, "Time Present," in *Travellers in Time*, ed. B. Levin (CLNE, 1990), p. 72.

8. Margaret and Michael Rustin, *Narratives of Love and Loss: Studies in Modern Children's Fiction* (London: Verso, 1987), p. 35.

REFERENCES

Boston, Lucy. *The Children of Green Knowe*. London: The Bodley Head, 1954.

Inglis, Fred. *Ideology and the Imagination*. London: Cambridge University Press, 1975.

Kipling, Rudyard. *Puck of Pook's Hill*. 1906. Ware, Hertfordshire: Wordsworth, 1994.

Lively, Penelope. *The House in Norham Gardens*. London: Heinemann, 1974.

Lowerson, John. "The Mystical Geography of the English." In *The English Rural Community: Image and Analysis*. Ed. Brian Short. Cambridge: Cambridge University Press, 1992.

Nesbit, E. *The House of Arden*. 1908. London: Dent, 1967.

Pearce, Philippa. *Tom's Midnight Garden*. Oxford: Oxford University Press, 1958.

———. *The Children of Charlecote*. First pub. as *The Children of the House*, 1968. London: Gollancz, 1989.

18

The Past Reimagined: History and Literary Creation in British Children's Novels after World War Two

Adrienne E. Gavin

The past is prominent in British children's literature of the post-World War Two period from the 1950s to the 1970s, often referred to as the second Golden Age of children's literature. Many children's novels written during these decades are concerned with time and with the effect of the past on the present. In one of his books on children's literature, Humphrey Carpenter notes how striking it is that "the greater part of [English] children's fiction produced in this period has the same theme: the discovery or rediscovery of the past."[1] Another specialist writer, John Rowe Townsend, clusters together some texts of this nature under the heading "Modern Fantasy . . . On the Margin."[2] As he indicates, the past is often introduced into these otherwise realist novels through fantasy. Writers such as Joan Aiken create historical fantasies in which the entire setting is historical, while other authors like C. S. Lewis or Alan Garner create pasts which are mythical or fantastic. The novels by Lucy M. Boston, Philippa Pearce, Penelope Farmer, and Penelope Lively discussed here adopt a different strategy; in these an ostensibly realist past is introduced into a realist present. Links to the past occur through quirks of fantasy or possible fantasy, by means of the supernatural, time-slips, dreams, or the power of the imagination.

The past so frequently present in postwar, quasi-historical, semi-fantasy children's novels has usually been seen in one of three ways. The first view sees the past as enabling the child (character and reader) to realize that time cannot be halted, that the child, too, must grow up and in turn pass into old age and history. The second view sees the past—often in the form of the history of family or place—as allowing the child character to better understand or endure his or her present. The third view sees the past as representing an idyllic lost or imagined Britain and thus provides nostalgic escape from a postwar period marked by austerity and change.

An examination of works by Boston, Pearce, Farmer, and Lively shows that the past in these novels is also linked in several ways with literary creation and the literary imagination; three such links are considered here. The first stage in the argument is that in these works the past is a metaphor for the creative act, for imagination. In other words, the child protagonist's experience of the past is the equivalent of the writer's experience of writing and the reader's experience of reading. Secondly, the suggestion follows that the past represented in these novels is drawn from literature rather than from history as we traditionally view it. Thirdly, the past in the novels selected reflects a significantly female literary imagination.

In Boston's Green Knowe series (1954–1976), Pearce's *Tom's Midnight Garden* (1958), Farmer's *Charlotte Sometimes* (1969), and Lively's *The House in Norham Gardens* (1974) and *A Stitch in Time* (1976), the past and time are crucial elements. Clocks tick, trees grow, and time expands and contracts in the world and mind of the child protagonist. Loneliness or fear of being alone is, similarly, a conspicuous feature of the child's existence in these novels. In *The Children of Green Knowe* we are told in the first paragraph that Tolly "was alone as usual."[3] He wishes "he had a family like other people."[4] *Tom's Midnight Garden* begins with an angry Tom being sent away from his brother and parents. In quarantine for measles, he is restricted from mixing with anyone other than his Aunt Gwen and Uncle Alan. *Charlotte Sometimes* opens with Charlotte alone on her first night at boarding school. Clare and Maria, appearing respectively in Lively's *The House in Norham Gardens* and *A Stitch in Time*, have no siblings. Clare, an orphan, is increasingly fretful about the approaching deaths of her elderly great-aunts while Maria, painfully aware that she is "'an only'" and lacking companionship, carries on conversations with objects and animals.[5] From these solitary positions each character moves on to experience the past through the intervention of fantasy, which both relieves the loneliness and gives the child an understanding of his or her place in the continuum of time.

A question often raised in reference to these novels, particularly given the prominent theme of loneliness, is whether the child character's experience of history—through ghosts, time-slips, or dreams—is real or imagined. One answer is that it is no more "unreal" than any other elements of the novel. Everything in the story is created and unverifiable. As readers we only get to the past through layers: the layer of the writer writing the story, of the character experiencing the past, of the stories told by historical characters. As we peel each layer off we are no more certain of "truth"; each layer is a creation, a fictional act.

A related answer involves looking at the corollary of loneliness: solitude. Solitude in at least some measure is a requirement for literary creation. Solitude for both child protagonist and writer results in acts of imagination or creation. Like writers, the child characters inhabit two co-existent time periods: the present and the past, the real and the imagined, the day-to-day and the literary. In this way these novels are metafictional; we can read the child as writer and his or her re-creating of the past through fantasy as the act of writing fiction. In Lively's *A Stitch in Time*, for example, Maria "writes" the life of the historical Harriet and has imaginary conversations just as a writer might create dialogue. That time and the past are central to Maria's literary creation is symbolized by the significance she grants to one of her non-human conversants: "[f]or a real heart-to-heart you couldn't do much better than a clock."[6] The past is similarly the key to literary creation for Tolly in the Green Knowe books who "writes" the fictions suggested to him by the stories of the past his great grandmother tells him. Clare in Lively's *The House in Norham Gardens* also creates a fiction of the past through her "writing" the story of a Stone-Age tribe of New Guinea; she enters into that world through her dreams just as a novelist enters into a fictional world through writing.

These child characters can be read as symbolic authors, but they are also symbolic readers. The world of the past operates upon them in the same way a novel works upon a reader; it causes suspension of disbelief. The past lifts the characters out of themselves, literally in *Charlotte Sometimes*, into a world of the imagination where the speed and continuity of time is disrupted. When the child protagonists enter a world of the past, present time often pauses. Tom, for example, spends his time in the midnight garden during the magical thirteenth hour of night. Tolly in *The Children of Green Knowe* wakes after dreaming and hears time start again: "suddenly, as if it had only just begun after being asleep itself, the slow tick-tock of the clock came to his ears, almost as loud as a hammer."[7] Clare in her clock-filled house in Norham Gardens similarly experiences time stopping as she enters her dream-world: "[h]er watch had stopped, and so had the hall clock."[8] This stopping or slowing of time reflects the capacity of imagination or memory to move through decades in moments and of books to cover years within the hours in which they are read.

If the past acts as a metaphor for literary creation, it is also notable that the past discovered or created by characters in these novels is also in itself predominantly literary. As the Marxist critic Fredric Jameson has suggested, "history is *not* a text, not a narrative, master or otherwise, but . . . as an absent cause, it is inaccessible to us except in textual form, and . . . our approach to it and to the Real itself necessarily passes through its prior textualization, its narrativization in the political unconscious."[9] Similarly, Penelope Lively writes that "[a]wareness of the past is an achievement of the imagination."[10] Both Jameson's and Lively's claims are significant in relation to the children's novels under discussion. The child protagonists, as "writers," re-create through their imaginations a history they have never experienced while in turn their creators, the novelists, in Jameson's terms, necessarily rely on textualized narrativizations of history in order to create their own imagined versions of the past. The narrative texts of history relied upon most heavily in these novels are in themselves fictional literary creations of the past. *Tom's Midnight Garden*, for example, owes more to Victorian novels than to "strict" Victorian history. The pasts created by writers such as Pearce are based not on the specifics of events found in traditional history books but are drawn from earlier fictions. These pasts, in other words, are re-imaginings of already imagined pasts.

That writers' and characters' conceptions of the past are literary is not surprising; fictional representations of history naturally influence the literary imagination. And perhaps, as Joan Aiken, the distinguished author of gothic fantasies, has claimed, "[o]nly fiction, or truly perceptive biography, can communicate [a] real appreciation of how the past looked, sounded, felt and smelt."[11] Literary influences also add to the palimpsestic qualities of novels which are deeply concerned with layers of time and history. History in these novels draws little on dates, political leaders, or exact chronology. Some facts of history are mentioned: a great freeze, a world war, a landslide, but their significance is individualized and made personal. The final months of World War One are the specific period of the past that Charlotte is exchanged into as Clare in *Charlotte Sometimes*, but it is the war (inter-)textualized by works of fiction rather than "fact." We are told in Farmer's novel of elements of the past familiar to us from literary, not historical, texts: old toys, the family who have lost their son, the teacher who has lost her fiancé. The pasts in the Green Knowe novels are similarly situated by date, but those pasts are strongly reliant on the tales told to the children by their grandmothers. These stories are presented as family history but hold strong literary echoes of ghost stories, adventure books, animal literature, and domestic novels. Similarly it is fiction that has made us familiar with the tediousness to a Victorian girl of having to sew samplers. Lively uses this literary stock at the heart of *A Stitch in Time* where it gives rise to Maria's mistaken belief that the Victorian Harriet, because she did not finish her sampler, has died young. In Victorian literature such a belief would be entirely plausible, but Lively re-imagines this past (and Maria "re-writes" her ending) to create a conclusion with a twist.

The past in these novels is pervaded by the ubiquitous attributes of Victorian fiction, many of which had strong echoes in postwar Britain: orphanhood, dead family members, prescribed behavior for children, children being sent to live elsewhere, and large rambling houses which hold secrets. Of all literary influences on the pasts and in some cases on the presents in these books, those of the Brontë sisters are perhaps strongest. Aspects of *Jane Eyre* and *Wuthering Heights,* such as orphanhood, loneliness, nervous emotion, the need to escape through the imagination, houses with secrets, family history, and the interplay of realism and the supernatural, influence the depiction of the past in the work of all these postwar writers. Jane Eyre's solitariness is reflected in the position of all the child protagonists as is her strength, imagination, and suppression of emotion. Hatty in *Tom's Midnight Garden,* like Jane Eyre, is an orphan who is unwanted by, and maltreated by, her aunt and cousins. Tom in the same novel experiences feelings of anger and injustice similar to Jane's. In *Charlotte Sometimes,* Charlotte is sent to boarding school as Jane is. Clare in *The House in Norham*

Gardens, an orphan who is carrying a copy of *Jane Eyre* in her bicycle basket when we first meet her, feels shut in by the snow and her nerves suffer in a way reminiscent of Charlotte Brontë's protagonists, both Jane Eyre and *Villette's* Lucy Snowe. Houses in all the novels hold mysteries connected with the past which in turn influence the present, just as Bertha Rochester's hidden presence in the attic at Thornfield Hall affects the course of Jane Eyre's life. The Brontëan influence has further significance when we consider the third link between the past and literary creation in these novels: the female literary imagination (or perhaps one particular one).

Written by women during a period of postwar retrenchment of traditional gender roles, these novels take as their focus the traditionally female sphere of home and family. The history that appears within their pages is closely linked to family or place and usually to domestic space as represented by large, many-roomed, often Victorian houses. The world presented in these novels is English and middle class, and the literary pasts it is influenced by are similarly English and middle class. The history presented in these works is also predominantly female even in novels with boy protagonists, and it is notable how many of these "realist with a twist" novels are written by women.

The female writers discussed here use literary patterns, characters, and settings drawn in particular from the work of Victorian women writers. This provides a link in literary imagination and in history. The Brontës, for example, as well as Boston and Pearce all wrote during periods of increased restriction and expected domesticity for women: the mid-nineteenth century and the post-1945 period. The idealized domestic sphere of middle-class womanhood during these periods also encompassed the world of children below a certain age; their world too was domestic and defined. Houses and domestic settings are thus fittingly central in each of these novels written by a woman for children.

The pasts the houses open up offer physical space and freedom. Tom in Pearce's novel wanders through a spacious Victorian house and garden at night while he is restricted to an oppressive small flat during the day. Clare in *The House in Norham Gardens* feeling trapped inside her present-day house by the snow, thinks "things slide agreeably from what is real to what is not" as she enters her New Guinean dream world.[12] The houses' pasts offer space for the imagination and empower domesticity by offering escape not necessarily from the domestic world the children and women live within, but escape within the domestic world through time, ghosts, or dreams.

In these houses the key with which the child character unlocks the door to the past is the imagination or memories of an older woman or women. These older women characters act as conduits to the past and enable readers and the child protagonists to enter the past through the female imagination. They demand through their storytelling or dreaming that the child characters suspend disbelief and in so doing open themselves up to the potential of the past and of fiction. Like the child characters, these conduits are usually solitary figures. They are women who are literary creators sustained by their own memories and reimaginings. Mrs. Oldknow, herself once an orphaned child with no brothers or sisters, has perhaps made up all her stories, but her literary imagination makes

Tolly believe, visualize, and imagine just as a writer empowers a reader to do the same. Through telling Tolly old stories of Green Knowe and family history, she gives him confidence enough in his own imagination to escape into the past just as she had done herself as a child. "'I like this house,'" says Tolly. "'It's like living in a book that keeps coming true.'"[13] It is made true by an act of the female imagination which reveals to him "the others" who live in the house.

In *Tom's Midnight Garden* Tom experiences the past because Mrs. Bartholomew is dreaming of her childhood. In *Charlotte Sometimes* Charlotte becomes Clare in part because of Emily's memory or imagination. In *A Stitch in Time* Maria's sensing of the Victorian Harriet is stimulated through Mrs. Shand. Clare's dream world in *The House in Norham Gardens* is provoked by thoughts about her great-aunts' pasts and her family history. The domestic setting of a house in conjunction with the power of female memory and imagination provoke fantasy and invoke the past.

The importance of female re-imagining of history is expressed powerfully in the conclusion to *The House in Norham Gardens*. Aunt Susan has told Clare: "'you can't carry a museum round with you. Neither will you need to. What you need, you will find you already have to hand. . . . You are a listener. It is only those who have never listened who find themselves in trouble eventually.'"[14] Clare realizes that she cannot carry facts around with her, nor can she physically keep as mementoes all the objects owned by her aunts, but she can remember and then recreate the past. History in this way becomes story. Clare looks at her elderly great-aunts "intently, at their faces and their hands and the shape of them. I'm learning them by heart, she thought, that's what I'm doing, that's all I can do, only that."[15] All she can do is remember history and recreate it through her imagination. It is only in memories or in literary creation that time can pause and the dead be brought back to life.

NOTES

1. Humphrey Carpenter, *Secret Gardens: A Study of the Golden Age of Children's Literature* (Boston: Houghton Mifflin, 1985), p. 217.

2. John Rowe Townsend, *Written for Children: An Outline of English-Language Children's Literature*, 6th ed. (London: Bodley Head, 1995), p. 238.

3. Lucy M. Boston, *The Children of Green Knowe*, 1954 (Harmondsworth: Puffin, 1975), p. 7; this edition is used for all subsequent citations.

4. Ibid., p. 9.

5. Penelope Lively, *A Stitch in Time*, 1976 (London: Mammoth, 1994), p. 2; this edition is used for all subsequent citations.

6. Ibid., p. 3.

7. Boston, *The Children of Green Knowe*, p. 127.

8. Penelope Lively, *The House in Norham Gardens*, 1974 (London: Mammoth, 1994), p. 80; this edition is used for all subsequent citations.

9. Fredric Jameson, *The Political Unconscious: Narrative as a Socially Symbolic Act*, 1981 (London: Methuen, 1983), p. 35.

10. Penelope Lively, "Bones in the Sand," in *Innocence and Experience: Essays and Conversations on Children's Literature*, ed. Barbara Harrison and Gregory Maguire (New York: Lothrop, Lee and Shepard, 1987), pp. 13–21: 14.

11. Joan Aiken, "Interpreting the Past: Reflections of an Historical Novelist," in *Only Connect: Readings on Children's Literature*, ed. Sheila Egoff, Gordon Stubbs, Ralph Ashley, and Wendy Sutton, 3rd ed. (Toronto: Oxford University Press, 1996), pp. 62–73: 67.

12. Lively, *The House in Norham Gardens*, p. 38.

13. Lucy M. Boston, *The Chimneys of Green Knowe*, 1958 (Harmondsworth: Puffin, 1976), p. 19.

14. Lively, *The House in Norham Gardens*, p. 154.

15. Ibid., p. 154.

REFERENCES

Aiken, Joan. "Interpreting the Past: Reflections of an Historical Novelist." In *Only Connect: Readings on Children's Literature*. Eds. Sheila Egoff, Gordon Stubbs, Ralph Ashley, and Wendy Sutton. 3rd ed. Toronto: Oxford University Press, 1996: 62–73.

Boston, Lucy M. *The Children of Green Knowe*. 1954. Harmondsworth: Puffin, 1975.

——. *The Chimneys of Green Knowe*. 1958. Harmondsworth: Puffin, 1976.

Carpenter, Humphrey. *Secret Gardens: A Study of the Golden Age of Children's Literature*. Boston: Houghton Mifflin, 1985.

Farmer, Penelope. *Charlotte Sometimes*. 1969. Harmondsworth: Puffin, 1992.

Jameson, Fredric. *The Political Unconscious: Narrative as a Socially Symbolic Act*. 1981. London: Methuen, 1983.

Lively, Penelope. "Bones in the Sand." In *Innocence and Experience: Essays and Conversations on Children's Literature*. Eds. Barbara Harrison and Gregory Maguire. New York: Lothrop, Lee and Shepard, 1987: 13–21.

——. *The House in Norham Gardens*. 1974. London: Mammoth, 1994.

——. *A Stitch in Time*. 1976. London: Mammoth, 1994.

Pearce, Philippa. *Tom's Midnight Garden*. 1958. Puffin Modern Classics. Harmondsworth: Puffin, 1993.

Rowe Townsend, John. *Written for Children: An Outline of English-Language Children's Literature*. 6th ed. London: Bodley Head, 1995.

19

England's Dark Ages?
The North-East in Robert Westall's *The Wind Eye* and Andrew Taylor's *The Coal House*

Pamela Knights

Who are the guardians of history and culture? Whose forms of knowledge and language shape the future? If the novel is always a battleground for contesting voices and values, the children's past-in-present narrative stages the dramas of cultural reproduction in especially acute form. Two late twentieth-century English samples of the genre are considered in this chapter, both popular books in the schools of North-Eastern England: Robert Westall's *The Wind Eye* (published and set in 1976) and Andrew Taylor's *The Coal House* (published in 1986, and set during the miners' strike of 1984). With both narratives centering on a sensible teenage daughter and a disturbed middle-class father—Westall's, a Cambridge professor, Taylor's, a university consultant who writes poetry textbooks for schools—these novels raise troubled and troubling questions about what adults pass on to young people and texts to readers.

Other candidates for the role of authoritative voice in these novels include Saint Cuthbert, striking miners, amateur gardeners, television newsmen, a man without a mouth, and an ambitious woman lecturer in the Durham University English department. The arena for their contest is the North-East of England, a contemporary time/space which keeps alive England's "dark ages": the grim spirituality and bloodlust of Westall's seventh-century Northumbria, and the more recent austerities and savageries of Taylor's Victorian coal-mining County Durham. Constructed from a repertoire of North/South binaries locked deep in English culture, it represents dangerous territory where incomers must earn acceptance in an older, stronger, land. Fathers prepare their children, and the readers: "'This place will harden you up'" or "'it's honester up there. Cleaner.'"[1] Coded as purer, violent, beyond the law, it is the realm of "authenticity," asserted through painful narratives of exposure and renewal, promising access to "truths" unavailable in the one-dimensional South.

This North-East is pristine, even prelapsarian: "God's own undiscovered country,"[2] terrifyingly empty in Westall, dazzlingly fresh in Taylor. At the same time, it is dirty, with polluted air, dense with fearful histories—of saints and Vikings, pitmen and managers—"soaked," as in the Coal House, "into its very stones" (p. 30). It is rich in chronotopes: meeting points of space and time, which interfuse present and past, cultural and personal histories: Norse place-names, artefacts, documents, scars on the land itself. Their force is concentrated in the strange house, a sprawling architectural palimpsest, which both figures the interior stresses of the characters and reactivates larger cultural tensions suppressed in the complacent Southern English base. Westall's Monk's Heugh, on the borders of land and sea, a house which "went on forever" (p. 25), preserves a space for the spiritual, lost in secular modern England. Taylor's Coal House, built by an industrial magnate, and labelled the "Bad House," the "castle," and the "Manor," embodies a record of privilege and injustice from the early 1800s to Thatcher's post-industrial Britain. Even its balcony, viewed by one child as "'Like *Gone With the Wind*'" (p. 9), by another as a "verandah" (p. 36), signals wider legacies of dispossession and imperialism.

Both texts, conventionally, deploy the region's past as the sphere of healing for the dysfunctions of the present. Involving readers in powerful emotional materials, here the academic's daughter begins to understand, and to mend, divisions in the house: of the psyche, the family, the culture, the nation. With intertexts that evoke Bede's and Symeon's chronicles in Westall and D.H. Lawrence and Elizabeth Gaskell in Taylor, these novels seem to endow their heroines with a significant place in England's continuing stories. But just how empowering are they?

THE DAUGHTER'S PLOT

In many ways, the novels recount what I label "the daughter's plot": in open texts that offer young readers room for negotiation, they assign the heroine authority. As in much young-adult fiction, the teenager is the sensitive consciousness who carries the weight of the conflicts. The text, by implication, extends this care-taking role to the reader. It suggests that even well-meaning adult authorities are limited, but it encourages viewpoints beyond the immediate horizons of the adolescent, presenting itself as a space which invites multiple perspectives, multiple voices.

The heroine's encounters with North-Eastern history model for the reader engagement with complex discourses. Here, "history," whether a Viking raid on a monastery, or fighting on a 1980s' picketline, is not simply a matter of a fixed event or fact, but one of its textual construction, an act in which the observer, too, is implicated. When Westall's Beth meets St. Cuthbert, "Her head seemed to split down the middle, and her two eyes saw things from two different viewpoints" (p. 125). The image breaks apart "reality," representing history as open to revision. Both texts enact this suggestion, most obviously, by distributing the focalization between teenage and adult characters, but also in self-reflexive moments which cast doubt on fixed ways of representing past or present. In *The Wind Eye,* is a white streak on Inner Farne island a vein of white marble, bird-lime, or waste carbide from the lighthouse (p. 34)? Are characters projecting the past out of the subjective histories of the present? What is the relationship between belief, legend and chronicle and how do these square with science and rationalism?

In *The Coal House,* heroine and reader thread their way through similar questions. From Alison's first tourist view of Durham as "a stylised drawing . . . in one of her history books" (p. 16), we negotiate a range of debased representations of history, from gossip to gravestones. For Alison, the most pernicious is that which purports to be the most immediate, the most truthful: the live reportage of a colliery picket through the eye of the television news. The episode picks up the intense real-life confrontations and bitter debates of August 1984, when the miners' strike daily occupied the British news media.[3] Alison's outburst against the cameramen vocalizes the text's repeated concern with the dangers of the camera image, a theme dramatized elsewhere in Alison's empathy with a dying Victorian girl, captured by chance on a photograph. Now Alison seizes power. Gate-crashing the cameras, she finds a public voice, reminding the nation of personal responsibilities within the political: "'You're making it worse! You're just—just vultures! Can't you see? These are people's Dads!'" (p. 91). The text, it is implied, respects her account, avoiding its own exploitation of North-East tragedy, embodying instead a superior "truth," where all voices and viewpoints are honored.

Here, no single discourse is infallible, least of all the discourses of the powerful. The time-shifts unfold the hidden histories of the silenced, and the heroines begin to understand their own self-construction as well as the oppressions of their own times through glimpsing the cramped lives of men and women from England's past. But if these texts authenticate the daughter's plot, they do so above all by seeming to validate forms of knowledge and language outside the Symbolic Order, the realm of rationality coded by the father. Readers take from *The Coal House* images of patriarchy in its grimmest form, in the capitalist industrial machine which rapes the land and breaks its children. In contrast, the heroine's home seems a haven. Here, in 1984, in the house erected from the aspirations of the Industrial Aristocrat, the text places a New Man. Aware of his didacticism, his urge to command, Alec begins to reshape himself, acknowledging different modes of understanding: "reasons . . . quite unknown to the head" (Epigraph). The text explores these further. It unsettles its own dominant realism, particularly on a first reading, with hints of the uncanny, unstable narrative focus, and uneasy metaphors, blurring nature and non-nature, past and present. It calls up the green realm of nursery rhyme and fairy tale, the nostalgia of childhood picture-books, the double-world of Gothic fiction, instructing the reader, but working most powerfully through emotion, suspense, and symbol.

In *The Wind Eye*, Westall presents the man's cognitive domain in virulent form. He figures the father as a "heartless masculine millstone" (p. 129) grinding the life out of his daughter. Numerous episodes focus on Bertrand's "utterly maddening reasonableness" (p. 33), his stifling empiricism, his ferocious repressions, his scorn for the unconscious, his ruthless insistence on his supreme right to name and to know. ("'God,'" thought his stepson, "'it's like living with the Encyclopaedia Britannica'" [p. 34].) The narrative thoroughly discredits this Law of the Father, representing its effects on his daughters as the darkest kind of abuse. Its marks are visible in Sally's horribly mutilated hand, in Beth's painful worries about not living up to academic expectations. Though Robert Westall and French Feminism might seem an unlikely coupling, *The Wind Eye*, like its exact contemporary Hélène Cixous' "The Laugh of the Medusa" (1976), finally posits the release of the daughter—to new forms of subjectivity, and to her "*great work*" (p. 131) on the earth—in the passing of the father's domination. Westall's time-slip narrative explodes the masculine world-order, confirming the fantastic, in all its subversive force. Through Sally, the youngest child, readers see marvels even the historian Bede only heard reported: St. Cuthbert's helpful birds and animals, visions of devils and heaven-bound souls. Affirming all the power of wonder, Sally's hand is healed, reinforcing the message of the chronicles with the truth of her own miracle.

THE FATHER FIGURE

However, I now wish to question such liberatory readings to suggest instead that what the texts enact, finally, is not the daughter's plot, but the father's: that a covert story reappropriates the young reader's novel for the adult's. In summary, these narratives dramatize crises of adult masculinity in the late 1970s and 1980s, embodied in the struggle for the control of history and culture. They "solve" their problems by restoring historical knowledge to the realm of the middle-class male, legitimating him as the rightful heir to the past, bringing the future safely under his sway. In so doing, they restabilize language, reasserting a hierarchy of the Word. And in the daughter's final, most significant, encounter, she meets at last a single "authentic" voice, which gives her direct access to "truth" and ties her to tradition.

Now to expand this. Through the figure of the father, these texts voice adult problems, symptomized in adult terms: in Westall, by Bertrand's bad faith, his dangerous anger; in Taylor, by Alec's drinking, sexual doubts and writer's block. This male intellectual is faced, in England's North-East, with an alien culture that exposes him as the guilt-ridden liberal, insecure about his role in history. The man's anxiety seems, primarily, class-based, figured in the superior strength and integrity of Northern working-class "natives": artisans, fishermen, miners, even Vikings. As Bertrand's wife taunts him, these are "'*real* people . . . who work with their *hands*'" (p. 13). Both texts are intrigued by hands, working or fighting. Alec patronizes, but is fascinated, by Peter, his gardener: "'God, his hands were like rough iron'" (p. 38). We may recall, too, Westall's memory of his craftsman father: "When I got my degree the only thing he said was, 'Well, you'll never have to get your hands dirty now.'"[4] Keeping his hands clean, how can the writer, the teacher, avoid complicity with social forces he purports to despise? (Bertrand goes white if anyone calls him *bourgeois* [p. 13].) What is this man's title to the Northern house? What right has Bertrand, the atheist, the Cambridge scholar, to colonize its history? How can Alec write schoolbooks in the Big House while miners' families suffer the strike? "'All that for two people,'" as Tommy, the miner's son, reminds Alison (p. 36).

But class also marks gender. Above all, these are fiercely masculine histories. Before the fight on Holy Island, Beth lingers uneasily as women and children are sent home. On the picket-line, Alison feels herself "in the way of a masculine venture" (p. 87): an episode linguistically marked by "some of the ripest language" (p. 89) she had ever heard. Women's lot is to wait and endure. But where does this place the writer? Does he have any part in this culture? As *The Wind Eye* asks, is he even a *"real* man" (p. 137)? For Westall, remembering his father's love for model ships, "the mark of manhood was to make, make, *make,* every working hour."[5] When the professor sails a boat, or climbs into his diving-suit, "His hands were swift and sure" (p. 108). But the locals have no respect for Bertrand's "long words" (p. 16), his international reputation, his disruptive research. Alec has dropped out of the world of men in suits, but risks losing male definition altogether: his daughter amuses her friends by describing him as a "typist" (p. 49); a widower, he is now "a total parent" (p. 68), father and mother both.

Each narrative tracks the father's reinsertion into male histories. Bertrand's vicious, hand-to-hand attempts to prove himself in the male pack lead *The Wind Eye* dangerously near to the terrifying realm of Peckinpah's film, *Straw Dogs* (1971), an earlier story of a pacifist academic beleaguered in one of England's outposts.[6] (There, Cornwall, like Northumberland, seemed remote enough from London to suggest the extremities of life in the margins.) Although Westall disliked being regarded as "the Norman Mailer of Children's Books,"[7] colored by such moments, his work has never escaped the "macho" labels.[8] Read against *The Wind Eye*'s blood and anger, *The Coal House* seems gentler—Alec wants to bond with men in the pub, the garden, the Leek Club – but it is no less insistent. Taken as a whole, both novels suggest that if the writer separates himself from the world of men, he renounces his stake in history.

The texts reinforce the dangers, by producing still greater fears, concentrated in the feminine. If groups of men are threatening, female force is more frightening still. Bertrand is afraid of female solidarity, even of his own daughters sharing a bed. But the supreme threat is wild, uncontained, female energy: *"Radix malorum,"* as Beth knows, is "'the root of evil,' which was what the old monks called women" (pp. 124–25). This threat is carried in these narratives through the adult woman, who replaces the (safe) dead mother as sexual partner to the man and parent to his adolescent daughter. Anecdotes, legends and metaphor accumulate to paint her as Eve, siren, vixen—coded in extremes. Whether Westall's housewife, or Taylor's academic, she flaunts long hair and erotic dress (vivid pantsuits, fleshy peepholes, and fur a speciality—even in bed); she drives powerful sports-cars (in Westall, a Spitfire driven with "machine-guns firing" [p. 11]). All predatory sexuality and vigorous speech, she is a menace to male institutions and an agent of an unthinkable future.

In *The Wind Eye*, Madeleine (Magdalen?) is woman typed as hysteric: a non-stop talker, emotionally volatile, a failed suicide, with a "quick dancing mind" (p. 10) sabotaging male logic. Where Bertrand embodies the caution of a road-safety slogan, "Mr Green Cross Code" (p. 34), Madeleine strains against limits. The text presents her assertiveness as aggression, her politics as pathological anger. In Durham Cathedral, deliberately trespassing on St. Cuthbert's tomb, she repeats the offence of a "scarlet wumman" (p. 16) of local legend. Uttering stereotyped 1970s feminist slogans, "Chauvinist pig," "Women's Lib forever!" (p. 16), she upsets patriarchal order, triggering the shockwaves of the story.

In *The Coal House*, ten years on, red-haired Sue intensifies the danger. The text produces her explosively, half way through the novel, paralleling the first eruption of the miners' strike. In a world of unemployed men, the real hazard is the successful working woman. Seen by Alison as "The white boiler suit" (p. 99), she combines *femme fatale* with feminist fighter. Where Madeleine is undomestic, Sue rejects motherhood altogether. Viewing Alec and Alison as career accessories, she wants an instant family without pregnancy or labor. Constructed as the angel in the house, Alison's dead mother remains a wise voice at moments of crisis. Intent on displacing her, Sue becomes the demon of disruption, dividing man from man, father from daughter. Meeting her, Alec loses touch with his wife, quarrels with Alison, stops gardening and cannot write. Significantly, Sue commands language and opinions. Alec meets her in the University Library, the terrain of the Word ("'Terrible places, these libraries. Moral minefields,'" [p. 79]). She is "good at lectures, committees and politics" (p. 81); she appears on radio's "Any Questions," the quintessential British forum for laying one's judgements before the nation. A history don cautions Alec about Sue's sexual past, warning of her ambitions to lead the University English Department and shine in the media. As Alison muses, "This woman was clever and that usually meant dangerous" (p. 102). Here, woman has infiltrated the male realm of rationality itself, and threatens to usurp the father as gatekeeper of culture and authority in the family.

In *The Wind Eye,* the disturbance lasts until Madeleine is content with home—baking cakes, driving at twenty miles an hour—her anger erased. In *The Coal House*, Sue's contempt for country rituals condemns her to life alone in the modern city, possibly even to "exile" in a North American university. The teenage girls remain notionally at the centre, but the narratives block their stories. Beth's quest on the island leaves her stripped naked on the rocks, bloody, covered in guano and fish slime. Alison speaks on television, but never becomes a "national phenomenon" (p. 91); the narrative forgets the incident, her politics evaporate.

Both narratives tame, humiliate, or expel transgressive women, and the social forms they promise. Instead, they shape the future out of the past through the figure of the enduring old man, who emerges out of the dark as a link with more ancient histories and mediator of more "authentic" forms of knowledge. This is the oracle figure of so many past-in-present novels. Here, in Westall's St. Cuthbert and in Taylor's Old Shotton (a man given the name of a notorious colliery), readers at last encounter the quintessential spirit of the North-East.[9] For most of the novel, he remains a presence in the shadows; but frightening though he is, he is generated to drive back the deeper fears of the narrative, as the structural counter to the contemporary woman. This figure embodies a realm without the feminine. He is a self-resurrecting saint, an owl-like man, who speaks to animals, a recluse, misogynist ("Cuddy"—St. Cuthbert—"couldn't stomach a wumman" [p. 16]), a celibate, robed as a priest, inquisitor and confessor. Crucially, he is all but silent. The narrative requires a tongue uncontaminated by women and modernity. So, Shotton, an injured miner, is a man with no mouth; St. Cuthbert, unseen, talks inside Beth's head in Latin. This voice redeems language. Through mumbles, hissed monosyllables, iconic signs, drawings, and startlingly material visions, this figure reaffirms the power of the patriarch, the force and fullness of the Word.

THE TROUBLED LIBERAL AS RIGHTFUL CUSTODIAN

Finally, the narratives endorse the troubled liberal as rightful custodian of the North-Eastern house, the house of England's significant histories, and guardian of its future. The endings reconstitute older families, reconciling past and present in reassuring continuities. In *The Wind Eye*, the final chapter is the father's. Bertrand, we suddenly learn, has a photographic memory, and this begins to replay the key scene of piety from Symeon's Chronicles: the flight of the devout monks with Cuthbert's coffin in 875 A.D. This act of remembering drives back cultural amnesia. As Bertrand sees himself in history, the text both resurrects and endorses the North-East's sacred past. Finding his beginning in his end, Bertrand, the atheist, follows the mystic path. He learns his true nature through finding his true name, the name of his fathers, present but invisible to readers in the novel's very first sentence. "Professor Bertrand Studdard" signs him as disciple not to a dead rationalist, say Bertrand Russell, but to a living saint. The paternal "Studdard" is "Stitheard" (or Stoutheart?), one of St. Cuthbert's inner brotherhood. Bertrand will follow his uncle's choice: to leave academia and stay in the inherited house, researching, but with reverence. Inheriting Cuthbert's shoes, and affectionate tokens from the saint, he steps into past and future.

In *The Coal House*, the prize-winning leek, grown on Alec's land through "horny handed" (p. 38) Peter's work, recapitulates older relations of management and labor, but in benign form. Exploitation becomes cornucopia. Politics turn to pastoral. Alec restores the betrayed wasteland, living on in the Big House, his conscience freed. He, too, becomes a full North-Eastern man; in Sue's words, he goes "native" (p. 114). Celebrating his Leek Show triumph, at the center of male "adulation" (p. 123), he is initiated into its language, uttering "the traditional formula": "'Gentlemen. I'll fill the bar!'" (p. 123). This text, too, concludes with gifts, which bond the men, absolve middle-class guilt and heal the scars of history. Miners' sons, past and present, enter the house and family, annealing the wounds of class division. Alison stitches her father a rabbit-skin cloak, investing him as nursery-rhyme king of the Coal House, blessing his work. Old Shotton's drawing transforms the Bad House from a site of cultural conflict into a Christmas card image. The text itself does the same. In the snow on Christmas night, Alec blows "a perfect smoke ring" (p. 143) at the stars. The circle excludes change and progress, a life in the city with Sue, to preserve the perfect unit of the father-daughter relation, in contact with the voice of the dead mother, and the living past.

Accepted in the alien land, heir to the name of its fathers, having earned his place within the virile community of working North-Eastern men, the male author can rest confirmed in his masculinity, his knowledge and his fatherhood. Under the influence of the wise Patriarch, in touch with history, so these texts suggest, his daughter (and the young reader) will be safe. As St. Cuthbert tells Beth, "*Femina bona es!*'" (p. 126); she will be a "virtuous woman" who will reproduce the word and the culture of the father, secure from England's truly dark ages: the dark forms of a feminist future.

NOTES

1. Robert Westall, *The Wind Eye* (1976; reprint, Harmondsworth: Penguin, 1989), p. 19. Andrew Taylor, *The Coal House* (1986; reprint, London: Lions-Collins, 1990), p. 7. Subsequent references in the text are to these editions.

2. Taylor is quoting a traditional term for County Durham: *The Coal House*, dustjacket.

3. The moment also echoes Elizabeth Gaskell's treatment of the strike in *North and South* (1855).

4. Cited by Peter Hollindale in "Westall's Kingdom," *Children's Literature in Education.* 25, 3 (1994), p. 147.

5. Robert Westall, "The Author in the Classroom," *Use of English* 31 (1979–80), p. 5.

6. Roman Polanski's *Macbeth* (1972) adopted Holy Island (Lindisfarne) similarly for the witches' opening sequences.

7. Cited in Hollindale, "Westall's Kingdom," p. 151.

8. See, for example, David Rees, *Painted Desert, Green Shade: Essays on Contemporary Writers of Fiction for Children and Young Adults* (Boston: Horn, 1984), pp. 115–25.

9. See, too, William Mayne, *Cuddy* [St. Cuthbert's local nick-name] (London: Cape, 1994).

REFERENCES

Bede. "Life of Cuthbert." c.761. Translated by J. F. Webb. In *The Age of Bede.* Ed. D. H. Farmer. Harmondsworth: Penguin, 1988: 41–102.
Cixous, Hélène. "The Laugh of the Medusa." Translated by Keith Cohen and Paula Cohen (1976). In *New French Feminisms: An Anthology.* Ed. and introd. Elaine Marks and Isabelle de Courtivron. Brighton: Harvester, 1980: 245–64.
Gaskell, Elizabeth. *North and South.* London: Chapman, 1855.
Hollindale, Peter. "Westall's Kingdom." *Children's Literature in Education.* 25, 3 (1994): 147–57.
Macbeth. Dir. Roman Polanski. Playboy/Caliban. 1972.

Mayne, William. *Cuddy*. London: Cape, 1994.

Rees, David. *Painted Desert, Green Shade: Essays on Contemporary Writers of Fiction for Children and Young Adults*. Boston: Horn, 1984.

Straw Dogs. Dir. Sam Peckinpah. Talent Associates/Amerbroco, 1971.

Taylor, Andrew. *The Coal House*. 1986. Reprint, London: Lions-Collins, 1990.

Westall, Robert. "The Author in the Classroom." *Use of English* 31 (1979–80): 5–13.

———. *The Wind Eye*. 1976. Reprint, Harmondsworth: Penguin, 1989.

Part VII

Masculine, Feminism — and the History of Fantasy

20

Re-Presenting a History of the Future: Dan Dare and *Eagle*

Tony Watkins

D an Dare, Pilot of the Future was constructed as a national hero to be a moral "pilot" for the young during the 1950s. The science fiction strip cartoon, which first appeared in the *Eagle* comic in April 1950, makes an interesting case study of a deliberate intervention to provide children at a specific moment in history with "a history of the future." John W. Campbell published a scheme for a "future history" in the magazine *Astounding Science Fiction* and the author, Robert A. Heinlein, attempted to construct such a history with a series of stories which mapped "the interplay of technological innovation and political response."[1] The future history provided by Dan Dare carried clear moral and ideological ways of seeing the present, the past and the future, ways of seeing which grew out of a combination of nationalism, idealism and a mythology of national identity shaped by Britain's experience of the Second World War, for, as Jeffrey Richards argues, "War always brings the question of national identity into sharp focus."[2]

In interpreting an historical, popular-cultural text such as "Dan Dare—Pilot of the Future," there are at least *three* histories to take into account. First, there is the history out of which the science fiction comic strip emerged; second, the future history of the world represented in the strip; and third, an account of the present in which the text is received. The approach in this critique has been influenced by theories of the relationship between text and history proposed by New Historicism, and by the semiotic approach to culture associated with Clifford Geertz. "Historical reality," either of the past or the present, is constructed by means of cultural fictions—metaphors and stories—which we employ to make sense of so-called reality. Some of these cultural fictions are historically located (but nevertheless long-lasting) myths of national identity which, because they "take on the character of collective representations that reconcile and unite many contradictory aspects of the past . . . come to form parts of . . . a common heritage."[3]

It is now clear to most analysts that comics' visual narratives embody ideological and moral structures,[4] and analysis reveals that the Dan Dare strip is characterized by moral and ideological discourses around heroism and, to a lesser extent, around gender and ethnicity. The strip also re-works the Romantic debate about technology and human values, while politically it displays a liberal form of nationalism and imperialism, tempered by faith in the United Nations. In turn, these values and ideologies are worked through the mythic discourses of national identity, in particular what the writer Angus Calder calls "the myth of the Blitz,"[5] which was born out of "the experience of Britain at war, when Britain stood alone against Hitler."[6] The myth continued to shape the experience of postwar deprivation and is still active today. Dan Dare can be seen as a British hero, and specifically a very English hero, re-presenting myths of national identity through the fantasy mode of a history of the future that links the comic strip to the liberal-minded utopianism of the planners of British postwar reconstruction and of the 1951 Festival of Britain on the South Bank in London.

The problem for such postwar utopian thinking was the fact that any "Brave New World" had to be built on what has been described as the "'Cruel Real World' of a bankrupt Britain with a ruined export trade and vanished overseas investments."[7] The postwar period out of which Dan Dare was constructed as a national hero, was marked by an economic crisis in the balance of payments, homelessness, physical privations and food shortages, although, just prior to *Eagle*'s publication in 1950, there was a gradual change nationally towards a more hopeful situation. Nevertheless, by the beginning of the 1950s, with the growth of the Cold War, anxiety about the atom bomb and the hydrogen bomb, and the threat of a Third World War, the international situation still seemed very grim to most people. It was out of this complex social and political history that "Dan Dare—Pilot of the Future" was published in the first issue of *Eagle* on 14 April 1950; the comic and the strip were an almost instant success with both children and adults.

Eagle had its origins in the late 1940s when the Reverend Marcus Morris created the Society for Christian Publicity as a forum for Christian discussion. His prime concern was with children's moral education and he focused his anxiety on the horror comics being imported from America. In an article for the *Sunday Dispatch* in 1949, he condemned such comics and outlined a clear moral program of reform, including a call to construct national heroes of a particular kind for children: heroic adventurers who displayed Christian zeal. Although strongly opposed to horror-comics, Morris was not against the comic strip as such; he saw it as "a form which could be used to convey to the child the right kind of standards, values and attitudes, combined with the necessary amount of excitement and adventure."[8] In 1948, Morris met Frank Hampson who, during the war, had experienced the bombing of Antwerp by rocketbombs. In 1946, Hampson had enrolled on a course at Southport School of Arts and Craft. He was not religious in the same way as Morris, but he admired Morris and was "infected by his desire to . . . 'publish morality.'"[9] In early 1949 the two men began planning what Morris later described as an entirely new and original children's paper. The full title of the new comic was, significantly, *Eagle—The New National Strip Cartoon Weekly*. As Stuart Sillars points out, the word "'weekly' stressed its orderly regular appearance and its superiority over 'fly-by-night horror comics' while 'National' suggested the embodiment of British values, as well as rebutting the overseas elements implicit within the transatlantically influenced comic books."[10]

Morris and Hampson were determined to produce an important, long-lasting character for the front page of *Eagle* and after wrestling with the ideas of a woman detective called Dorothy Dare, a fighting parson from the East End of London and "a flying padre" called Lex Christian, they settled on the Space Fleet Commander, Dan Dare, Pilot of the Future. The careful construction of the name, the genre, and the role of the character in guiding the young and giving them a hope for the future, were quite deliberate, as Hampson explained in an interview in 1974: "when Dan was finalised it was as a *Pilot* of the Future, which had an apt double meaning. . . . I . . . felt that young people were getting a rough deal in those years so soon after the end of the war. Everything was so pessimistic, what with the Bomb and all . . . I wanted to give them something that made the future more hopeful in human terms."[11] In his foreword to *Dan Dare's Spacebook*, Hampson explains how his dreams for the future were shaped by his experience of the past: "Most of Dan Dare's adventures take place in 2000 A.D. But they all began, really, in Belgium in 1944. . . . 'Rocketbombs' pounded the city. . . . On the quays of Antwerp you could watch the birth of Space Travel."[12] So, Dan Dare, Pilot of the Future, was a character constructed partly out of the past (especially the mythic and heroic discourses surrounding the experience of the Second World War) and partly out of the present of 1950 (in particular, the contradictory discourses of despair and hope that surrounded technology, food supplies, and the possibility of a Third World War), but he was presented as a character living about 50 years in the future.

The contemporary nature of what purports to be the future is shown in the very first frame of Dan Dare (*Eagle*, No. 1, 14 April 1950) which depicts "the Headquarters of the Interplanet Space Fleet" in 1996, over which flies a jet-propelled vehicle resembling a helicopter. Sillars comments on this "filmic establishing shot": "buildings recognisable from recent British originals like Tecton's Finsbury Health Centre make the scene credible, and above it flies a jet capsule which looks remarkably like the cockpit of a Westland Dragonfly, then the latest British military helicopter."[13] Space Fleet headquarters appears to be in London and Space Fleet itself is staffed largely by "Englishmen wearing cast-off British army uniforms dyed green."[14] The British Cabinet is meeting because of the threat of world-wide food shortages: the world government has ended wars and poverty, nearly all diseases have been conquered, but there is no food. In a clear extrapolation from the late 1940s, the character called "Sir Hubert Guest" explains that world population has doubled since 1950 and food supplies have grown less because "vast areas of the earth have been exhausted by bad farming in the past,"[15] while newspaper headlines announce food riots all over the world. As the critic Edward James puts it: "the world inhabited by Dan Dare, Sir Hubert Guest and their colleagues was in one sense not far removed from the austerities of Britain of 1950. Indeed, rationing was even worse in 1996 than in 1950."[16]

As for Dan Dare, he embodies many of the qualities associated with the male hero of nineteenth-century boys' adventure stories, while displaying others which arise from the ideological discourses of postwar Britain. In many respects, Dare incorporates and continues the code of the nineteenth-century chivalrous gentleman. Chivalry was deliberately promoted in the nineteenth century to "provide a code of life for the young, based on the virtues of the gentleman: courtesy, bravery, modesty, purity and compassion, and a sense of responsibility towards women, children, the weak and the helpless."[17] A gentleman was a natural leader of men, fearless in war and excelling in all manly sports.[18] Such a character, displaying "a mixture of stoicism with medieval lay chivalry, and of both with unconscious national ideals, half Puritan and half secular," came to represent, in the words of the polymath Sir Ernest Barker in 1947, "the character of England,"[19] and much of this language is echoed in the description of Dan Dare as "a natural leader and a man who inspires those around him to give of their best. His word is his bond no matter how treacherous his adversaries are."[20] However, Dan Dare is not the conventional superhuman male soldier-hero who defeats his enemies through violence and killing: he prevails, as Hampson intended, "by intelligence, common-sense, and determination."[21]

Through its display of male camaraderie, the comic strip carried on the tradition of "masculine romance" associated with the nineteenth-century adventure story. Even though Dan Dare's friends and colleagues are types, they are not all stereotypes of the male adventure story: on the one hand, there are the unproblematic figures such as Sir Hubert Gascoigne Guest, ex-R.A.F, who is Controller of the Interplanet Space Fleet and father-figure to the group; on the other hand, there are the representative "ally figures," Pierre and Hank. (Hampson had also wanted to have a Russian in his space fleet, but "the cold war was bitter in 1950 and he was dissuaded from introducing the character, who would have been called Boris."[22]) Digby, the joker in the group, is described by Hampson as "Dan's batman and faithful companion," and by Sillars as "a working-class northerner, the kind of supporting figure familiar from Ealing films of the war years."[23] Nevertheless, Digby is reasonably intelligent and "quite capable of piloting a spaceship."[24] But it is not an all-male club: in the first adventure, a Professor Peabody joins the crew of the spaceship bound for Venus. They are expecting "some old greybeard" but Professor Peabody turns out to be a woman—Professor Jocelyn Peabody—whose first words are: "I don't see what all the fuss is about. . . . I'm a first class geologist, botanist, agriculturalist and the cabinet agree I'm the best person to reconnoitre Venus as a source of food—I'm a qualified space pilot as well."[25]

The late nineteenth-century boys' adventure story was bound up with the ideology of a dominant imperialism; however, Dan Dare was a hero constructed out of the decline of Britain's imperial position in the world (during the late 1940s and early 1950s, the colonial empire almost vanished). So the historical context of this comic strip's construction gives it a more complex post-imperial quality. In the first adventure, the evil Treens are eventually defeated at the Battle of Mekonta by an international United Nations force consisting of cavalry made up of Texan cowboys, British Lifeguards, South West African police, Sikhs, Canadian Mounties, and archery club members, led by UN Police Commandant Bunche, who is African or Afro-Caribbean. The imperialism in the strip is the imperialism of the United Nations, rather than of Britain. In Dan Dare's second adventure, Hampson devotes a full page frame to a utopian vision of the faces of people from all over the world staring at the threatening asteroid, Red Moon. The caption reads: "These self-governing people have been engaged in a mighty drive to end poverty and squalor. Individual liberty and equality is secure, regardless of race, colour or creed, under the elected World Federal Government and the protection of the incorruptible UN Police."[26] However, in true imperialist (and evangelical) fashion, such liberal-democratic ideology must be spread to all corners of the universe. In the fifth adventure, "Prisoners of Space," Dan Dare reminds Digby that, "the whole purpose of our peaceful penetration into outer space has been to show dwellers on other planets that earth's code is the finest way of life. . . . We've got to set an example of truth and honour to the rest of the universe *at whatever cost*."[27]

Ideologies concerning gender and a form of imperialist adventure are combined in the strip with nineteenth-century cultural debates about mechanism and technology, and mythological discourses of national identity. The evil race of the Treens and their leader, the Mekon, represent the worst aspects of "the mechanistic rationalism of science."[28] The Mekon (born, interestingly, around 1750, roughly at the beginning of the Industrial Revolution), Hampson explained, "was meant to show the depths that a scientifically-based society could sink to. A specially bred superbrain with no emotions at all. All that mattered was the advance of Mekon science and universal domination by the Treens." The Mekon's name was "arrived at by thinking about something mechanical . . . mech-an, Mek-on . . . ";[29] the Treens were made "slightly reptilian to add to [the] cold, ruthless, scientific image"; and, Hampson finally reveals, "basically we were fighting the Second World War again . . . the Treens were the Nazis."[30] The fight between the liberal-democratic allies and the forces of Fascism is replayed in "Dan Dare," but as a conflict between the imperialism of a liberal humanism that must be spread to all parts of the universe under the control of the United Nations World Government, and the Fascistic imperialism of the Mekon and Treens who use their "scientific rationality" to try to enslave earth's inhabitants and make them obedient automata.

Dan Dare is a British hero, with ancestors from England and Scotland. But it is English national identity, embodied in the English landscape, that is under threat from the Treens. What is at stake is articulated in an issue of August 1951, in which the leading frame shows a peaceful village green on a sunny afternoon and, in the background, a thatched cottage and a church flying the flag of St. George on its spire. Unknown to the villagers, Treen spaceships are invading the

English countryside; a boy sees the alien spaceships coming in to land but refers to them as "Flying Saucers."[31] On the village green, the 94th Annual Cricket match between Nether Wallop and Picrust Parva is taking place; cricket, as Angus Calder argues, is "the most 'English' of games and perhaps the most 'mythological.'"[32] The "Englishness" Dan Dare must defend is defined in terms of an eccentric rural simplicity combined with political stability and continuity.

One final historical point is that "Dan Dare" was part of the "powerful sense of beleaguered hope" that characterized, not only the campaign against horror comics, but many other aspects of British postwar culture. Because "a country's culture is the means both of expressing national identity and maintaining . . . political consensus," the greatness of postwar, post-imperial Britain had to be asserted not "through Empire, but through carrying our culture to the world" and one of the main ways of doing this was the Festival of Britain in 1951.[33] The Festival, "suitably backward-looking as well as forward-looking," was a "celebration of past and present" held to commemorate the Great Exhibition of 1851.[34] Not only did it express the values of the radical middle classes and the utopian idealism of the planners of postwar reconstruction, it was also a way of "propagandising modern styles."[35] The ideologies of the Festival and those of the "Pilot of the 1950s," Dan Dare, were remarkably similar. Indeed, by 1951, much of the utopian idealism and many of the "modern styles" had already appeared in the pages of "Dan Dare" and James suggests that, to some readers of *Eagle*, who "by this time were familiar with the symmetries of Treen city architecture, and the lush Utopian architecture of the Therons, much of [the Festival of Britain] must have seemed rather dull."[36]

Lastly, what significance does Dan Dare, the pilot of the 1950s have at the beginning of the twenty-first century? To undertake that analysis fully is beyond the scope of this chapter. It would involve our becoming aware not only of the history from which "Dan Dare" was produced, aware not only of the "history of the future" that it presents, but aware also of ourselves as historically and culturally situated readers. In other words, it would involve our becoming "dialectically historicist."[37] However, it is significant that the figure of Dan Dare has survived as an iconographic hero for a half-century, in spite of the comments of people such as the publisher, Chris Lowder, at IPC (International Publishing Corporation), who justified stopping publication of *Eagle* in 1969 by arguing that, "Looked at with a cold unprejudiced eye, *Eagle* was merely a symbol of its time, and no more."[38] Yet for many, the creator of Dan Dare, Frank Hampson, was "the creator of a new 21st-century mythology and a great artist in [an] extraordinary, powerful medium."[39]

NOTES

1. John Clute and Peter Nicholls, eds., *The Encyclopaedia of Science Fiction* (London: Orbit, 1993), p. 857.

2. Jeffrey Richards, *Films and British National Identity: From Dickens to Dad's Army* (Manchester: Manchester University Press, 1997), p. 14.

3. Ernest J.Yanarella and Lee Sigelman, "Introduction: Political Myth, Popular Fiction, and American Culture," in *Political Mythology and Popular Fiction*, ed. Ernest J. Yanarella and Lee Sigelman, Contributions in Political Science, 197 (Westport, Conn.: Greenwood Press 1988), p. 4.

4. Stuart Sillars, *Visualisation in Popular Fiction 1860–1960: Graphic Narratives, Fictional Images* (London: Routledge, 1995), p. 133.

5. Angus Calder, *The Myth of the Blitz* (London: Jonathan Cape, 1991).

6. Edward James, "The Future Viewed from Mid-Century Britain: Clarke, Hampson and the Festival of Britain," *Foundation: The Review of Science Fiction* 41 (1987), p. 43.

7. Ibid., p. 44.

8. Marcus Morris, "Introduction," in *The Best of Eagle*, ed. Marcus Morris (London: Michael Joseph and Ebury Press, 1977), p. 3.

9. Alan Vince, *The Frank Hampson Interview* (Cambridge: Astral Publications in association with the Eagle Society, 1994), p. 13.

10. Sillars, p. 134.

11. Vince, *Interview*, p. 13.

12. Quoted in Norman Wright and Mike Higgs, *The Dan Dare Dossier* (London: Hawk Books, 1990), p. 5.

13. Sillars, *Visualisation*, p. 137.

14. James, *Future*, p. 49.

15. *Eagle*, No. 4, 5 May 1950.

16. James, *Future*, p. 48.

17. Richards, *Films*, p. 12.

18. Mark Girouard, *The Return to Camelot: Chivalry and the British Gentleman* (New Haven: Yale University Press, 1981), p. 260.

19. Sir Ernest Barker, ed., *The Character of England* (Oxford: Oxford University Press, 1947), p. 566–67, quoted in Richards, *Films*, p. 12.

20. Wright and Higgs, *Dossier*, p. 16.

21. Vince, *Interview*, p. 21.

22. Alistair Crompton, *The Man Who Drew Tomorrow* (Bournemouth: Who Dares Publishing, 1985), p. 187.

23. Sillars, *Visualisation*, p. 136.

24. Vince, *Interview*, p. 27.

25. *Eagle*, No. 5, 12 May 1950.

26. *Eagle*, Vol. 3, No. 2, 18 April 1952.

27. *Eagle*, Vol. 5, No. 31, 30 July 1954.

28. John Tulloch and Manuel Alvarado, *Doctor Who: The Unfolding Text* (London: Macmillan, 1983), p. 45.

29. Vince, *Interview*, p. 22.

30. Ibid., p. 21.

31. *Eagle*, Vol. 2, No. 18, 10 August 1951.

32. Calder, *Myth*, p. 3.

33. Robert Hewison, *Culture and Consensus: England, Art and Politics since 1940* (London: Methuen, 1995), pp. xvii–xviii; Martin Barker, *The Haunt of Fears: The Strange History of the British Horror Comics Campaign* (London: Pluto Press, 1984).

34. James, *Future*, p. 44.

35. Paul Addison, *Now the War Is Over: A Social History of Britain 1945–51* (London: Pimlico, 1995, [1985]), pp. 208–9.

36. James, *Future*, p. 45.

37. Jeremy Hawthorne, *Cunning Passages: New Historicism, Cultural Materialism and Marxism in the Contemporary Literary Debate* (London: Arnold, 1996), p. 84.

38. Quoted in Crompton, *Tomorrow*, p. 190.
39. Quoted in Crompton, *Tomorrow*, p. 211.

REFERENCES

Addison, Paul. *Now the War Is Over: A Social History of Britain 1945–51.* 1985. London: Pimlico, 1995.

Barker, Sir Ernest, ed. *The Character of England.* Oxford: Oxford University Press, 1947.

Barker, Martin. *The Haunt of Fears: The Strange History of the British Horror Comics Campaign.* London: Pluto Press, 1984.

Calder, Angus. *The Myth of the Blitz.* London: Jonathan Cape, 1991.

Clute, John, and Nicholls, Peter. *The Encyclopaedia of Science Fiction.* London: Orbit, 1993.

Crompton, Alastair. *The Man Who Drew Tomorrow.* Bournemouth: Who Dares Publishing, 1985.

Geertz, Clifford. *The Interpretation of Cultures.* London: Hutchinson, 1975.

Girouard, Mark. *The Return to Camelot: Chivalry and the British Gentleman.* New Haven: Yale University Press, 1981.

Hawthorne, Jeremy. *Cunning Passages: New Historicism, Cultural Materialism and Marxism in the Contemporary Literary Debate.* London: Arnold, 1996.

Hewison, Robert. *Culture and Consensus: England, Art and Politics Since 1940.* London: Methuen, 1995.

James, Edward. "The Future Viewed from Mid-Century Britain: Clarke, Hampson and the Festival of Britain." *Foundation: The Review of Science Fiction*, 41 (Winter 1987): pp. 42–51.

Morris, Marcus. "Introduction." In *The Best of Eagle.* Ed. Marcus Morris. London: Michael Joseph and Ebury Press, 1977.

Richards, Jeffrey. *Films and British National Identity: From Dickens to Dad's Army.* Manchester: Manchester University Press, 1997.

Sillars, Stuart. *Visualisation in Popular Fiction 1860-1960: Graphic Narratives, Fictional Images.* London: Routledge, 1995.

Tulloch, John, and Alvarado, Manuel. *Doctor Who: The Unfolding Text.* London: Macmillan, 1983.

Vince, Alan. *The Frank Hampson Interview.* Cambridge: Astral Publications in association with the Eagle Society, 1994.

Wright, Norman, and Higgs, Mike. *The Dan Dare Dossier.* London: Hawk Books, 1990.

Yanarella, Ernest J., and Sigelman, Lee. "Introduction: Political Myth, Popular Fiction, and American Culture." In *Political Mythology and Popular Fiction.* Eds. Ernest J. Yanarella and Lee Sigelman. Westport, CT: Greenwood Press, 1988.

21

The "Masculine Mystique" Revisioned in *The Earthsea Quartet*

Yoshida Junko

Ursula K. Le Guin published *The Earthsea Quartet*, which includes *A Wizard of Earthsea* (1968), *Tombs of Atuan* (1972), *The Farthest Shore* (1973), and *Tehanu* (1990), during the turbulent years of changing conceptions of gender in the United States. Le Guin honestly admits in her essay, *Earthsea Revisioned* (1993), that she "lived under the spell" (p. 17) of the myth of masculinity, like most Americans, when she wrote the first three books of Earthsea. The myth is based on a narrow image of white middle class heterosexual males, and expects men to conform to it. *The Earthsea Quartet* can therefore be placed in its social and cultural context, by reading the four books as novels about changing conceptions of masculinity in the 1960s, 1970s, and 1980s.

In *A Wizard of Earthsea*, the apprentice wizard Ged conjures up a shadow in order to prove himself. Because the shadow is nameless and therefore out of his control, his whole existence is threatened. Hunted by the shadow he travels around the world. After his critical failure in dealing with the shadow, Ged learns from his mentor, Mage Ogion, that he has to pursue it instead of fleeing from it. He finally confronts the shadow and integrates it into himself by calling it "Ged," thereby becoming whole himself. The shadow can be viewed as gendered construct, because Ged's attitude toward it is closely connected with his masculine identity. The shadow represents the dark side of his conventional masculinity which has features of being power-hungry, always "in harness" (suppressing human feelings), disturbing the balance of nature (exploiting nature), and excluding the feminine from his gender construct (using and exploiting femininity).

Ged's first contact with the shadow comes after he becomes an apprentice of Ogion, his initiator into manhood. In other words, the shadow appears after the shift of his role model from his harsh and violent father to the silent and mild father figure who respects the balance of nature and is reluctant to use power. Ged's confused and irritated reaction to Ogion's passivity is described as follows: "when it rained Ogion would not even say the spell . . . [but he] let the rain fall where it would. He found a thick fir-tree and lay down beneath it. . . . Ged wondered what was the good of having power if you were too wise to use it" (pp. 26–27).

Around the same period, Ged is challenged by the daughter of the Lord of Re Albi to summon a spirit of the dead. Out of "a desire to please her, to win her admiration" (p. 28) and to "prove himself for her" (p. 30), he eventually conjures up a shadow, which is actually "the foreboding of the shadow, or the shadow of a shadow" (p. 120). According to the sociologist Arlene Skolnick, American society in the 1950s was already haunted by a "masculinity crisis." Skolnick (1991) says, "the ideology of the strong male was at odds with the ideology of togetherness" (*Embattled Paradise*, p. 71), and "social critics feared that women were powerful and growing more so, and that men were weak and becoming ever more effeminate and emasculated" (p. 111). Like the protagonist, Jim, in the 1955 film *Rebel Without a Cause* who mocks and rebels against his "weak" father, Ged sneers at Ogion's typically feminine and ineffectual attitude while attempting to master the most difficult art of magic, and he chooses to go to Roke, the place at the top of the hierarchy of wizardry. Like many teenage boys in the 1950s, Ged is beginning to feel a nameless fear caused by the "masculinity crisis." It is of metaphorical significance that the ship that carries Ged to his ambition is named "Shadow" (p. 33) and that when he enters the School of Roke, the shadow stealthily follows him through the gate (p. 40).

The real shadow is released when Ged competes with Jasper, a similarly power-hungry apprentice wizard at the school. Jasper challenges Ged to perform "the highest of the Summoner's art and the mage's power" (p. 57) to summon up a spirit from the dead. Ged, again out of his arrogant desire to prove himself, calls up the spirit of Elfarran, a legendary beautiful lady. The prominent children's literature critic Perry Nodelman (1995), in his interpretation of this scene, uses Eve Kosofsky Sedgwick's analysis of "male homosocial desire" (*Between Men*, p. 1) and maintains that Ged and Jasper "develop their bonds and establish their hierarchies of power" through the exchange of the woman ("Reinventing the Past," p. 191). However, I would rather emphasize femininity in discourses of manhood than homosocial men's bonding, as Le Guin writes:

In the realm of male power, there is no interdependence of men with women. Manhood . . . is obtained and validated by the man's independence of women. . . . Women in that world are non-people, dehumanized by a beautiful, worshipful spell—a spell which may be seen, from the other side, as a curse. *(Earthsea Revisioned*, p. 16)

The sociologist Anthony Rotundo (1993) maintains that the concept of conventional masculinity is defined by the idea of a "separate sphere" and has been accepted as the norm by American society. This sphere excludes any attributes that are thought to be feminine, such as the nurturing, caring, intimate, passive and emotional.[1] Therefore, women as a full embodiment of the feminine are useful in "the male traffic" in the sense that men are exempted from taking the feminine elements into their manhood. This scene paradoxically exemplifies the omission of femininity from the conventional masculine construct. Ironically, Elfarran helps Ged disclose the dark side of conventional manhood, which costs him a high price. He is physically and psychologically wounded.

The year of the publication of *A Wizard of Earthsea,* 1968, was an eventful one. In February the greatest number of U.S. troops was dispatched to Vietnam despite the rising anti-war movement throughout the country. In April the Reverend Martin Luther King, Jr., was assassinated, setting off widespread riots in urban areas. In September a group of feminists demonstrated against the Miss America Pageant in Atlantic City, attracting much attention from the mass media. In this social and cultural climate Ged releases the shadow and tracks it down in his shipwrecked boat with water seeping in everywhere, continually casting a weakening spell on the boat to keep it from sinking (pp. 134–37). This desperate quest reflects the social and cultural situation around 1968 when America's masculine authority and justice came into question. In addition, Ged's Odyssey reminds us of that of Holden Caulfield in J. D. Salinger's *The Catcher in the Rye,* who roams around New York psychologically weakened and wounded after he becomes disillusioned with "phony" masculinity.[2] Ged, who has confronted the cultural anxiety that has no name, is a successor to Holden. In the closing pages, when Ged approaches the shadow, it starts to transform from one image into another including images of his father and Jasper. They all represent conventional manhood. Thus, Ged successfully overcomes the masculine identity crisis by integrating conventional masculinity into his consciousness. He does not escape into the world of innocence as Holden does. He sees "phony" masculinity not in others but in himself.

Tombs of Atuan (1972), from the perspective of Ged's masculinity, deals with his fear of the feminine. Though Ged once felt threatened by and escaped from the female power—"the Old Powers of earth" that locked the Stone of Terrenon in the first book—he enters the Tombs of Atuan, a female world, which is governed by the same biding-spell. Trapped in the womb-like maze under the tombs, the magelight of his staff, his masculine symbol, becomes feeble. Here he encounters Arha/Tenar, a priestess who has been sacrificed for the female power, and he meekly accepts Tenar's food and water (female nurturing). As Le Guin (1980) admits, the focus of this novel is on a girl's coming of age (*The Language of the Night,* 55), but in the background it narrates how Ged, after overcoming his fear of femininity, establishes an egalitarian relationship with Tenar and plays the role of midwife/witness in the rebirth of the female adolescent. It is symbolically represented in the reunification of the broken ring of Erreth-Akbe and Tenar's exit from the world of the dead with Ged. Skolnick says that several studies recognize a dramatic turning point in sex role beliefs in the early 1970s, when the traditional concept of the female role was replaced by a more egalitarian attitude (*Embattled Paradise*, p. 105). In other words, many women rejected the gender-based division of labor and the role of the Earth Mother, that is to say the externalized and institutionalized feminine nature.

It is not surprising then that many men who had excluded feminine nature from their construction of masculinity started to develop various men's movements in order to reconfigure their masculinity. The First National Conference on the "Masculine Mystique" and the first "Men and Masculinity" conference were held, respectively, in 1974 and 1975. In the following years, there was a rush of publications on masculinity including Herb Goldberg's *The Hazards of Being Male* (1976), a national best seller, which proclaimed: "Earth Mother is dead and now macho can die as well. The man can come alive as a full person" (p. 20).

Le Guin's third *Earthsea* novel, *The Farthest Shore*, was published in 1973 after the Vietnam War had ended and there were widespread rumors of the Watergate scandal. In this novel masculinity really starts to change. Cob, a self-proclaimed Lord of the dead and the living, inflicts a "wound" on Earthsea that has caused the decline of power. The story unfolds through the dangerous voyage of Ged, the Archmage, and Arren, the young prince, to the Dry Land. There Ged faces up to Cob, another shadow, and consumes all his magic power in healing the wound. In the meantime Arren, guiding Ged, comes back across the Dry River and is thus initiated into manhood. The central theme in this novel is the generational shift from Ged to Arren, or Arren's coming of age.

In reading this novel from the perspective of masculine development, we should note one keyword, "sword," a masculine symbol. We learn in the opening pages that Arren's name means "Sword." He possesses a hereditary sword that has never been wielded except for justice, but he usually wears a knife. Later we learn that this seventeen-year-old "girlish lad" cannot use even this knife effectively to protect Ged and himself in a crisis. When Arren finally gets a chance to wield the sword, he destroys the wraith of Cob only in vain (p. 466). Arren's development of masculinity is at odds with the traditional and magnificent sword. Read in the social and cultural context of America in the late 1960s, this is reminiscent of the awkward and strained relationship between American youth and the national masculine authority, typically witnessed in the counter-culture and radicalism. However, Ged does not mind this tension and rather admires Arren's innocence while encouraging him to learn passivity. Ged says, "You are my guide. In your innocence and courage, in your unwisdom and your loyalty, you are my guide. . . . It is your fear I follow" (p. 411). Arren, beset by anxiety and fear, suffers recurring nightmares and hears a voice that beckons to him throughout his journey. Ged says to Arren:

You stand on the borders of possibility, in the shadowland, in the realm of dream, and you hear the voice saying *Come*. As I did once. But I am old. I have made my choices, I have done what I must do. I stand in daylight facing my own death. And I know that there is only one power worth having. And that is power, not to take, but to accept. (p. 424)

In order to heal the wound inflicted by Cob, Ged needs Arren as his guide to the Dry Land. In the early 1970s, according to the historian Peter N. Carroll, America was suffering a "raw, painful, unhealing wound" (*It Seemed Like Nothing Happened*, p. 20) or "a gaping crack in the American identity" (p. 20) inflicted by the "dishonesty of the Vietnam War" and the Watergate scandal (p. 159). Carroll further maintains that, during the 1970s, millions of Americans came to share the hopeful vision that the young were trying to remake America in their own image (p. 21). If we genderize the wound, the young, and America as masculinity, we can say that the new manhood embodied in Arren is a guide and hope to heal America's wounded masculinity.

As they enter the Dry Land, Arren takes his sword while Ged lifts up his staff to cast a light in the darkness. What is significant here is that it is Ged's staff that is responsible for healing the wound, not Arren's sword. When the job is done, "there [is] no more light on Ged's yew-staff" (p. 467). As Arren's awkwardness in wielding his father's sword shows, the new manhood of the early 1970s did not meet the approval of the general public and found an unstable home only in hippies' masculinity. In other words, the concept of new manhood had just entered an "adolescent" phase and, in order to be recognized as mature, needed to "grow up" through discussion and men's movements. In this sense Arren's new manhood anticipates the "New Man" who stimulated an active discourse on ideal images of new masculinities in the late 1970s and the early 1980s.

The final novel, *Tehanu* (1990), although it foregrounds female issues, is concerned with how to revitalize Ged, whose power has been totally consumed. Ged already anticipated this problem in *The Farthest Shore*: "It is time to be done with power. To drop the old toys. . . . It is time that I went home. I would see Tenar. . . . And maybe there I would learn at last what no act, or power can teach me, what I have never learned" (p. 441). After coming back from the Dry Land, Ged is carried to Ogion's house on a dragon's back where he meets the middle aged and widowed Tenar and her adopted daughter, Therru, who had been abused by her father. Tenar nurses Ged as well as Therru, who later identifies herself as a daughter of dragon-people and also the future Archmage at Roke. Therru is the key in this book, as Le Guin writes, "Raped, beaten, pushed into the fire, disfigured, one hand crippled, one eye blinded, this child is innocence in a different sense of the word. This is helplessness personified: disinheritance, a child dehumanized, made Other" (*Earthsea Revisioned*, p. 19). Because Therru is a female, a child, and a dragon (representing nature), marginalized and exploited by the world of men, she is the "Other" on all three points. The encounter with Therru is vital for Ged because he had believed, "Both men and magery are built on one rock: power belongs to men" (p. 664), and now he must face up to the ugly reality that male power has created.

At first Ged's attitude toward Therru is one of indifference, even though he displays no overt aversion. Ged says, "I don't know . . . why you took her, knowing that she cannot be healed. Knowing what her life must be . . . we must live on into the new age with the spoils of our victory over evil. You with your burned child, and I with nothing at all" (p. 547). Unable to find any correlation between the burned child and himself, Ged regresses to his childhood by retreating to the mountain in Gont where he used to tend goats as a boy. It is not until he comes down from the mountain that Ged marries Tenar, after fighting burglars with a farmer's fork, not with a wizard's staff. Then Ged accepts Tenar as his wife and Therru as his adopted daughter. In this way Ged learns what Roke cannot teach him: by nurturing and loving others he can reconcile his masculine identity with the feminine aspects buried within himself, such as the nurturing, intimate, and emotional, and thereby can heal his wound.

Turning our attention to American society in the 1980s, we see that the Reagan presidency marked the emergence of a new conservatism and a backlash against radicalism. The social analysts Rabinowits and Cochran maintain that "masculinity that defined the male psyche as a simplistic, achievement-oriented black box" returned in the 1980s (*Man Alive*, p. xvi). Some young men who found no appropriate masculine model felt a need to protect themselves from the possible confusion and came to identify with a narrow and rigid masculinity. The machismo portrayed in Sylvester Stallone's films during this period exemplifies this trend. Therefore, it is not by accident that a "spiritual perspective" group in the men's movement became active during the same period, and many of their writings appeared in "New Age" publications. Its activities were mostly grounded in Carl Jung's theory that men's psychological wounds could be healed by searching the archetypes buried in their unconscious and recovering their psycho-spiritual health.

John Rowan's *The Horned God* (1987), a politicized and feminist contribution to the debate, offers insight into Ged's trajectory of psychological healing. Rowan acknowledges that many men have repressed or excluded their feminine elements. The rejection of the feminine, he maintains, worsens the wounds men receive when the reality of their masculinity is debunked. Rowan claims that men can heal their wounds by reconnecting with the feminine buried in their unconscious.[3]

We should note that Ged appears in the first book—published in 1968 while the civil rights campaign was being waged—as a dark-skinned hero. This suggests that Le Guin's attitude toward the hero's manhood in this fantasy was subversive from the beginning. Le Guin writes, "I was making him an Outsider, an Other, like a woman" (*Earthsea Revisioned*, p. 8). Therefore, it is natural that she should further decentralize the hero's masculinity. If we think of Ged and Arren as one man in the discourse of manhood, then we can say that Arren who once was a premature New Man in *The Farthest Shore* has matured into Ged in *Tehanu*. Seen from a pro-feminist man's viewpoint, Le Guin seems to follow social trends rather than lead them, taking four volumes and 25 years to transform Ged's masculinity.

NOTES

1. Anthony Rotundo, *American Manhood: Transformations in Masculinity from the Revolution to the Modern Era* (New York: Columbia University Press, 1985), pp. 22–25, 253–54, 264–65.

2. J. D. Salinger, *The Catcher in the Rye* (1951; Boston: Little Brown, 1991), pp. 40–52. Note that Holden's flight from Pencey comes after his fight with Stradlater, who represents a stereotypically conventional type of masculinity and can conform to the norm of masculinity at prep school during that time.

3. John Rowan, *The Horned God: Feminism and Men as Wounded and Healing* (New York: Routledge, 1987), p. 1, pp. 93–94.

REFERENCES

Carroll, Peter N. *It Seemed Like Nothing Happened: America in the 1970s.* New Brunswick, NJ: Rutgers University Press, 1982.

Clatterbaugh, Kenneth. *Contemporary Perspectives on Masculinity: Men, Women, and Politics in Modern Society.* Boulder, CO: Westview Press, 1997.

Goldberg, Herb. *The Hazards of Being Male: Surviving the Myth of Masculinity Privelege.* New York: Sanford J. Breenburger Associates, 1976.

Kosofsky Sedgwick, Eve. *Between Men: English Literature and Male Homosocial Desire.* New York: Columbia University Press, 1985.

Le Guin, Ursula K. *A Wizard of Earthsea.* 1968. Reprinted in *The Earthsea Quartet.* Harmondsworth: Penguin, 1992.

———. *Tombs of Atuan* 1972. Reprinted in *The Earthsea Quartet.* Harmondsworth: Penguin, 1992.

———. *The Farthest Shore.* 1973. Reprinted in *The Earthsea Quartet.* Harmondsworth: Penguin, 1992.

———. *The Language of the Night.* New York: Perigee Books, 1980.

———. *Tehanu.* 1990. Reprinted in *The Earthsea Quartet.* Harmondsworth: Penguin, 1992.

———. *Earthsea Revisioned.* Cambridge, Massachusetts: CLNE/Green Bay, 1993.

Nodelman, Perry. "Reinventing the Past: Gender in Ursula K. Le Guin's *Tehanu* and the Earthsea 'Trilogy,'" *Children's Literature* 23 (1995): 179–201.

Rabinowitz, Fredric E., and Cochran, Sam V. *Man Alive: A Premier of Men's Issues.* Belmont, CA.: Brooks/Cole, 1994.

Rotundo, E. Anthony. *American Manhood: Transformations in Masculinity from the Revolution to the Modern Era.* New York: HarperCollins, 1993.

Rowan, John. *The Horned God: Feminism and Men as Wounded and Healing.* New York: Routledge, 1987.

Salinger, J. D. *The Catcher in the Rye.* 1951. Boston: Little Brown, 1991.

Skolnick, Arlene. *Embattled Paradise: The American Family in an Age of Uncertainty.* New York: Basic Books, 1991.

22

Witch-Figures in Recent Children's Fiction: The Subaltern and the Subversive

John Stephens

The witch—a figure drawn into the present from real and imagined pasts—is a remarkably widespread motif in literature for young readers. Books in which a major character is identified as a "witch," of one kind or another, range from picture books through to young adult fiction. This chapter examines the schemata for witches as they appear in children's literature of the past dozen years or so, beginning with some speculations about what needs and desires in contemporary Western society might be met by the witch and hence produce so many witch-figures.

Texts pivoting around witch-figures are always intertextual, existing in a dialogic relationship with history, historiographic discourses, scholarly research and popular culture, religious belief, and classic literary works (especially fairy tales and Shakespeare's *Macbeth*). Whether implicitly or explicitly, books for young readers engage with how these discourses have figured and regulated the shape and boundaries of cultural formations: the nature of belief; the antithesis of scientific positivism and myth; the delineation of subaltern groups at the margins of sociality; the role of the feminine in patriarchal societies, and so on.

Witches, then, are commonly depicted as people finding their own way outside the boundaries of mainstream society, and their representation is a way of looking at the relationships between past and present and the nature of cultural paradigm shifts. In many late twentieth-century children's books the witch-figure has undergone rehabilitation, though this is not universally so. There are probably several cultural factors that underlie the rehabilitation, but two in particular seem to be the most influential. They are also interlinked.

First, and perhaps the more obvious, is the influence of feminist social and literary analysis and of the women's movement more generally. In drawing attention to the discourses and power structures which are dominant in a given society, feminist analysis has enabled a revaluation of the nature of female "others," of women who choose or endeavor to lead lives outside the gendering frame of establishment discourses. In other words, it creates the possibility of validating what hegemonic patriarchy has rendered marginal, of giving a voice to the subaltern. In her judicious treatment of the rise and discursive deployment of the twentieth-century myth of "the Burning Times," the cultural historian Diane Purkiss has pointed to the connection of ahistorical feminist accounts of witch persecutions with "contemporary questions of authority, authenticity and public politics," and the rhetorical function of pseudo-histories "not as a reconstruction of the past, but an account of the way things *always* are."[1] However, the evocation of the suffering female body characteristic of this rhetoric makes only rare appearances in children's literature. The extended representation of the motif in Donna Jo Napoli's *The Magic Circle* (1993) is thus unusual, although its concomitant affirmation of traditional feminine roles and domestic space is not. Fiction for children has, rather, one of two foci, depending on a novel's temporal setting. First, fictions set in the past may attempt to invert historical representations by depicting a witch-figure from a sympathetic perspective. Thus Monica Furlong's *Wise Child* (1987) is narrated by a young girl who, having been left without any adults to take care of her, is given a loving home by Juniper, the local "witch," and quickly becomes embroiled in the difference between actuality and representation. The other children, the village adults, and especially the village priest place Juniper in the subject position of the traditional evil witch. Wise Child, who as narrator embodies the novel's most authoritative perspective, soon learns that Juniper is the most upright and meritorious member of the community. Second, fictions set in the present, such as Theresa Tomlinson's *Summer Witches* (1989), are apt to deal with the theme of escaping from the limiting and confining structures of the past in the process of forming a contemporary female subjectivity.

The second cultural factor instrumental in the depiction of witches is really a bundle of attitudes; it seems to derive its represented witch-schema and its somewhat New Age grounding philosophy from several streams. One is a myth derived from elements of Margaret Murray's hypothesis about witches as devotees of an ancient pre-Christian fertility religion.[2] While the "Murrayite" hypothesis has been generally discredited since its enunciation in 1921,[3] it has also been enormously influential and appears to inform many of the modern representations of witches; it endures as an example of how people construct alternative pseudo-histories in order to challenge familiar representations in history. Subsequently wrapped in with this image is that of the midwife-healer, which, as Purkiss points out, originated as recently as 1973.[4] An attractive effect of such an alternative history is that it inverts the conventional, Enlightenment, probably masculine, privileging of history over myth. The entry for "Witchcraft" in Barbara Walker's *The Woman's Encyclopedia of Myths and Secrets* (1983, pp. 1081–1091) is a convenient symptomatic example of how history, anecdote and fancy become inextricably imbricated.

For contemporary fictional representations of witchcraft, however, discriminations between fact and fancy are less important than the pervasiveness of the pseudo-history as an enabling myth. Other, often related, recent influences shaping the modern witch-schema are neo-paganism, goddess-worship, eco-feminism, and the late twentieth-century mania for Celtic traditions. All of this yields up a bundle of ideas centered on a quasi-pantheistic conception of the cosmos as an ordered and coherent universe in which all parts are interrelated but from which most human beings are alienated. This bundle of ideas is used to interrogate or reject Western historical traditions and cultural metanarratives of various kinds, ranging from the ethics of individualism to the social codes which regulate sexual practice and its meanings. It is often an effective mode of analogical thinking, but can also slip into discourses that are little more than sentimental essentialism. A crucial function of the modern witch-schema is that it is used to fill a gap opened up by the other strand of this second cultural factor, a pervasive unease with or anxiety about (post-)modernity.

To recognize that reality is socially constructed, along with the conceptual categories used to order and reproduce it—history, science, reason, self, subject, sex, sanity[5]—is to destabilize the ground of children's literature. It is no accident that Kenneth Lillington's *An Ash-blonde Witch* (1989), for example, problematizes all of those conceptual categories just listed, or that other books reaffirm from various perspectives the existence of immanent, as opposed to transcendent, good and evil prior to the social construction of experience. Within the surface-without-depth, fragmented culture of post-Christian postmodernism, witches can be used to evoke an important function: to offer visions of wholeness, and to reassert certain values either present in or ascribed to the past, and to suggest that those values are recuperable in our mundane modern world. Witches such as Juniper, or the two very different witches depicted in *An Ash-blonde Witch*, are positioned on the outside of both patriarchal institutional religion and patriarchal secular society, and they either practice or move toward new versions of spirituality. What such a witch stands for is a neo-humanistic protest against postmodernism's denial of ethical values and a resistance to late twentieth-century human indifference. As a figure (self-)excluded from patriarchal, "old humanist" society and belief, she embodies the inverted hierarchical oppositions of modernity, but invests them with ethical and aesthetic value. Thus she sees others as fellow human beings rather than strangers, and privileges the other over the self, the object over the subject, society over the individual, myth over history, emotion over reason, intuition over knowledge, female knowledge over male knowledge, nature over culture, and immanence over transcendence. In her embodiment of these emphases, and her conversion of them into social praxis, she makes her world both meaningful and a better place.

One of the problems implicitly attributed to late modernity is that it separates people from their cultural history and alienates them from their own selves. In this context the witch-figure can be used as a counterweight to cultural paradigm shift. This seems to me to be the basis for Tomlinson's *Summer Witches*, an overtly simplified rethinking of the traditional idea of witch as crone and its cultural transmission, presented through a story about the evolution of young female friendship and subjectivities. It is a story about two girls—Sarah and Susanna—who are thrown together and negotiate friendship as they convert an old air-raid shelter into their own special place, inadvertently replicating what two female neighbors had done there during World War Two. The girls have identified one of these women—Miss Lily—as a witch because she is speech-and hearing-impaired, and have used her perceived otherness as a basis for a misconstruction in terms of the witch of fairy-tale imagination, especially in *Hansel and Gretel* and *Rapunzel*. The novel does not merely falsify and expel the girls' misconstruction, as happens elsewhere, as, for example, in Helen Griffiths' *The Mysterious Appearance of Agnes* (1975), a historical novel which debunks ideas about witchcraft as mere unreasoned prejudice and suspicion of otherness. Rather, *Summer Witches* replaces the crone stereotype with the "wise woman" schema. This happens quite overtly toward the end of the book, when Chapter 11 is entirely given over to a conversation about constructions of "witchiness." The positive image offered here is that of the conventional "green" witch, the woman in touch with the natural world and its cycles and with her own instinctual responses. In the following chapters the girls apply their new knowledge, first by deconstructing the life-size representation of a crone-witch found in a local history museum, and second by using their own newly discovered witchiness to help Lily overcome the trauma of her wartime memories. The novel thus builds in a double recuperation of the past—of the near past of the mid-twentieth century and of the deeper past of cultural misogyny and subaltern womanhood, presenting now an image of witches as conservers of nature and tradition, healers, and agents of renewal.

Summer Witches explores the idea of the witch by contrasting two schemata familiar from the historiographical discourses about witches, encapsulated here by "Horrid, ugly old things who ate children and rode broomsticks" and "wise women . . . [who] grew herbs and made medicines that often worked well" (p. 69). These are the schemata which tend to dominate contemporary representations in children's books, though by the 1970s the crone-schema of an old woman wearing the conventional uniform of black clothing, pointed hat, and boots, and travelling by broomstick, or "borrowing" the bodies of animals, was falling out of serious use. It was being dismantled in three ways: by being rendered comic, by being dismissed as a stereotype, and by becoming supplanted as versions of the Murrayite wise witch emerged within children's literature. In opposition to the wise witch is the third witch-schema, that of the sorceress-witch; fascinating, young, beautiful, but malevolent, the sorceress-witch expresses the dark, wild and subversive elements of female desire, female pain, and female nature more generally. In the "Witches" sub-series within his Discworld novels, Terry Pratchett develops a sustained humorous effect by evoking all three schemata but interchanging various elements. More characteristically, though, the depiction of the sorceress-witch is apt to be tinged with misogyny, perhaps best illustrated by the 1996 film, *The Craft*.

A text generally identifies its witch-figure as such, most usually by the suspicious, prejudiced and hostile attitudes of other characters toward her, and this enables exploration both of the nature of otherness and of the functions of historical patriarchy in deploying ideas about witchcraft to induce female conformity and docility. The wise-witch schema is therefore always an intertextual representation and often overtly presented as a contrast with or even deconstruction of the crone- and sorceress-witch schemata, so that the three possibilities are brought into dialogic relationships with one another and into relationships with historiography. Because witches have been constructed, historically, as possessing an evil disposition that sets them apart from common humanity, narratives about good witches will seek either an overt recuperation of the term, as in *Summer Witches*, or a substitute term. Thus Furlong introduces the word *doran*, and endows it with the now conventional wise-witch attributes; a *doran*, she writes, is "someone who loves all the creatures of the world . . . the animals, birds, plants, trees and people and who cannot bear to do any of them any harm. It is someone who believes that they are all linked together and that therefore everything can be used to heal the pain and suffering of the world. It is someone who does not hate anybody and is not frightened of anyone or anything" (*Wise Child*, p. 240). As a character type, and in intertextual contrast with the received notions attached to her less savory sisters, the wise witch conforms with a bundle of conventional schematic attributes. Further, the three principal components of the wise-witch schema as deployed in recent fiction—her place in the community, her personal appearance, and her spiritual beliefs—function as social critique.

As Lucy Mair (1973) points out, in social practice witches belong to certain social categories—"people who in some sense or other are not full members of the community."[6] The identification of witchiness with strangers, outsiders and nonconformists is also virtually absolute in children's literature. This otherness is commonly a catalyst for story events, but it also has a significant thematic function in that it constitutes a site from which the excluding community can be evaluated and judged. Her apparently eccentric behavior both marks her as an object of suspicion and defines the host community as narrow-minded, petty and malicious.

In appearance, the wise witch is apt to be young, healthy and handsome. Her overall wholesomeness contrasts both with the extreme ugliness of the crone and with the "bewitching" beauty of the sorceress-witch. She is nevertheless usually comely enough to be an object of desire, envy, or slander. Moreover, she tends to be sexually active in a community with a patriarchal social structure, and this contributes to community representations of her as "witch" and "evil"—as Mair puts it, "A witch . . . is a person who does not control the impulses that good members of society must keep in check."[7] When, in *An Ash-blonde Witch*, the crone-witch Dorcas wants to eliminate the beautiful newcomer, Sophie, her method is to promulgate an insinuation attributing to Sophie the perverted, insatiable, and destructive sexuality of the sorceress-witch. Because Sophie is no such thing, and as the novel's principal focalizing character, the effect of such attributions is to interrogate the cultural formations which shape and regulate sexual practices, whether in the past or the present.

The wise witch is most set apart from the local community by her spiritual beliefs. She does not conform with, or subscribe to, the beliefs of whatever contemporary, hegemonic religion prevails (usually a form of Christianity), but either has an ecumenical view of religion, or is a pantheist, a polytheist, or a Goddess-worshiper. This makes her an inevitable object of suspicion, and sometimes a target for pulpit-oratory, and in *Wise Child*, for example, where such attacks are presented as unjustified, the effect is to separate spiritual experience and insight from organized religion. Juniper's ecumenical adherence to a broad-based spiritual immanence challenges other characters, and readers, to think about the nature of spiritual experience and the bases for religious pronouncements about such issues as gender.

The propensity for community members to attribute evil supernatural affiliations to all witch-figures is more than an important plot catalyst. The schemata for crone and sorceress are, of course, predicated on the assumption that witchcraft derives its power from its link with the "forces of darkness" (demons, and so on), and that the witch has explicitly or implicitly exchanged her soul for that power. What is perhaps really at issue is the principle of magic-working in itself. Not just for characters within fictions, but for authors and audiences as well, it is possible that any kind of magic will be problematic because of what it might symbolize: the subversion of religion, rationality, patriarchy, sanity, and science.

Recent re-readings of the role of the witches in Shakespeare's *Macbeth* as a radical otherness which challenges and is repudiated by official society offer a pertinent comparison with the representations of witches in books for young readers. In *Summer Witches* the wise witch is a liberating force and agent of change, but in *Wise Child* and *An Ash-blonde Witch* she is subjected to expulsion by "official society." The crone, as I observed earlier, is commonly rendered as a comic non-conformist figure with subversive potential, notably in the novels of Pratchett,[8] and in picture-books and junior fiction. Where official society most forcibly reasserts traditional hegemonic structures and values, especially gendered behaviors, is in the depiction of the sorceress-witch. When positioned as a supplementary participant, as with Wise Child's evil sorceress mother, Maeve, she tends to represent femininity gone wrong, choosing to evade the hegemony of patriarchy by exercising her power in a dangerous and destructive manner. In Donna Jo Napoli's exquisitely written retelling of the Rapunzel story, *Zel* (1996), the stepmother-witch has traded her soul to the devil in return for the power to ensnare Rapunzel's parents and gain possession of their child. She escapes her contract, redeems herself, and loses her power by yielding her claim to the prince's, and so is instrumental in returning the young lovers to the hegemony of a romantic outcome under patriarchy, where Zel exemplifies "good" femininity. The implications of *Zel* seem quite mild, however, when compared with *The Craft* (1996), a popular film for late adolescent audiences and upward, marketed as "a hip, sexy, supernatural thriller." Mair observed that, "The stronger the belief that the world ought to be a moral order, the greater the need for the idea of the witch,"[9] so that the deviant can be identified and expelled. This idea seems to underlie the linking of witchcraft and femininity gone wrong in *The Craft*, and hence the film's not very subtle reaffirmation of the wisdom of official society's control over the lives and bodies of young women, of remaking the subversive into the subaltern, a view powerfully encapsulated in the final images of Nancy, the truly malevolent (and so most expendable) witch of the four: insane, deluded, self-mutilating, she lies sedated and strapped to a bed in a psychiatric hospital.

The three witch-schemata deployed in recent texts for young audiences answer to a variety of needs and desires, but in general they bring past and present into relationship in two ways. The comic crone and the wise witch can be used to critique or even subvert contemporary social attitudes and practices; the sorceress, however, despite having the most potential for disrupting common social assumptions is represented in such a way as to reinscribe traditional social values and hierarchies.

NOTES

1. Diane Purkiss, *The Witch in History* (London: Routledge, 1996), pp. 10–11.
2. Margaret A. Murray, *The Witch-Cult in Western Europe* (Oxford: Oxford University Press, 1921).
3. See especially Lucy Mair, *Witchcraft* (London: World University Library, 1973), pp. 226–231; Norman Cohn, *Europe's Inner Demons* (St Albans, Herts.: Paladin, 1976), pp. 107–120; Carlo Ginzburg, *Ecstasies: Deciphering the Witches' Sabbath* (New York: Pantheon Books, 1991), pp. 8–9. Purkiss offers a more balanced analysis, *The Witch in History*, pp. 62–63.
4. In Barbara Ehrenreich and Deirdre English, *Witches, Midwives and Nurses: A History of Women Healers* (London: Writers and Readers Publishing Cooperative, 1973).
5. The list is drawn from Geraldine Finn, *Why Althusser Killed His Wife: Essays on Discourse and Violence* (New Jersey: Humanities Press, 1996), p. 98.
6. Mair, *Witchcraft*, p. 46.
7. Mair, *Witchcraft*, p. 38.
8. See John Stephens, "Not Unadjacent to a Play about a Scottish King: Terry Pratchett Remakes *Macbeth*." *Papers* 7, 2 (1997), pp. 29–37.
9. Mair, *Witchcraft*, p. 230.

REFERENCES

Barry, Margaret Stuart. *The Witch on Holiday*. London: Collins, 1983.
Baum, L. Frank. *The Wizard of Oz*. New York: Holt, Rinehart and Winston, 1982.
Briggs, Robin. *Witches and Neighbours: The Social and Cultural Context of European Witchcraft*. London: HarperCollins, 1996.
Brink, André. "The Writer as Witch." In *The Dissident Word: The Oxford Amnesty Lectures 1995*. Ed. Chris Miller. New York: BasicBooks, 1996, pp. 41-59.
Cohn, Norman. *Europe's Inner Demons*. St Albans, Herts.: Paladin, 1976.
The Craft. Dir. Andrew Fleming. Columbia Pictures Industries Inc., 1996.
Eagleton, Terry. *William Shakespeare*. Oxford: Blackwell, 1986.
Eco, Umberto. "The Sacred Is Not Just a Fashion." In *Travels in Hyperreality*. Translated by William Weaver. London: Pan Books, 1987, pp. 89-94.

Finn, Geraldine. *Why Althusser Killed His Wife: Essays on Discourse and Violence*. New Jersey: Humanities Press, 1996.

Furlong, Monica. *Wise Child*. London: Victor Gollancz, 1987. London: Corgi Books, 1990.

———. *Thérèse of Lisieux*. London: Virago Press, 1987.

Ginzburg, Carlo. *Ecstasies: Deciphering the Witches' Sabbath*. New York: Pantheon Books, 1991.

Griffiths, Helen. *The Mysterious Appearance of Agnes*. New York: Holiday House, 1975.

Lawrence, Louise. *The Earth Witch*. London: Collins, 1982.

Lillington, Kenneth. *An Ash-blonde Witch*. London: Penguin Books, 1989.

Mair, Lucy. *Witchcraft*. London: World University Library, 1973.

Murray, Margaret A. *The Witch-Cult in Western Europe*. Oxford: Oxford University Press, 1921.

Napoli, Donna Jo. *Zel*. New York: Dutton, 1996.

Nicoll, Helen and Pienkowski, Jan. *Meg and Mog*. London: Puffin Books, 1975.

Pratchett, Terry. *Lords and Ladies*. London: Victor Gollancz, 1992.

———. *Witches Abroad*. London: Corgi Books, 1992.

———. *Wyrd Sisters*. London: Corgi Books, 1989.

Purkiss, Diane. *The Witch in History*. London: Routledge, 1996.

Spivack, Charlotte. "Morgan Le Fay: Goddess or Witch?" In *Popular Arthurian Traditions*. Ed. Sally K. Slocum. Bowling Green: Bowling Green State University Popular Press, 1992, pp. 18-23.

Stephens, John. "Not Unadjacent to a Play about a Scottish King: Terry Pratchett Remakes *Macbeth*." *Papers: Explorations Into Children's Literature* 7, 2 (1997).

Stewig, John Warren. "The Witch Woman: A Recurring Motif in Recent Fantasy Writing for Young Readers." *Mythlore* 74 (1993): 48-53.

Tomlinson, Theresa. *Summer Witches*. London: Julia MacRae Books, 1989.

Walker, Barbara G. *The Woman's Encyclopedia of Myths and Secrets*. Cambridge: Harper and Row, 1983.

Yolen, Jane. *Here There Be Witches*. A collection of stories previously published between 1977 and 1995. Illustrated by David Wilgus. San Diego: Harcourt, Brace and Company, 1995.

Zipes, Jack. *Don't Bet on the Prince*. Aldershot: Gower, 1986.

Afterword

On the Future for Children's Literature

The Duty of Internet Internationalism: Roald Dahls of the World, Unite!

Jean Perrot

The friendly forum provided by our International Research Society allows me to plead for a new International and advocate another subversion: a cultural, rather than a political, revolution in the field of children's literature criticism. Hence the rather enigmatic title of my Afterword and the support I am expecting for my enterprise from the literary ghost of Roald Dahl, Britain's national emblem of international success.

If I had any misgivings about the choice of this highly controversial author to introduce my ideas, I was soon reassured on my way to York by the evidence of Dahl's tremendous popularity: I will never forget the window of the Albion Bookshop in Canterbury, where a summer children's reading competition was advertized by a quiz-game on *Charlie and the Chocolate Factory*, and I can still see the grinning and inviting faces of Verula Salt and Augustus Gloop, surrounded by George with his "medicine" and other well-known characters meant to entice future readers into the game. Surely this was a good way of persuading the greedy consumers of chocolate bars and the enthusiastic owners of Paddington or Winnie the Pooh, the perfect devotees of the English Teddy Bear Company, to transfer their appetites to more abstract nutrition! For the new worldwide cultural problem is this — how are we to get children (or their parents) to shift from the consumption of material goodies to the appreciation and practice of intellectual nimbleness? What "marvellous medicine" can we give them to promote reading? A brief survey in France, Japan and other post-industrial countries has shown me that Dahl has something to offer here. And technical changes in the international field can help countries, where books are not available, to develop effective literacy policies. Not that we should rely solely on market forces to achieve such real promotion, but other issues have to be raised before we can answer such difficult questions.

READING AND THE CATCHWORD
OF THE "POLITICALLY CORRECT"

Contemporary reading has shown us that "surfing the Internet is fine for whizz kids,"[1] but it calls for skilled navigators, as Judith Elkin puts it in her Esme Green Lecture, published in *The New Review of Children's Literature and Librarianship*. New modes of literacy also require greater international cooperation and understanding between nations. We have had an example of this recently, when the American Supreme Court overturned the Communication Decency Act on constitutional grounds. The Court concluded that the Act, which was partly intended to protect children, "endangers free speech and threatens . . . a large segment of the Internet community." The Court finally restored freedom in the field,[2] yet the question of censorship and its consequences for creative writing highlight the contradictions of our complex societies and can be felt both in and outside the world wide web.

Therefore I wish at the outset to echo Paul Hazard's words in his ground-breaking book, *Books, Children and Men,* published in 1932, when he hailed the "The World Republic of Childhood" initiated by children's literature.[3] At that time, the circle of the elect consisted of "the happy few." Hazard, who was a navigator after his own fashion, indulged in more traditional journeys; he liked the *Tour de France par deux enfants* [Two children's journey around France], *Don Quixote, Uncle Tom's Cabin*, and *Baron Munchausen* but, like Roald Dahl who spent several years in East Africa, he also had been to Africa. He had not seen the "Ompas Loompas" but, as he wrote: "I visited the pigmy country in Africa, which did not seem strange to me, as I was familiar with Lilliput."[4] Of course, Dahl in his satire, *Charlie and the Chocolate Factory,* has shown us how pigmies could be made to serve the capitalist system, here representing the symbolic benefit and greedy enjoyment of the world's happy children.

Children nowadays are more demanding and want more exotic science fiction cruises to the moon and even like to make dangerous experiments; some of them, indeed, have tried to hack into the Pentagon webnet system with the help of their personal computers. Postmodern art also is "sustained by collective processes of technological reproduction," more seriously wrecking Walter Benjamin's "angel of History," as Joseph Tabbi has it in his introduction to *Postmodern Sublime, Technology and American Writing from Mailer to Cyberpunk.*[5] Under such conditions, what are the general characteristics of the critical international field which could enlarge and broaden the contemporary World Republic of Childhood? This "Republic" saw its rights proclaimed in 1989, and is being inhabited by children from more and more distant countries, as we saw at the Fourth Asian Conference for Children's Literature held in Seoul in 1997. Everywhere, be it in Russia or in the Native People's Reservations in Canada, new readers are eager to acclaim the new international bestsellers. These books do not tend to emanate from the Disney market system or the Goosebumps series and if future "classics" are to see the light of day, they will have to take into account the expectations of television, videogame and CD-Rom enthusiasts. And where are we critics to stand? I do not mean as a corporate body of people whose interests are linked to the object of their study, but as a group of citizens of the world, who wish to support the new trends of excellence in the field and, if mass production offers ways of sharing with more potential readers, to make the most of what it offers to current non-readers.

I consider these issues to be of the highest importance, because "the challenge of the new media—electronic, multimedia, the Internet—can impact hugely on the development of the child," to quote again from Judith Elkin's Lecture.[6] It seems necessary for researchers of every country to pool their reserves and promote real international intellectual acuity and a clear understanding of what we mean by "children's literature." To put it bluntly, I would like to challenge the special link which an increasing number of academics, from across the Atlantic in particular, make between children's literature criticism and the concept of what is "politically correct." This obsession, or bias, to my mind, is not simply a literary methodological approach which has become a fashion, and on the altar of which every researcher feels bound to sacrifice and abandon her or his intellectual vigilance. It has its habits and mannerisms, or rather manias, and compulsory procedures, which I propose to examine and which are new symbolic responses to the pressures of the intellectual market.

The new moralism of the "p.c." (politically correct), a form of Puritanism in my opinion, is a screen behind which the assessment of texts, all too often unwittingly, leads to "international incorrectness," literary blindness, the neglect of historical perspective and even cross-cultural insensivity. It is, as we will see, sometimes based on so-called progressive assumptions or the worn-out Marxist theories of the 1960s, long since abandoned in the field of general literature, but still in use in children's literature criticism even after the Berlin Wall has come down. It ignores the specific playfulness of a child's reading and the essence of literature is warped by ideological prejudice usually expressed in cramped rhetorical terms and biased methodological leaps from one field to another. This is worrying, not only because of the personal misunderstandings it may involve between colleagues from different countries, but because of the danger of cultural uniformity; I will even risk calling it the standardization of a new totalitarianism.

This may be very obnoxious indeed, especially within the new forms of literacy involved in the modern media and the development of the Internet, where English is the dominant language. On the Net, as we know, a specific manipulation of time and space, along with the combination of text, image and sound, and the fragmentary mode of reading tend to lessen the reader's awareness of historical perspective or questions of style, and call for greater vigilance from the critical mind. New responsibilities and international obligations are needed if we are to avoid any unbalanced, peremptory condemnations or the negation of the reader's right to respond freely to the literary qualities of the text. As we shall see, respect for history is precisely the first rule that these critics break in their rash attacks on the cultures of other peoples.

ZU HILFE! ZU HILFE! ROALD DAHL!

To alleviate the suspense raised by such preliminary considerations, I would like to imitate Mozart's Tamino when oppressed by the monster and call for Dahl's help now and say that his selection as a reference arose out of my appreciation of this author's successful presentation of the tumultuous and incongruous premises of postmodern experience. Dahl's achievement (and that of Quentin Blake, who so beautifully illustrated his books) is characterized by the new attitude of "storming the Reality Studio," to use the title of Larry McCaffery's "Casebook on Cyberpunk and Postmodern Fiction."[7] It consists of blurring the distinction between man and machine in *Charlie and the Chocolate Factory* (1964), for instance, or in *Charlie and the Great Glass Elevator*. It deals with the problem of modern representation in *The Wonderful Story of Henry Sugar* (1977), which tries to present the unpresentable and, by using the post-Carrollian habit of playing with people's sizes in *George's Marvellous Medicine*, it heralds the cyberpunk compression of beings, exhibited for instance—as Carole Scott has shown us[8]—in Susan Cooper's *The Boggart,* and in Alexandre Jardin's *Cybermaman,*[9] a French cyberpunk fantasy in which the quest for a dead mother leads to the core of hard disk of a computer, where her virtual remains are stored.

Dahl's literary world heralds a new facetious fantasy and genuine international sensitivity. His exploitation of the imaginary world is entirely in harmony with the specificities of the child's imagination, which I believe draws on particular sections of the general cultural codes. My view of the socio-psychological foundations for successful literariness for children is explained in depth in my book *Du jeu, des enfants et des livres* [On play, children and books] and I give a brief outline of it in my essay "Play Prepares Father Christmas's Future."[10] My idea is that literary play in children differs from the imaginative play of adults, in so far as it is stretched more specifically between the two poles of "surprise" (the fusional dependence on adults and gleeful acceptance of the law and of its "magical" gifts), on the one hand, and of "mischief-making" (the playful transgression of cultural codes leading to liberty and autonomy), on the other. Within such a framework, the varieties of fiction develop in a complex field, mapped by the grid lines set by the concepts of the child, by the supposed functions of literature, and by the moral or political outlook of the writer, and her or his conception of style and of literary address.

This special transitional and even "transactional" space is what makes Dahl so successful in his books, ranging from *James and the Giant Peach* or Charlie's "surprises" to *The Twits*' highly caricatured mischief-making. What I hope we will see is the transfer and adaptation of such gems into future works in a form which we cannot yet predict, but which will be founded on a genuine exchange with the Internet generation of children. And this is where Dahl's *Matilda* comes in to provide a clearer picture of what I consider to be an international literary classic. The reader, who no doubt knows the story very well, will remember how it ends: Matilda, the witty little genius who—while she was between four and five—had read all the available books in the local library, is abandoned by her shameless parents. Her father, significantly called Mr. Wormwood, is a dishonest second-hand car-dealer, who puts sawdust into the engines to sell the cars as new. When this shady practice is discovered, the couple mean to fly to Spain to avoid prosecution by the police, never to return. The last scene is particularly appealing and moving. Matilda is left in the arms of her teacher, Miss Honey, who has grown fond of her and who takes care of her in the absence of the girl's natural parents.

Let me quote Roald Dahl's last paragraph to illustrate the vignette with which the reader is left after closing the book:

Matilda leapt into Miss Honey's arms and hugged her, and Miss Honey hugged her back, and then the mother and father and brother were inside the car and the car was pulling away with tyres screaming. The brother gave a wave through the rear window, but the other two didn't even look back. Miss Honey was still hugging the tiny girl in her arms and neither of them said a word as they stood there watching the big black car tearing round the corner at the end of the road and disappearing for ever in the distance.[11]

Now, this may be a good illustration of what the psychoanalyst D. W. Winnicott means by positive "child-holding," but it is also a surprisingly new baroque representation of the Holy Virgin and Child; the "postmodern sublime," to use the title of Joseph Tabbi's book mentioned above, breaks through this ecstatic yet humorous and illuminating vision of innocence. And the "sublime," as Tabbi has it, is "the very possibility of symbolization,"[12] what exceeds any rational thought, what is left of art or nature beyond any explanation or logical system.

One also notices how the dramatic intensity of the moment is conveyed through the repetitions of the word "hugged," through the insistence on the reciprocal attitude of the girl and of her teacher, illustrating a kind of aesthetic Batesonian "double-bind," and through the contrast established between the concentration of the motionless pair and the tearing haste of the others, all of which is enforced by the stylistic use of a series of short notations culminating in one apparently twisted and convoluted sentence.

HENRY JAMES ALSO COMES TO THE RESCUE

This pathetic ending has many similarities with Henry James's concluding chapter in *What Maisie Knew*. In the final scene of the 1897 novel, a little girl is also left to the hugging of her governess, the old, widowed and child-bereft Mrs. Wix, whose name suggests witchcraft and evil thoughts. James's text stresses the powerlessness of the little "prisoner": "The next thing the child knew she was at that lady's side with an arm firmly grasped," he writes.[13] This grip offers Maisie an escape from her stepmother's "wild snatch."[14] Eventually the girl and her governess catch the steamer to France and escape from the step-parents and parents. James very cleverly leaves a subtle ambiguity as to the nature of what Maisie "saw," while adults were fighting to "possess" her, but he is fully aware of the "inclusive" child-adult relationship, since the story transforms what was at first a casual educational bond into Maisie's fate. As he writes using a vivid metaphor:

Embedded in Mrs. Wix's nature, as her tooth had been socketed in her gum, the operation of extracting her would have been a case for chloroform. It was a hug that fortunately left nothing to say, for the poor woman's want of words at such an hour seemed to fall in with her want of everything.[15]

Embedded? This is precisely the word used by Sandra Beckett in her presentation of *Reflections of Change*, the Proceedings of the 1995 Stockholm IRSCL Congress. Beckett introduces us to Perry Nodelman's opening plenary paper on Paul Hazard, "Fear of Children's Literature: What's Left (or Right) After Theory?" and, commenting on early "conservative critical approaches," underlines that Nodelman's contribution showed "how developments in literary theory in the ensuing fifty years have led to the understanding that children's literature embeds its readers in ideology."[16]

As we can see, James also understood the adult-child bond as a twofold matter of conscious and unconscious, and physical as well as complex ideological involvement or "embedding." This will help us in our reader's response to *Matilda* as a very subtle and significant transformation of the Victorian novelist's vision.

Like Maisie, cast off without hope by her immoral and scandalously behaved parents and by their successive lovers, her stepfather and stepmother, and left to the furiously hysterical grip of the stern old lady, Matilda actively determines her own future and happiness. Yet, whereas Maisie, a substitute for her governess's dead child, "knew" and "saw," but—apart from her intellectual astuteness— remained hopelessly dependent on adults, Matilda, the modern heroine, does not use chloroform, but acts through the very strength of her eyes. She is not "displaced" from one corner to the other of the social field like Maisie. She is no mere "shuttlecock" in her parents' modern family game. She indeed can displace objects: first a glass, then a piece of chalk, and she can finally banish her parents and rout the terrifying Miss Trunchbull, the school headmistress, described as a kind of Nazi Kapo, who uses children as a "hammer" for her physical exercise. While Maisie is being grabbed and hugged by the necrophilic ogress, Matilda commits her future to the sweet Miss Honey, Miss Trunchbull's ward, who had been defrauded of her inheritance after her father's death. A last feature of Dahl's system of transformation in his modern "fairy tale" deals with the child's displacement: Maisie's flight to France is matched by the symmetrical escape of Matilda's parents to Spain.

These contrasting literary constructs of child and adult relationships are in both cases very telling about the whole conception of writing as linked to the dominant art forms of the time. We see that James, with his complex sentences espousing the workings of the child's supposed imagination, constructed scenes that are wholly controlled by the playwright's outlook, just as the stage—and more particularly Octave Feuillet's melodrama—were the reference for literary success in the closing decades of the nineteenth century.

Dahl's conclusion, on the contrary, is a satire inspired by television dramas and detective series. Both stories are inspired by the desire to fight social evil (James was scandalized by the divorce cases of his times) and are provided as illustrations of the dominant relationship which unites children and adults in the symbolic social order. Obviously, Dahl brings in his own view of the modern frail but daring child of his own desires. No doubt also both novelists put much of their own personalities into these constructs and it is difficult to tell where their consciousness of personal involvement ended, so far as sexual implication was concerned in these scenes. But we will leave this for the Trunchbull to decide. Also, the episode of Miss Honey's house resounds with singular echoes of what we know about Dahl's own Rousseau-like home and lifestyle and, as I have shown elsewhere, Maisie can be read as a literary image of the representative intellectual of the times, namely the young Gustave Flaubert, whose letters were being published when James, a great reader of his work, was writing *What Maisie Knew*.[17]

And so, Dahl's book, publicized as a "national bestseller" on the title page of the Puffin edition, has won a considerable readership in a paradoxical manner: despite deriding television fans, it is based on the technical devices of the favorite medium of the children of our times. Similarly James has taken his little heroine to the fair and given her "point of view" through the fantastic prism of her fairy-tale imagination; thus the child's father is seen as a wolf with flashing teeth.

One final feature links the authors of these two stories: their cosmopolitanism. James was an American expatriate who, after an unsuccessful start in France, settled in England in 1876, 20 years before writing *What Maisie Knew*, while Dahl, in *Boy, Tales of Childhood*, has told the story of his parents who came from Norway. Of particular significance to me is the story of his father and of his uncle, who both initially came to France, then separated, the uncle investing all his energies in the furniture business near Bordeaux, where "he acquired a wife from a good family and a magnificent town house, as well as a large château in the country,"[18] and the father crossing the Channel to have the son we know. So France got the furniture dealer and Britain got the writer; I can only wonder what would have happened if the opposite choice had been made.

I now seem like an actor playing the part of the dispossessed, envious younger brother in a fairy tale: the international fairy tale of literary success, as James considered it, in which the inevitably conflicting interests of artists do not prevent them from also being the repositories of their nation's symbolic power.

LITERATURE AND THE SYMBOLIC ORDER

But, you will exclaim quite justifiably, literature is not a matter of furniture, nor of ideology or of mere market factors. As the literary theorist Gérard Genette has shown in *Palimpsestes* [Palimpsests], a "hypertext" always implies a hypotext and any piece of writing is sure to be an "answer" to another, as well as a sociological construct based on contemporary facts.[19] The very process by which classics develop in children's literature, or in any literature, is grounded on such historical exchanges between international comparative minds and on such rich intertextuality as to transcend any national barriers or partiality.

Most significantly, both Dahl's and James's stories illustrate this trait, as they are similarly shaped through the equation (or is it a dilemma?) formulated by Jean Baudrillard in the title of his book, *L'échange symbolique et la mort* [Symbolic exchange and death].[20] Maisie and Matilda illustrate the literary alternative to spiritual death for children of the middle class, and even the text of their stories participates in the symbolic order, as an escape from the economic system of value exchanges. The symbolic order implies the complete reversibility of the gift into the counter-gift; it rules bodies, words, images of love, families and art, in which the laws of the market have no reason to exist. Literature here is seen as the resolution of a destructive fantasm through the projection of the fictional body onto the imaginary literary space and style. The beneficial transfer of the crisis to aesthetic codes is the first step toward its resolution, as Didier Azieu has shown in his book *Le corps de l'œuvre* [The body of the work],[21] in which he investigates artistic creation.

This global scientific perspective, which gives us some insight into literary works and helps to evaluate the refinements of style, is precisely what the critics I mentioned at the beginning of this chapter tend to forget and fail to take into consideration. Let me return to a first example of what I now call "literary Trunchbulling," which I criticized at the Children's Literature Association's Annual Conference in 1996, that of Herbert Kohl in his book, *Should We Burn Babar?* (1995).[22] A written version of my communication, "Why We Should Not Burn Mickey Mouse" has appeared in the 1998 collection of essays, *Critical Perspectives on Postcolonial African Children's Literature.*[23] Let me just sum up its main point in a few words: in the chapter dealing with Jean de Brunhoff, Kohl criticizes what he calls "the colonialism, the implied racism and sexism"[24] of *The Story of Babar, the Little Elephant* and wonders whether such a book should not be destroyed because of the negative influence it may have on young readers. In my answer, I demonstrated that Kohl had overlooked the historical context in which the book was published and was therefore blind to its avant-garde quality, to its defence of the child's symbolic order through the stylized representation of the "garden cities" developed by architects of the period; this is a cliché today, but not devoid of all relevance for anyone who knows the black ghettos.

By dwelling on money matters, and viewing Babar's friendship with the old lady as a case of human bondage or of "glorifying the ruling class," Kohl reduced *The Story of Babar* to mere "propaganda" and a legitimization of capitalist and colonialist ideology.[25] He ignored the playful imagination which is eminently capable of involving the reader and was insensitive to the succesful transfer from the happy relationship with a natural mother tragically killed by a hunter, to a new mystic bond uniting him to his cousin Céleste. The baroque treatment of the plot and the insistence on the generous attitude of all the protagonists toward the young elephant are not only a convention of the literary genre, but are also related to the "symbolic exchange" which rules family life and to the positive "holding" of the good-mother substitute, which, according to Winnicott, are absolutely necessary if children are to achieve balanced maturity.

P.C. AND THE APPRECIATION OF STYLE

A more obvious drift from literary questions to a biased sociological analysis is perceptible in Kohl's comment on another important children's classic from Southern Europe, namely Collodi's *The Adventures of Pinocchio*; this leads him to a major conclusion: "The implication is that boys and men are mischievous, full of adventure, apt to get into trouble, but ultimately redeemed through their ability to help, when help is needed. . . . 'Boys will be boys' is a dangerous attitude, one that leaves sanction for male violence."[26]

Here we feel the discreet figure of some feminist Trunchbull looming in at the back of Kohl's mind's eye, for he finds himself forced to side with girls and to infer that they are excluded from such a formation and "denied the pleasure of sin, as well as saved from the punishments."[27] Nothing in the book, which was concerned with other matters, called for such a claim. But quite naturally Kohl then concludes with a canonical condemnation, saying that, "Despite their delight with Pinocchio, the troublemaker, my kindergarten and first-grade students clearly saw the sexism in the story."[28]

Blind to any literary quality of the text in his fanatical condemnation of immorality, Kohl, who in his book indulges in a 40-page "plea for Radical Children's Literature,"[29] never draws his students' attention to the problems of history nor to questions of style; he is only concerned with social and moral issues and considers that "stories are tools to approach and investigate these moral issues with students." His definition of Radical Literature shows his complete disregard for what constitutes the essence of literature, namely the unique flavor and quality of the artist's voice; a book, in his opinion, is radical, when it is "partisan" and when "it presents a vision of solutions that are not merely individual, but affect entire groups."[30]

For him, literature is but an implement in a defense of the "very enterprise of public education," which—as he writes in his conclusion—is "threatened by Right-wing and corporate attacks."[31] It is not surprising that he ends his book with a chapter telling the story of the "Left-wing and progressist" teaching movement, dwelling upon the fact that the Sputnik episode of Soviet science had the effect of focusing "educational concern on the development of excellence."[32]

But with what results! Most curiously, along the same lines as Kohl's, I have come across another surprising reader's response to *Pinocchio* in a recent essay published by Patricia Merivale in the special issue of the periodical *Ariel* on postcolonial literature. Here too, I was taken aback to read that "in postcolonial terms, Collodi lacks the political courage of his artistic convictions."[33] The conclusion of the paper also seemed implacable: "So *Pinocchio* cannot help but be, one supposes, a pre-postcolonial children's story, employing the savage pedagogy of the School of Hard Knocks."[34] Miss Trunchbull again! Such an approach in my opinion stresses the acute need for the Internet to have systematic translations of children's books, backed by critical editions, if we want to avoid the complete cultural regression of future readers obsessed by an immediate shortsighted use of literature. Here English-speaking scholars are fortunate, since they can profit from Ann Lawson Lucas's 1996 translation of *Pinocchio*, on the cover of which, however, we read that this very complete version is "far more sophisticated, funny and hard-hitting than many abridged versions!"[35] Hard-hitting? The commercial Trunchbull again? Certainly, but in this case a mild and humorous one, and one standing in defense and respect of the text and of its unity and coherence; indeed it clearly underlines the fact that Collodi was a tough critic of social and political matters and far from the conservative writer that inconsiderate reviewers of his work would like him to appear.

FEAR OF WHICH THEORY?

Yes indeed, Herbert Kohl's theory makes me "fear theory," as our colleague Perry Nodelman put it in his Stockholm plenary session paper. Quite surprisingly in Nodelman's case, a Freudo-Marxist coalition of theoreticians, even more ominous than the radicals mentioned by Kohl, including "Antonio Gramsci, Louis Althusser, Raymond Williams"[36] and Jacques Lacan, is called up in support of the plea he registers against Hazard, resorting on that occasion to the sociological concept of "Ideological State Apparatuses" (a concept which is too limited to account for the complex reality of post-industrial multinational capitalism) as the basis of his literary demonstration.

Can I say here that Nodelman belongs to the same school of criticism as Kohl himself and evinces the same biased approach to literature mainly as some kind of reductive ideological discourse? Indeed even more so! Relying on critics like Williams, who wanted to integrate an historical perspective into the study of Literature, as we are reminded by David Lodge's seminal remarks in *Modern Criticism and Theory*,[37] Nodelman achieves the paradoxical feat of passing very severe judgments on books that he considers outside their historical context.

This is what baffled me when I listened to his oral communication a few years ago, but I was not then able to answer or refute what he himself called his "attack" on Paul Hazard's *Books, Children and Men,* published in 1932 in France and translated in the USA in 1944. So I would like to answer it now, as the debate may help us clarify our research and make us notice Nodelman's own perplexity when he writes: "you might well wonder why I have spent so much time attacking such an obvious target."[38] I share this perplexity myself, but not for the same reasons, and it will not be difficult to show that Nodelman's demonstration follows the same drift as Kohl's in its assessment of other people's works. Nodelman begins by questioning Hazard's conception of the child as "innocent" and writes at the very outset: "It's hard to imagine that children could have ever been so innocent, or that children's books could ever have been so innocent—or above all, that an adult could have been so innocent— as to believe so wholeheartedly in that child's innocence."[39] Now this is a very deep remark, which he should have weighed more carefully, for he has felt that such an assumption on Hazard's part was a rhetorical construct of "the implied reader," but he has not grasped the fact that such "innocence" provides a basis for a strategy of persuasion conveying exactly the opposite view of children. We will come to this later in our counter-reading of Hazard's book, but we can assume that the author of the *Crise de la conscience européenne* [The crisis of conscience in Europe] was not as naive as Nodelman appears to think. The

American critics of the 1960s were already very much aware of this when they wrote in *The Library Quarterly* the words quoted on the back of the fourth edition in 1960:

Paul Hazard brought to the fascinating subject of children's literature the scholarly enthusiasm of a man read in the literature of the world, who informed his knowledge by direct experience of life in the countries whose written expression he studied. He saw literature for children in relation to the driving, universal force of creative writing, whenever it appears in the world, whether it be addressed to children or adults.[40]

But this is not the case with Nodelman, who, having first stated that the child's supposed innocence was but a means to gain power over him by limiting his faculties of expression, writes: "I conclude that children's literature is best understood as a means by which adults claim power over children and force them to accept our repressive versions of what they really are."[41] This is a spurious conclusion, for Hazard, far from accepting children as ready victims of adults' manipulations, actually highlighted their faculty to resist. The heading of the second part of his book reads: "Children have defended themselves."[42] Even if the titles of the books he selected as classics may seem rather difficult for our contemporary young readers, Nodelman, who claims to know "real children," is not entitled to contest their acceptability to children of that earlier period. The foreword to the first American edition, written by Horatio Smith on August 1, 1944, stressed the fact that Hazard was a great master of the art of symbolic exchange with children. He wrote: "I had known how gracious and successful a host he could be with children in the case of my own, whom he once entertained in Gisors, showing them just enough of the old town to amuse them without strain. . . . He had the same gift for understanding his students."[43]

Hazard, an expert in the art of evaluating children's reading, could indeed appreciate the faculty of "inertia," applied by children to books they do not like, to the books with which adults have tried to "stifle a young heart," imposing "limits, rules and constraints."[44]

It is not fair to reduce the list of books he proposed to children, as Nodelman does, solely to stories "that offer to children an intuitive and direct way of knowledge, a simple beauty capable of being perceived immediately, arousing in their souls a vibration which will endure all their lives."[45] Paul Hazard wanted children to read other books, as well, books "that enable them to share in great human emotions," books "which understand that the training of intelligence and reason cannot, and must not always have the immediately useful and practical as its goal."[46] This, on Hazard's part, looks like a good practical illustration of the necessity of the symbolic order of literature.

Nodelman's reading then proceeds by devious selections, approximations and risky generalizations: for instance, he gets support from James Kincaid, who in his book *Child-Loving: The Erotic Child and Victorian Culture*, equated the supposed "purity" of children to "emptiness"[47] and writes: "And so Hazard, I see, constructed it (the child) to his taste—which was mostly to privilege and celebrate its emptiness."[48] There is no "purity" in Hazard's children (the word does not appear in the text), but again a good intuitive understanding of the symbolic order, and a greater complexity than such a rapid shift from one concept to another might entail. Similarly, Nodelman resorts to Lacan's theory to give a psychological basis to his objections and goes back to the celebrated analysis of the "mirror stage." But he misinterprets it when he writes that in the mirror the child "perceives that it exists as a separate being, only inside a context that is larger than itself, and that makes the child feel small in relation to it."[49] That conclusion is a far-fetched generalization and expresses a Puritanical projection and lack of self-assurance. Neither can we accept the strained affirmation that under such conditions, "we are always conscious of ourselves as diminished, lacking a wholeness we once had." On the contrary, "healthy" children do not feel such diminution and always derive from the sense of self an incentive to grow and to imitate adults.

Lastly we will note that for Nodelman, "this pre-Oedipal stage sounds very much like Hazard's vision of childhood, a prelapsarian paradise before knowledge of distinction and divisions intervene."[50] But Hazard's children always look to the future as a means of achieving a wider unity, so that Nodelman's "very much" hints at some regrettable imprecision. So too does the extrapolation based on the argument that "children are innocent, and imaginative, where adults have lost the ability to imagine, playful, when adults insist on serious purposes even in their play."[51] It does not entitle one to decree that Hazard, himself an "analytical adult," is sick, "Or to put it another way, adults are all sick." A more serious and deplorable logical leap occurs finally, when Nodelman rounds off his plea with the following sentence: "Thus another thing Hazard's view of childhood shares with certain forms of racism or sexism is praise of those qualities that mark the other and opposite to oneself as a stick with which to beat oneself and one's kind."[52] Here is Trunchbull's "hammer" once more, but used in a terrifying manner! The big hackneyed catchwords of conventional trendy criticism, "sexism, racism," are let out and Nodelman even suggests that Hazard's answers betray "a profound degree of self-hatred," and share the dominant alienating wish to make children feel "guilty." Standing in defense of the child's freedom, Nodelman can now turn toward Althusser (whose sickness, if one followed Nodelman's line, is evident on other grounds, as the distinguished Marxist theoretician killed his wife). Quoting the article "Ideology and Ideological State Apparatuses," he denounces the "fearful potential to repress and envelop us," or to "embed," which ideological representations possess.[53] He finally claims that the task of adults is to make children more conscious of such possible alienation: "In other words, we must teach them to be divided subjects in their reading and in their lives—to be involved as both implied readers of texts and critical observers of what texts demand from them in that process."[54]

This is, of course, a good definition of the teacher's duty, but not a fine exposition of the functions of literature, which does not only mean to "teach," but which is an art imparting complex aesthetic feelings. Literary theory here is at stake, and we have seen that Roald Dahl was providing a more suggestive answer, with the last scene of *Matilda*.

Finally one should note that Hazard was an advocate of something, which is sorely missing in Nodelman's approach, and which characterized the post-First World War period: *Books, Children and Men*, as I already hinted, is concluded by a chapter on "The Republic of Childhood," from which we can extract two significant sentences: "Yes, children's books keep alive a sense of nationality; but they also keep alive a sense of humanity."[55] Far from relying on insularity, Hazard saw children's literature as a space devoted to the establishment of closer and closer international relationships: "each of them is a messenger that goes beyond mountains and rivers, beyond the seas, to the very ends of the world, in search of new friendships. Every country gives and every country receives."[56]

The symbolic order, again and again! Like Jean de Brunhoff, Hazard shared in the new spirit of the League of Nations. Living half of the year in Connecticut for several years before World War II, he was able to witness the dynamism and openness of the American publishers of that time: "We have Japanese books on our shelves for the children of Boston, our young publishers send people all over the world to hunt stories to translate."[57] For the interest was in style and in the text, and not only in censorship. This "hunt," we can say, is not common, nowadays, with the exception of a few small publishers, such as The Creative Company (Mankatto, MN), whose editorial policy I explored recently at the Fourth Asian Worldwide Symposium in Seoul; after all, most American publishing houses go to the Bologna Book Fair not to "buy," but to "sell."

In his "attack," it is also as a representative of the protectionist American publishing system that Nodelman, implicitly sharing Kohl's view, stood before us in 1995, although he returned to Hazard in the last part of his paper, when he considered that adults had to help young readers establish "enriching connections with other human beings." Nodelman may have been half conscious of his aggressive symbolic function, for he declared at the end of his communication that he was "aware how the faces one puts on are mere masks, how there is always more to us than whatever particular way we've decided to represent ourselves to others (and presently to ourselves) at any particular moment."[58] So that the mask I am wearing is now perfectly clear: Literature, and children's literature as well, is not a place where only intellectual "capital" accumulates, it is also a conflictual situation, within which the erasure of significant contributions drawn from the past of other countries is not innocuous and may have some imperialistic market impact on international friendships: political correctness must extend worldwide.

IS THERE ONLY ONE CENTER?

It is still too early to know whether the Internet system will change this state of things and introduce a new sort of international friendship. So far only a few significant CD-Roms for children have been produced from which to judge. In France, a few CDs point to this new internationalism: *Kyeko and the Night-Robbers* by Vladimir Hulpach,[59] for instance, runs in five languages and is adapted from the South American folktale, "The Serpents that Robbed the Night". It can be read both as a work of fiction and as a documentary on the flora, climate, and so forth, of the Amazon. It is narrated by Kyeko, a young

Yanomami, who tells about the life of his tribe and helps us discover "the Other." Exoticism and humanism unite to increase the reader's curiosity and pleasure by making it possible to reconstruct another people's view on what life and civilization mean at the start of the millennium. A second example turns toward the past and deals with the Second World War. *Opération Teddy Bear,* by Edouard Lussan,[60] is graphically based on a comic strip and depicts the landing of the Allies in Normandy in 1944; a German war reporter, an English officer and an American parachutist compete to recover secret Nazi plans which a French Resistance group has hidden within 12-year-old Marcel's teddy bear. Here again the story can be explored as a documentary or as a work of fiction. The teddy bear is a fine symbol of the international friendship, which the toy or "transitional object," can harbor. In addition, CD-Roms are a meeting point for different intellectual disciplines, from science to history.[61]

But, more than CDs, many novels nowadays exploit the imaginary world of the Web in a very original way, as was thoughtfully demonstrated by Joseph Tabbi. An interesting issue arising out of the debate that followed Tabbi's contribution was the challenge to the exponent of Marxist theories, Fredric Jameson. Contesting the views laid out in his famous essay, "Postmodernism or the Cultural Logic of Capitalism" (1984),[62] Tabbi considered that, as a result of lack of knowledge, Jameson had missed the significance of cyberpunk fiction, and was not really describing the innovative literary works of the time, but "rather the majority fiction being published by an industry that, as a result of a series of unprecedented mergers, was in the process of becoming an oligarchy."[63] Tabbi ascribed this blindness to Jameson's "assumption of the existence of a single hegemonic system rather than many possible and conflicting systems."[64] It would take too long to go into the details of the debate; let us simply say that to support his thesis Tabbi did quote Curtis White taking Jameson to task in 1992 for not seeing "the scene that had been emerging on the margins of corporate publishing in the preceding decade."[65]

These remarks, far from taking us away from our theme, challenge the theoretical position of Maria Nikolajeva in her recent book *Children's Literature Comes of Age* in which, relying on the "poly-system" theory of the 1960s like Zohar Shavit in *Poetics of Children's Literature* (1986),[66] she holds that children's literature is ruled by a similar supposed "center," writing for instance, that "Sweden, which has been a peripheral country as far as children's books are concerned, has recently gained international acknowledgement for, among other things, its excellent picture-books."[67] Without denying the excellence of Swedish picture-books, I have discussed this issue in a review of *Children's Literature Comes of Age* in *Ariel*[68] and I am not going to rehearse my argument here. I will just repeat the question I pose in it and ask whether such a centre is not "some other hidden literary Wall Street Stock Exchange," which excludes the Bologna Book Fair and other important international book events? But what would we do then with some of the excellent picture-books we have seen in Korea or in Brazil? Are these to be judged by the same criteria as the no less excellent Italian books?

What I would like to stress through this point is the damaging effect such implicit assimilation of market-oriented forces to literary excellence can have on our literary judgments. What the Internet can show us is precisely that, whatever and wherever the material and economic center may be, there will now no longer be any literary polarization: aesthetic centers of excellence are to be found everywhere and can be identified and accessed from any point of the Web by any reader. There is as much literary "sublime" in *Grandfather Drum*,[69] a small picture-book by the Ojibwa author and artist Ferguson Plain from the Sarnia Indian Reservation (Ontario) or in the oral legends from Brazil transcribed by Clarice Lispector,[70] as in any of the works we have just mentioned.

NO PASARÀN: THE ULTIMATE GAME

In fact, the danger now comes from other causes, political or cultural ones from which, while waiting for the new multimedia literature, a few novelists from the Gutenberg Galaxy draw the best literary effects. To illustrate the situation thus enacted, let me conclude by quoting a French novel just about to be translated into German and English and written by Christian Lehmann in 1996, *No pasaràn, le jeu* [No pasaràn, the game].[71]

The story starts in London, in a shop owned by a former Nazi camp prisoner, and is about Internet fans of video games. Through the dramatic weaving of his plot, Lehmann shows the ambiguities of the Nazi ideology which they covertly express. The teenage hero of the story, Eric, has to face Andreas, a young Fascist, whose father, like Matilda's parents, is a shady businessman. Through the Internet Eric ends up getting involved in the "Guernica" video game, in which players have to relive "on line" this dreadful episode of 1936 in the Spanish Civil War.

Andreas, who speaks German and whose code name is "Condor," plays the part of the Franco supporter. Lehmann, who is himself partly of English descent, very cleverly shows the blurring of the line that divides the make-believe of the game and the real working of the player's imagination. Andreas is a future male Trunchbull, a killer, who resorts to the game to express his deeper impulses and project his hatred of foreigners (here for a young girl exiled from Serbia) onto the virtual characters. In this confusion between fact and fiction, Andreas will meet an ironically tragic end; in a last game, "The Ultimate Trial," he is chasing a young Jew in 1942, the year the Jews were deported from France with the connivence and support of the authorities. Strangely enough, the young man he is chasing appears to have the voice of the London owner of the video-game shop we saw in the first scene. Andreas is about to have him arrested, when a French collaborator asks him for his identity papers and, taking Andreas himself for a Jew, sends him to the Nazi camp. This is a perfect ironical reversal of situation and another illlustration of the necessity for "the symbolic exchange." The title of Lehmann's book comes from the motto of the Spanish Republicans, who lost the war: "No pasaràn," (Fascism will not get through). Like Dahl's story, and reversing James's ending, Lehmann's novel is an attempt to rewrite history from a positive point of view and to deal with Nazi ideology in a subtle and questioning way.

Surely the future Internet literature of the "global village" will need more subjects and plots of this kind as well as pleasant cruises for young navigators. Ones similar, for instance to Dahl's *The Child Who Talked to Animals* or to *The Hitchhiker*[72] with its paradoxical denial of the laws of the market and the triumph of symbolic exchange. This is a short story suffused with postmodern Dickensian humor in which a successful novelist, who owns a wonderful "toy," a BMW, the acme of social symbolic power, discovers the secret "genius" of an unknown artist in a kind of boyish adventure along the motorways of England. He is no pickpocket—what the man actually is—but a fantastically dextrous person, "a fingersmith," as he calls himself. Both the novelist and the artful dodger are masters of illusion, Dahl suggests, but the make-believe of literature englobes that of its material counterpart and so confers on the artist a dignity rewarded by real social recognition. Let us hope that fingersmiths on the Net, as in Dahl's story, will give way to practiced authors for the pleasure of numerous "nimble readers."[73] That is why once more I will utter my magic watchword: "Roald Dahls of the World, Unite!"

NOTES

1. Judith Elkin, "Looking to the Future: The Esme Green Memorial Lecture," *The New Review of Children's Literature and Librarianship*, 2 (1996), pp. 1–13.

2. Stephen Levy, "On the Net, Anything goes," *Newsweek*, (7 July 1997), p. 44.

3. Paul Hazard, *Des livres, des enfants et des hommes* (Paris: Flammarion, 1932); trans. and published in the USA in 1944, with a publisher's preface (pp. v–vii) by Bertha E. Mahony, a translator's preface (pp. ix–xii) by Marguerite Mitchell and a presentation of Paul Hazard by Horatio Smith (pp. xiii–xix), under the title, *Books, Children and Men* (Boston: The Horn Book, Inc., March 1944; 3rd version, 1947; 4th ed., October 1960; 5th printing, 1963), p. 144.

4. Paul Hazard, *Books, Children and Men*, 5th printing, 1963, p. 145.

5. Joseph Tabbi, *Postmodern Sublime: Technology and American Writing from Mailer to Cyberpunk* (Ithaca: Cornell University Press, 1995), p. 27.

6. Elkin, "Looking to the Future," p. 3.

7. Larry McCaffery, ed., *Storming the Reality Studio: A Casebook of Cyberpunk and Postmodern Fiction* (Durham, NC: Duke University Press, 1991).

8. Carole Scott, "High and Wild Magic, the Moral Universe, and the Electronic Superhighway: Reflections of Change in Susan Cooper's Fantasy Literature," in *Reflections of Change: Children's Literature Since 1945,* ed. Sandra L. Beckett (Westport, CT: Greenwood Press, 1997), pp. 94–96.

9. Alexandre Jardin, *Cybermaman* (Paris: Gallimard-Jeunesse, 1996).

10. Jean Perrot, "Play Prepares Father Christmas's Future," *ChLA Quarterly* 19, 3 (Fall 1994), pp. 128–133. See Chapter 1, "La dynamique imaginaire: entre surprise et bêtise" in *Du jeu, des enfants et des livres* (Paris: Editions du Cercle de la Librairie, 1987), pp. 23–66.

11. Roald Dahl, *Matilda*, 1988 (Harmondsworth, UK: Puffin, 1990), p. 240.

12. Tabbi, *Postmodern Sublime*, p. 13.

13. Henry James, *What Maisie Knew*, 1897 (Harmondsworth, UK: Penguin, 1969), p. 247.

14. Ibid., p. 245.

15. Ibid., p. 34.

16. Beckett, *Reflections of Change*, p. X.

17. Jean Perrot, "Du texte contre des dents de lait: Henry James et l'écriture," in *Le récit d'enfance*, ed. Denise Escarpit and Bernadette Poulou (Paris: Editions du Sorbier, 1993), p. 74.

18. Roald Dahl, *Boy, Tales of Childhood*, 1984 (Harmondsworth, UK: Puffin, 1986), p. 15.

19. Gérard Genette, *Palimpsestes: La littérature au second degré* (Paris: Le Seuil, Coll. Poétique, 1982).

20. Jean Baudrillard, *L'échange symbolique et la mort* (Paris: Gallimard NRF, 1976).

21. Didier Anzieu, *Le corps de l'oeuvre* (Paris: Gallimard NRF, 1982).

22. Herbert Kohl, *Should We Burn Babar? Essays on Children's Literature and the Power of Stories*. Intro. Jack Zipes (New York: The New Press, 1995).

23. Jean Perrot, "Why We Should Not Burn Mickey Mouse," in *Critical Perspectives on Postcolonial African Children's Literature*, ed. Meena Khorana (Westport, CT: Greenwood Press, 1998), pp. 45–52.

24. Kohl, *Should We Burn Babar?* p. 17.

25. Ibid., p. 18.

26. Ibid., p. 97.

27. Ibid.

28. Ibid., p. 98.

29. Ibid., pp. 56–97.

30. Ibid., p. 67.

31. Ibid., p. 170.

32. Ibid., p. 163.

33. Patricia Merivale, "The Telling of Lies and 'the Sea of Stories': *Haroun, Pinocchio* and the Postcolonial Artist Parable," *Ariel*, 28, 1 (January 1997), pp. 193–197: 193.

34. Merivale, "The Telling of Lies," p. 194.

35. Carlo Collodi, *The Adventures of Pinocchio*, trans. and intro. Ann Lawson Lucas (Oxford: Oxford University Press, 1996).

36. Perry Nodelman, "Fear of Children's Literature: What's Left (or Right) After Theory?" in Beckett, ed., *Reflections of Change*, p. 9.

37. David Lodge, ed., *Modern Criticism and Theory: A Reader* (London: Longman, 1988), pp. 384, 400.

38. Nodelman, "What's Left," p. 9.

39. Ibid., p. 3.

40. Hazard, *Books, Children and Men* (4th Ed., 1960), back cover.

41. Nodelman, "What's Left," p. 4.

42. Hazard, *Books, Children and Men* (5th printing, 1963), p. 45.

43. Ibid., p. xvii.

44. Ibid., pp. 3, 49.

45. Nodelman, "What's Left," p. 3.

46. Hazard, *Books, Children and Men* (5th printing, 1963), p. 43.

47. James Kincaid, *Child-Loving: The Erotic Child and Victorian Culture* (New York: Routledge, 1992), pp. 70–72.

48. Nodelman, "What's Left," p. 9.

49. Ibid., p. 10.

50. Ibid.

51. Ibid., p. 4.

52. Ibid., p. 6.

53. Ibid., pp. 7–8, 12.

54. Ibid.

55. Hazard, *Books, Children and Men*, (5th printing, 1963), p. 146.

56. Ibid.

57. Ibid., p. 147.

58. Nodelman, "What's Left," p. 12.

59. Vladimir Hulpach, *Kyeko and the Night-Robbers* (Paris: Ludi Media Ubi-Soft, CD-Rom, 1995).

60. Edouard Lussan, *Opération Teddy Bear* (Paris: Ludi Media Ubi-Soft, CD-Rom, 1996).

61. See Joëlle Vadel-Séguillon, "Médias et culture d'enfance: émergence de nouvelles écritures." Mémoire de DEA d'Etudes Littéraires Francophones et Comparées (Université Paris 13, Villetaneuse, 1997), p. 84.

62. Fredric Jameson, "Postmodernism, or the Cultural Logic of Capitalism," *New Left Review* 146 (1984), pp. 53–82.

63. Tabbi, *Postmodern Sublime*, p. 214.

64. Ibid.

65. Ibid., p. 215.

66. Zohar Shavit, *Poetics of Children's Literature* (Athens: The University of Georgia Press, 1986).

67. Maria Nikolajeva, *Children's Literature Comes of Age, Toward a New Aesthetic* (New York: Garland Publishing, 1996), p. 25.

68. Jean Perrot, "A review of *Children's Literature Comes of Age* by Maria Nikolajeva," *Ariel*, 28, 1 (January 1997), pp. 209–220.

69. Ferguson Plain, *Grandfather Drum* (Winnipeg, Canada: Pemmican Publications, 1994).

70. Clarice Lispector, *Como nasceram as estrelas, Doze lendas brasilieras*, ill. Ricardo Leite (Rio de Janeiro: Editora Nova Fronteira, 1993).

71. Christian Lehmann, *No pasaràn, le jeu* (Paris: L'école des Loisirs, 1996).

72. Roald Dahl, *The Hitchhiker* (London: Jonathan Cape, 1977), p. 36.

73. Roderick McGillis, *The Nimble Reader, Literary Theory and Children's Literature* (New York: Twayne, 1996).

REFERENCES

Anzieu, Didier. *Le corps de l'oeuvre*. Paris: Gallimard, NRF, 1982.

Baudrillard, Jean. *L'échange symbolique et la mort*. Paris: Gallimard NRF, 1976.

———. "Simulations." In *Storming the Reality Studio: A Casebook of Cyberpunk and Postmodern Fiction*. Ed. Larry McCaffery. Durham, NC: Duke University Press, 1991.

Beckett, Sandra L., ed. *Reflections of Change: Children's Literature since 1945*. Westport, CT: Greenwood Press, 1997.

Collodi, Carlo. *The Adventures of Pinocchio*. Translated and ed. by Ann Lawson Lucas. Oxford: Oxford University Press, 1996.

Dahl, Roald. *Boy. Tales of Childhood*. 1984. Harmondsworth, UK: Puffin, 1986.

———. *Matilda*. 1988. Harmondsworth, UK: Puffin, 1990.

———. *The Hitchhiker*. London: Jonathan Cape, 1977.

Elkin, Judith. "Looking to the Future: The Esme Green Memorial Lecture." *The New Review of Children's Literature and Librarianship*, 2 (1996): 1–13.

Genette, Gérard. *Palimpsestes: La littérature au second degré*. Paris: Le Seuil, Coll. Poétique, 1982.

Hazard, Paul. *Des livres, des enfants et des hommes*. Paris: Flammarion, 1932. Translated by Marguerite Mitchell as *Books, Children and Men*. Boston: The Horn Book, 1944.

Hulpach, Vladimir. *Kyeko and the Night-Robbers*. Paris: Ludi Media Ubi-Soft, CD-Rom, 1995.

James, Henry. *What Maisie Knew*. 1897. Harmondsworth, UK: Penguin, 1966.

Jardin, Alexandre. *Cybermaman*. Paris: Gallimard-Jeunesse, 1996.

Kincaid, James. *Child-Loving: The Erotic Child and Victorian Culture*. New York: Routledge, 1992.

Kohl, Herbert. *Should We Burn Babar? Essays on Children's Literature and the Power of Stories*. Intro. Jack Zipes. New York: The New Press, 1995.

Lehmann, Christian. *No pasaràn, le jeu*. Paris: L'école des Loisirs, 1996.

Levy, Stephen. "On the Net, Anything goes." *Newsweek*. (7 July 1997): 44–45.

Lispector, Clarice. *Como nasceram as estrelas, doze lendas brasileiras*. Rio de Janeiro: Editora Nova Fronteira, 1993.

Lodge, David, ed. *Modern Criticism and Theory: A Reader*. London: Longman, 1988.

McCaffery, Larry, ed. *Storming the Reality Studio. A Casebook of Cyberpunk and Postmodern Fiction*. Durham, NC: Duke University Press, 1991.

McGillis, Roderick. *The Nimble Reader: Literary Theory and Children's Literature*. New York: Twayne, 1996.

Merivale, Patricia. "The Telling of Lies and 'the Sea of Stories': *Haroun, Pinocchio* and the Postcolonial Artist Parable." *Ariel*, 28, 1, (January 1997): 193–97.

Nikolajeva, Maria. *Children's Literature Comes of Age, Toward a New Aesthetic*. New York: Garland Publishing, 1996.

Nodelman, Perry. "Fear of Children's Literature: What's Left (or Right) After Theory?" In *Reflections of Change: Children's Literature Since 1945*. Ed. Sandra L. Beckett. Westport, CT: Greenwood Press, 1997: 3–14.

Perrot, Jean. "Du texte contre des dents de lait: Henry James et l'écriture." In *Le récit d'enfance*. Eds. Denise Escarpit and Bernadette Poulou. Paris: Editions du Sorbier, 1993: 63–88.

———. "Why We Should Not Burn Mickey Mouse." In *Critical Perspectives on Postcolonial African Children's Literature*. Ed. Meena Khorana. Westport, CT: Greenwood Press, 1998.

———. "A review of *Children's Literature Comes of Age* by Maria Nikolajeva." *Ariel*, 28, 1 (January 1997): 209–220.

———. "Play Prepares Father Christmas's Future." *ChLA Quarterly*, 19, 3 (Fall 1994): 128–133.

Plain, Ferguson. *Grandfather Drum*. Winnipeg, Canada: Pemmican Publications, 1994.

Scott, Carole. "High and Wild Magic, the Moral Universe, and the Electronic Superhighway: Reflections of Change in Susan Cooper's Fantasy Literature." In *Reflections of Change: Children's Literature Since 1945*. Ed. Sandra L. Beckett. Westport, CT: Greenwood Press, 1997: 91–97.

Shavit, Zohar. *Poetics of Children's Literature*. Athens: The University of Georgia Press, 1986.

Tabbi, Joseph. *Postmodern Sublime: Technology and American Writing from Mailer to Cyberpunk*. Ithaca, NY: Cornell University Press, 1995.

Vadel-Séguillon, Joëlle. "Médias et culture d'enfance: émergence de nouvelles écritures." Mémoire de DEA d'Etudes Littéraires Francophones et Comparées, 124 pp., Université Paris 13, Villetaneuse, 1997.

Select Bibliography

Ahrens, Rüdiger and Neumann, Fritz-Wilhelm, eds. *Fiktion und Geschichte in der anglo-amerikanischen Literatur*. Heidelberg: Winter, 1998.

Aiken, Joan. "Interpreting the Past: Reflections of an Historical Novelist." In Sheila Egoff, Gordon Stubbs, Ralph Ashley and Wendy Sutton, eds. *Only Connect: Readings on Children's Literature*. 3rd ed. Toronto: Oxford University Press, 1996: 62–73.

Barker, Martin. *The Haunt of Fears: The Strange History of the British Horror Comics Campaign*. London: Pluto Press, 1984.

Bator, Robert, ed. *Signposts to Criticism of Children's Literature*. Chicago: American Library Association, 1983.

Baudrillard, Jean. *L'échange symbolique et la mort*. Paris: Gallimard NRF, 1976. Translated as *Symbolic exchange and death*. London: Sage, 1993.

Beckett, Sandra L., ed. *Reflections of Change: Children's Literature Since 1945*. Westport, CT: Greenwood Press, 1997.

Bourdieu, Pierre. *Les règles de l'art: genèse et structure du champ littéraire*. Paris: Seuil, 1992. Translated as *The Rules of Art*. Cambridge: Polity Press, 1993.

Brantlinger, P. *Crusoe's Footprints: Cultural Studies in Britain and America*. New York: Routledge, 1990.

Butts, Dennis, ed. *Stories and Society: Children's Literature in its Social Context*. London: Macmillan, 1992.

Calder, Angus. *The Myth of the Blitz*. London: Jonathan Cape, 1991.

Canary, Robert H. and Kozicki, Henry, eds. *The Writing of History: Literary Form and Historical Understanding*. Madison: University of Wisconsin Press, 1978.

Carpenter, Humphrey. *Secret Gardens: A Study of the Golden Age of Children's Literature*. Boston: Houghton Mifflin, 1985.

———— and Prichard, Mari, eds. *The Oxford Companion to Children's Literature*. Oxford: Oxford University Press, 1984.

Clute, John and Nicholls, Peter. *The Encyclopaedia of Science Fiction*. London: Orbit, 1993.

Coghlan, Valerie and Keenan, Celia. *The Big Guide 2: Irish Children's Books*. Dublin: Children's Books Ireland, 2000.

Cox, J. N. and Reynolds, L. J. *New Historical Literary Study: Essays on Reproducing Texts, Representing History*. New Jersey: Princeton University Press, 1993.

Currie, Mark. *Metafiction*. London: Longman, 1995.

Eco, Umberto. "Postille a *Il nome della rosa*." *Alfabeta*, n. 49, giugno 1983. Translated as "Postscript" to *The Name of the Rose*. New York: Harcourt Brace, 1984. Translated into French as *Apostille au "Nom de la Rose."* Le Livre de Poche, Biblio Essais. Paris: Grasset, 1985.

Engler, Bernd and Müller, Kurt, eds. *Historiographic Metafiction in Modern American and Canadian Literature*. Paderborn: Ferdinand Shöningh, 1994.

Even-Zohar, Itamar. "Reality and Realemes in Narrative." *Poetics Today*, special issue, 11, 1. Durham, NC: Duke University Press, 1990: 207–218.

Fisher, J. *An Index of Historical Fiction for Children and Young People*. Aldershot, UK: Scolar Press, 1994.

Fisher, Margery. *The Bright Face of Danger*. London: Hodder and Stoughton, 1986.

Geertz, Clifford. *The Interpretation of Cultures*. London: Hutchinson, 1975.

Genette, Gérard. *Palimpsestes : La littérature au second degré*. Paris: Le Seuil, Coll. Poétique, 1982.

Green, Martin. *The Robinson Crusoe Story*. University Park: Pennsylvania State University Press, 1990.

————. *Seven Types of Adventure Tale: An Etiology of a Major Genre*. University Park: Pennsylvania State University Press, 1991.

Hawthorne, Jeremy. *Cunning Passages: New Historicism, Cultural Materialism and Marxism in the Contemporary Literary Debate*. London: Arnold, 1996.

Hewison, Robert. *Culture and Consensus: England, Art and Politics since 1940*. London: Methuen, 1995.

Hobsbawm, Eric, and Ranger, Terence, eds. *The Invention of Tradition*. Cambridge: Cambridge University Press, 1983.

Horowitz, C. "Dimensions in Time: A Critical View of Historical Fiction for Children." In *Horn Book Reflections*. Ed. E. W. Field. Boston: Horn Book, 1969.

Hunt, Peter. *Criticism, Theory and Children's Literature*. Oxford: Basil Blackwell, 1991.

————, ed. *The International Companion Encyclopedia of Children's Literature*. London: Routledge, 1996.

————, ed. *Literature for Children: Contemporary Criticism*. London: Routledge, 1992.

Inglis, Fred. *Ideology and the Imagination*. London: Cambridge University Press, 1975.

Jaffe, Steven H. *Who Were the Founding Fathers? Two Hundred Years of Reinventing American History*. New York: Holt, 1996.

Jameson, Fredric. *The Political Unconscious: Narrative as a Socially Symbolic Act*. 1981. London: Methuen, 1983.

Kaes, Anton. *From Hitler to* Heimat: *The Return of History as Film*. Cambridge: Harvard University Press, 1989.

Kerr, James. *Fiction Against History: Scott as Storyteller*. Cambridge: Cambridge University Press, 1989.

Kress, Gunter and van Leeuwen, Theo. *Reading Images*. Melbourne: Deakin University Press, 1990.

Lees, Stella and Macintyre, Pam. *The Oxford Companion to Australian Children's Literature*. Melbourne: Oxford University Press, 1993.

Lodge, David, ed. *Modern Criticism and Theory: A Reader*. London: Longman, 1988.

Lukacs, Georg. *The Historical Novel*. London: Merlin Press, 1962. Published in French as *Le Roman historique*. Paris: Payot, 1972.

McGillis, Roderick. *The Nimble Reader: Literary Theory and Children's Literature*. New York: Twayne, 1996.

———, ed. *Voices of the Other: Children's Literature in the Postcolonial Context*. New York: Garland, 2000.

Moeller, Robert G. "War Stories: The Search for a Usable Past in the Federal Republic of Germany." *American Historical Review* (October 1996): 1008–1048.

Myers, M. "Missed Opportunities and Critical Malpractice: New Historicism and Children's Literature." *Children's Literature Association Quarterly*, 13, 1 (1988): 41–43.

Nélod, Gilles. *Panorama du roman historique*. Paris: Editions SODI, 1969.

Nikolajeva, Maria. *Children's Literature Comes of Age: Towards a New Aesthetic*. New York: Garland, 1996.

Nodelman, Perry, ed. *Touchstones: Reflections on the Best in Children's Literature*. 3 vols. West Lafayette, IN: Children's Literature Association, 1985–89.

Otten, Charlotte F. and Schmidt, Gary D., eds. *The Voice of the Narrator in Children's Literature: Insights from Writers and Critics*. New York: Greenwood Press, 1989.

Purkiss, Diane. *The Witch in History*. London: Routledge, 1996.

Richards, Jeffrey. *Imperialism and Juvenile Literature*. Manchester: Manchester University Press, 1989.

Ricoeur, Paul. *Temps et Récit*. 3 vols. Paris: Seuil, 1983–85.

———. *Lectures on Ideology and Utopia*. New York: Columbia University Press, 1986.

Rose, Jacqueline. *The Case of Peter Pan, or: The Impossibility of Children's Fiction*. London: Macmillan, 1984.

Rotundo, E. Anthony. *American Manhood: Transformations in Masculinity from the Revolution to the Modern Era*. New York: HarperCollins, 1993.

Said, Edward W. *Culture and Imperialism*. New York: Knopf, 1993.

Seelinger Trites, Roberta. *Waking Sleeping Beauty: Feminist Voices in Children's Novels*. Iowa City: University of Iowa Press, 1997.

Shavit, Zohar. *A Past without a Shadow*. (In Hebrew.) Tel Aviv: Am Oved, Ofakim, 1999.

Smith, Bernard. *European Vision and the South Pacific*. 1960. Revised ed. Oxford: Oxford University Press, 1989.

Soriano, Marc. "Histoire et littérature pour la jeunesse." In *Guide de la littérature pour la jeunesse*. Paris: Flammarion, 1975.

Spaas, Lieve and Stimpson, Brian. *Robinson Crusoe: Myths and Metamorphoses*. New York: St. Martin's, 1996.

Stephens, John. *Language and Ideology in Children's Fiction*. London: Longman, 1992.

Sutcliff, Rosemary. *Blue Remembered Hills*. London: Bodley Head, 1983.

Veeser, H. A., ed. *The New Historicism*. New York: Routledge, 1989.

Vindt, Gérard and Giraud, Nicole. *Les Grands Romans historiques*. Paris: Bordas, 1991.

Wall, Barbara. *The Narrator's Voice: The Dilemma of Children's Fiction*. London: Macmillan, 1991.

Warner, Marina. *From the Beast to the Blonde: On Fairy Tales and Their Tellers*. London: Chatto and Windus, 1994.

————. *Joan of Arc: The Image of Female Heroism.* Harmondsworth: Penguin, 1983.

West, Mark I. *Trust Your Children: Voices Against Censorship in Children's Literature.* New York: Neal-Schuman, 1988.

White, Hayden. *Metahistory: The Historical Imagination in Nineteenth-Century Europe.* Baltimore: Johns Hopkins University Press, 1973.

————. *Tropics of Discourse: Essays in Cultural Criticism.* Baltimore: Johns Hopkins University Press, 1978.

Williams, Raymond. *The Politics of Modernism: Against the New Conformists.* London: Verso, 1989.

Worton, M. and Still, J., eds. *Intertextuality.* Manchester, UK: Manchester University Press, 1990.

Yanarella, Ernest J. and Sigelman, Lee, eds. *Political Mythology and Popular Fiction.* Westport, CT: Greenwood Press, 1988.

Young, James E. *Writing and Rewriting the Holocaust: Narrative Consequences of Interpretation.* Bloomington: Indiana University Press, 1988.

Zipes, Jack. *Breaking the Magic Spell: Radical Theories of Folk and Fairy Tales.* London: Heinemann, 1979.

————, ed. *The Trials and Tribulations of Little Red Riding Hood.* New York: Routledge, 1993.

Index of Names and Titles

About the Editor and Contributors

ANN LAWSON LUCAS, as Senior Lecturer in Italian at the University of Hull, UK, has taught literature from Dante to Calvino, specializing, however, in Modern Italian Literature, including nineteenth-century children's writers, and Translation; she also introduced the interdisciplinary teaching of European children's literature. Her principal research field is the "golden age" of children's literature in Italy, in particular the adventure novels of Emilio Salgari and Carlo Collodi's writings for children. She is the author of the first comprehensive, research-based monograph on Salgari: *La ricerca dell'ignoto: I romanzi d'avventura di Emilio Salgari* [The search for the unknown: The adventure novels of Emilio Salgari] (Florence, 2000), and has edited a volume of three Salgari novels, *Romanzi di giungla e di mare* [Novels of jungle and sea] (Turin, 2001). She was editor and translator of *The Adventures of Pinocchio*, unabridged, for Oxford University Press, and is an advisory editor for the *Oxford Encyclopedia of Children's Literature* (Editor, Jack Zipes), currently in preparation. The British Arts and Humanities Research Board recently made her a beneficiary of the Research Leave Scheme and she has been awarded a Visiting Research Fellowship at the Institute for Advanced Studies in the Humanities at the University of Edinburgh, UK. She served for two terms on the Board of the International Research Society for Children's Literature (1993-97) and was the organizer of the 13th IRSCL Congress, held in York, UK, in 1997.

FRANCESCA BLOCKEEL studied Romance Languages at the University of Ghent, Belgium, and obtained her master's degree in Spanish Literature at the University of Lille in France. In 2000 she was awarded a PhD at the University of Leuven, Belgium, with a thesis on identity and alterity in contemporary Portuguese youth literature. She is the author of a number of articles and of *Literatura Juvenil Portuguesa Contemporânea: Identidade e Alteridade* [Contemporary Portuguese youth literature: Identity and alterity] (Lisbon, 2001). She is a Lecturer in Portuguese at the School for Translators in Antwerp (Lessius Hogeschool) and in Spanish at the School of Management in Ghent (Artevelde Hogeschool).

CLARE BRADFORD is an Associate Professor in literature at Deakin University in Melbourne, Australia, where she teaches literary studies and children's literature. She researches and publishes mainly on children's literature, with an emphasis on colonial and postcolonial theory and visual texts. Her most recent book is *Reading Race: Aboriginality in Australian Children's Literature* (2001). She is the editor of the journal *Papers: Explorations into Children's Literature*, and has been president of the Australasian Children's Literature Association for Research.

PENNY BROWN is Senior Lecturer in Comparative Literary Studies in the Department of French at the University of Manchester, UK, where she teaches (among other things) a course on European children's literature. She has published books on twentieth-century women's novels of self-development and the portrayal of childhood in nineteenth-century English women's writing: *The Captured World: The Child and Childhood in Nineteenth-Century Women's Writing in England* (1993); she has written articles on French and English children's literature, notably on the authors Mary Wollstonecraft, Madame de Genlis and the Comtesse de Ségur. She is currently writing a critical history of French children's literature and working on illustrations in children's books.

DENNIS BUTTS teaches on the MA course in children's literature at the University of Reading, UK, and is a former chairman of the national Children's Books History Society. His research interests include the adventure story and early children's books, and recently he has been co-editing a study of popular children's literature.

PAULA T. CONNOLLY ia an Associate Professor at the University of North Carolina at Charlotte, USA, where she teaches courses in American and Children's Literature. She has published several articles and chapters on the depiction of slavery in children's books, and is currently completing a book-length study on the subject. She has also written on A. A. Milne in her book, *Winnie-the-Pooh and The House at Pooh Corner: Recovering Arcadia* (1995).

ADRIENNE E. GAVIN is a Principal Lecturer in English at Canterbury Christ Church University College, UK, where she is course director for Victorian

Literature and Children's Literature. A New Zealander who completed her PhD at the University of British Columbia, Canada, she has published on Elizabeth Gaskell, D. H. Lawrence, Anna Sewell, and Charles Dickens. She is co-editor of the collection of critical essays, *Mystery in Children's Literature: From the Rational to the Supernatural* (2001), and is currently writing a literary biography of Anna Sewell, author of *Black Beauty*.

LINDA HALL, as Senior Lecturer in English at Trinity College, Carmarthen, in Wales, UK, initiated MA programs in Women's Writing and Children's Literature, being director of the latter. She has published two books, *Poetry for Life* and *Tracing the Tradition: An Anthology of Poetry by Women*. She also reviews and writes regularly for *The Use of English* and *Children's Literature in Education*.

TINA L. HANLON is an associate professor of English at Ferrum College in Virginia, USA. She has published essays on folk-tale adaptations, children's plays, dragons in children's literature, picture books, Apalachian children's literature, and environmental literature for children. Her essay "The Art and the Dragon: Intertextuality in the Pictorial Narratives of *Dragon Feathers*" appeared in *Tales, Tellers and Texts* in 2000.

CELIA KEENAN lectures in English at St. Patrick's College Drumcondra, a college of Dublin City University, where she directs the MA program in Children's Literature. Her interests include contemporary Irish literature, especially fiction by women writers, personal narratives by people hitherto marginalized, and literature for children. She wrote on historical fiction for the special Irish edition of *The Lion and the Unicorn*, and co-edited, with Valerie Coghlan, *The Big Guide to Irish Children's Books* (1996), contributing its chapter on Irish historical fiction for children (*The Big Guide 2: Irish Children's Books* came out in 2000).

PAMELA KNIGHTS lectures in the Department of English Studies at the University of Durham, UK, where she teaches course on American Literature and on contemporary fiction for children. Her research focuses on regionality and constructions of identity, and she has published on a range of American authors, including Alcott, Lowrie and Faulkner. She has recently completed editions of Kate Chopin's *The Awakening and Other Stories* and of Edith Wharton's *Ethan Frome*, and is currently working on an introduction to *Lorna Doone*, as well as on a book on ballet fiction.

THOMAS KULLMANN studied English, French and Classical Greek literatures at the universities of Freiburg, Heidelberg and Dublin (Trinity College), obtaining his PhD from Heidelberg where he taught English Literature from 1987 to 1996; in 1996 he was appointed Professor of English Literature at the University of Göttingen, and has now moved to the University of Osnabrück. His publications include two books, on Shakespeare (*Abschied, Reise und*

Wiedersehen bei Shakespeare [Departure, journey and return in Shakespeare] 1989) and on the nineteenth-century English novel (*Vermenschlichte Natur* [Anthropomorphic Nature] 1995), as well as articles on various fields of English literature, including children's literature. His fields of interest are English Renaissance literature, Victorian literature and culture, and children's literature.

GILLIAN LATHEY lectures at the University of Surrey Roehampton where she is Deputy Director of the National Centre for Research in Children's Literature. She specializes in translated children's books and German children's literature. She is the author of *The Impossible Legacy*, a comparative study of recent German and English-language autobiographical children's literature set in the Second World War and the Third Reich.

ISABELLE NIÈRES-CHEVREL is Professor of Comparative Literature at the University of Rennes II, France. Her main interests are in children's literature from an historical and a social point of view, in adaptation and translation, and in the relationships between text and pictures. Her research has included work on publishers (Le Père Castor, François Ruy-Vidal) and major authors such as Madame Leprince de Beaumont, Madame de Ségur, Maurice Boutet de Monvel, Johanna Spyri, Beatrix Potter, Jean de Brunhoff, Maurice Sendak and Daniel Pennac.

JEAN PERROT, Emeritus Professor of Comparative Literature at Paris University, founded the Charles Perrault International Research Institute in 1994 for the advanced study of children's literature (e-mail: imagecom@club-internet.fr). His fields of interest are the picture book, the novel, and children's culture. In 2001 his book *Jeux et enjeux du livre d'enfance et de jeunesse* [Play and games: Books at stake for children and young adults] was selected as an IRSCL Honor Book and, in appreciation of his distinguished work, he has received the Osaka "Brothers Grimm Award."

ROLF ROMØREN is Associate Professor at Agder University College in Norway, where he researches and teaches in the Department of Nordic Literature and Media. His thesis in comparative literature was on the Norwegian modern poet Stein Mehren. He has published articles on children's literature in Norway and abroad, and his current research project concerns Norwegian boys' fiction between the two World Wars. He was elected to the Board of the IRSCL in 1997, serving as vice-president from 1999 to 2001.

ZOHAR SHAVIT, who is full Professor at the Unit for Culture Research, Tel Aviv University, Israel, has worked in the fields of children's culture, the history of Israeli culture, and the History of Hebrew and Jewish culture, especially as they bear upon relations between the German and Jewish cultures. She has written and edited books in Hebrew, English and German, and published over sixty articles in eight languages. Her award-winning work has included *Poetics of Children's Literature* (1986), *Just Childhood: Introduction to Poetics of*

Children's Literature (1996), a bibliographical work on books for Jewish children in the German-speaking countries: *Deutsch-jüdische Kinder- und Jugendliteratur* [German-Jewish Literature for Children and Adolescents] (1996), and a study of the construction of the image of the past in German books for children: *A Past Without a Shadow* (published in Hebrew in 1999).

DAVID STEEGE is Associate Professor of English and Associate Dean of Carthage College in Kenosha, Wisconsin, USA. He has published and delivered papers on American humorists, children's literature, core curriculum and classroom pedagogy, and has developed service/learning at Carthage. An essay on the connections between Harry Potter and *Tom Brown's School Days* will appear in a forthcoming essay collection.

JOHN STEPHENS is Professor in English at Macquarie University, Sydney, Australia, where he teaches and supervises postgraduate research in children's literature, as well as other literatures. He is the author of *Language and Ideology in Children's Fiction* (1992), *Retelling Stories, Framing Culture* (co-authored with Robyn McCallum, 1998), two books about discourse analysis, and over sixty articles about children's (and other) literature. More recently, he has edited *Ways of Being Male: Representing Masculinities in Children's Literature and Film* (2002). His primary research focus is on the relationships between texts produced for children and young adults (especially literature and film) and cultural formations and practices. He was the IRSCL president from 1997 to 1999.

DEBORAH STEVENSON is the editor of the bulletin of the Center for Children's Books, located at the University of Illinois' Graduate School of Library and Information Science, where she is also Assistant Professor. With Betsy Hearne, she is co-author of the third edition of *Choosing Books for Children: A Commonsense Guide* (1999) and she sat on the 2001 Caldecott Award Committee. She is a senior editor of the *Oxford Encyclopedia of Children's Literature* (in progress).

SUSAN TEBBUTT is now Head of German Studies at the Mary Immaculate College of the University of Limerick, Ireland, and was previously Senior Lecturer in the Department of Modern Languages at the University of Bradford, UK. She is author of *Gudrun Pausewang in Context: Socially Critical "Jugendliteratur"* (1994), and *Gudrun Pausewang and the Search for Utopia* (1994), as well as editor of *Sinti and Roma: Gypsies in German-speaking Society and Literature* (1998), and has published numerous articles on children's literature and German cultural studies. In 2001 she received a Charles H. Revson Fellowship to do research at the United States Holocaust Memorial Museum Center for Advanced Holocaust Studies in Washington DC.

DANIELLE THALER, originally from France, has lived in Canada for many years. She teaches at the University of Victoria in British Columbia and is a past president of the Canadian Association of College and University Professors of French. Her publications reflect her interest in the nineteenth-century novel— *Peuple, femme, hysterie: La Clinique de l'amour chez les freres Goncourt* [The working class, women and hysteria: Love as sickness in the works of the Brothers Goncourt] (1986)—and in children's literature: *Etait-il une fois? Panorama de la critique France-Canada* [Once upon a time? A survey of French and Canadian criticism] (1989). She regularly contributes reviews and articles to *Canadian Children's Literature* and has recently written (with A. Jean-Bart, for publication in Paris) a book on youth literature as a genre: *Les enjeux du roman pour adolescents* [The world of the novel for adolescents].

TONY WATKINS is Senior Lecturer in English, Director of the Centre for International Research in Childhood: Literature, Culture, Media (CIRCL) and Director of the MA Program in Children's Literature at the University of Reading, UK. He has lectured on children's literature in Europe, the USA and Australia and has been Research Fellow at the International Centre for Children's Literature Research in Osaka, Japan. He is currently convenor of CIRCL's international collaborative research project on "National and Cultural Identity in Children's Literature and Media" and supervisor of a study funded by the British Arts and Humanities Research Board on "Children's broadcasting and changing constructions of national and cultural identity c.1936-c.1955." He has published articles in various books and journals and has co-edited and contributed to a collection of essays entitled *A Necessary Fantasy? The Heroic Figure in Children's Popular Culture* (2000). He has a particular interest in representations of space, place and history in children's literature.

YOSHIDA JUNKO is Professor of English at Kobe College (and previously at Hiroshima University) in Japan, where she teaches American children's and adolescent literature. She is the author of *Amerika Jido Bungaku: Kazoku Sagashi no Tabi* [Family quest in American children's literature] (Kyoto: Aun-sha, 1992). Her English articles have appeared in several international journals including *Children's Literature* 26 ("The Quest for Masculinity in *The Chocolate War*: Changing Conceptions of Masculinity in the 1970s").